The Story Of The Diamond Necklace

Told In Detail For The First Time, Chiefly By The Aid Of Original Letters, Official And Other Documents, And Contemporary Memoirs Recently Made Public; And Comprising A Sketch Of The Life Of The Countess De La Motte, Pretended Confidant Of Marie-Antoinette, And Particulars Of The Careers Of The Other Actors In The Remarkable Drama (Volume I)

Henry Vizetelly

Alpha Editions

This Edition Published in 2020

ISBN: 9789354304231

Design and Setting By
Alpha Editions
www.alphaedis.com
Email – info@alphaedis.com

As per information held with us this book is in Public Domain.
This book is a reproduction of an important historical work. Alpha Editions uses the best technology to reproduce historical work in the same manner it was first published to preserve its original nature. Any marks or number seen are left intentionally to preserve its true form.

TO A. E. V.

THE LIGHT OF MY HOME, THE HAPPINESS OF MY LIFE,

I DEDICATE,

WITH MUCH AFFECTION,

THIS RECORD OF AN ERRING SISTER'S CAREER.

H. V.

The Countess de la Motte

PREFACE.

THE great scandal of the Diamond Necklace, which to the clear vision of Goethe presaged the coming Revolution, and in which the quick-witted Talleyrand saw the overthrow of the French throne, possesses an interest akin to that of the French Revolution itself. The story is one of which the world does not seem to tire, for it has been told scores upon scores of times, and more or less recently, by historians, biographers, essayists, memoir-writers, anecdotists, novelists, and dramatists, and in well nigh every European language. In the form in which it appears in the Memorials and Judicial Examinations of the parties accused of complicity in the fraud, it has been pronounced "the greatest lie of the eighteenth century," and numerous active brains have essayed to unravel its tangled web of truth and falsehood; nevertheless, there are many persons who still think that a certain mystery envelops the transaction which all the research hitherto bestowed upon it has failed to satisfactorily clear up.

The writer of the present work has diligently studied all the contemporary evidence, bearing in the smallest degree on the subject, which an active search enabled him to discover, and the bulk of which he has availed himself of in the course of the subjoined narrative. These include, for example, unpublished autograph letters and documents, written either by actual actors in the drama, or else by persons intimately associated with it, and derived chiefly from the valuable collection of M. Feuillet de Conches; the official records of the judicial proceedings to which the affair gave rise; all the memorials put forth on behalf of the accused and the memoirs subsequently issued by them, including the exceedingly scarce Mémoire by Rétaux de Villette, which the present writer is the first to quote from, and the curious Autobiography written in his old age by Count de la Motte; the discussions in the Paris Parliament; and the numerous memoirs penned by persons living at the time, some of which, and these of the highest importance—such as the interesting Memoirs of Count Beugnot—having been only recently made public, have not been at the command of previous writers. In addition to the foregoing sources of information may be mentioned the different biographies, and the various critical disquisitions of historians and essayists in which the subject has been so exceedingly fruitful, and of which considerable use will be found to have been made.

PREFACE. vii

With such materials at his command, the writer has been able to tell the story for the first time in all its fulness, and as he believes approximating more closely to the truth, in small matters as well as large, than any previous narrative of the transaction. He conceives that he has completely exonerated the French queen from the slightest suspicion of complicity in the miserable fraud. He has made a point of supplying missing dates to the more trivial as well as to all the more important incidents, of vouching every statement of the smallest consequence, and of giving the very language of the witnesses to the various facts which they are called upon to prove.

It is proper to mention, with regard to some few of the authorities referred to in the following pages, such as Madame Campan's and Weber's "Memoirs of Marie-Antoinette," Madame de la Motte's "Mémoires Justificatifs," and the "Mémoire pour le Comte de Cagliostro," that the French and English versions of these works have been indiscriminately used, and that the references given, if they do not apply to the one, will be found to belong to the other edition of the works in question.

Paris, Feb. 1867.

AUTHORITIES REFERRED TO IN THIS WORK.

Mémoire des joailliers Böhmer et Bassenge, du Août 12, 1785. Paris, 1786.

Mémoire pour Louis-Réné-Edouard de Rohan, cardinal, contre M. le Procureur-Général, en présence de la dame de la Motte. Paris, 1786.

Pièces justificatives pour M. le Cardinal de Rohan, déclarations authentiques selon la forme Anglaise. Paris, 1786.

Requête au parlement, les chambres assemblées, par M. le Cardinal de Rohan. Paris, 1786.

Réflexions rapides pour M. le Cardinal de Rohan, sur le sommaire de la dame de la Motte. Paris, 1786.

Mémoire pour dame Jeanne de Saint-Remy de Valois, épouse du Comte de la Motte. Paris, 1786.

Réponse pour la Comtesse de Valois-Lamotte au Mémoire du Comte Cagliostro. Paris, 1786.

Sommaire pour la Comtesse de Valois-Lamotte accusée, contre M. le Procureur-Général, accusateur, en présence de M. le Cardinal de Rohan et autres co-accusés. Paris, 1786.

Mémoires justificatifs de la Comtesse de la Motte, écrit par elle-même. London, 1789.

Ditto, English translation.

Mémoire pour la demoiselle le Guay d'Oliva, fille mineure, émancipée d'âge, accusée, contre M. le Procureur-Général. Paris, 1786.

AUTHORITIES REFERRED TO IN THIS WORK.

Seconde mémoire et pièces justificatives, pour Mademoiselle le Guay d'Oliva. Paris, 1786.

Requête pour le sieur Marc-Antoine Rétaux de Villette, ancien gendarme, accusé, contre M. le Procureur-Général. Paris, 1786.

Mémoire pour le Comte de Cagliostro, accusé, contre M. le Procureur-Général, accusateur, en présence de M. le Cardinal de Rohan, de la Comtesse de la Motte et autres, co-accusés. Paris, 1786.
Requête au parlement, les chambres assemblées, pour le Comte de Cagliostro, signifiée à M. le Procureur-Général, le 24 Février, 1786. Paris, 1786.
Mémoire pour le Comte de Cagliostro contre Maître Chesnon fils et le Sieur de Launay. Paris, 1786.
Memorial for the Count de Cagliostro. London, 1786.

Mémoire pour Jean-Charles-Vincent de Bette d'Etienville, bourgeois de Saint-Omer en Artois. Paris, 1786.
Deuxième Mémoire pour le sieur Jean-Charles-Vincent de Bette d'Etienville. Paris, 1786.
Collection complète de tous les Mémoires qui ont paru dans la fameuse affaire du Collier, avec toutes les pièces secrètes qui y ont rapport et qui n'ont pas paru. Paris, 1786.
Compte-rendu de ce qui s'est passé au parlement relativement à l'affaire de M. le Cardinal de Rohan. Paris, 1786.
Jugement rendu par le parlement de Paris sur l'affaire du Collier de diamants, avec le détail de ce qui s'est passé aux séances du parlement les 30 et 31 Mai, 1786, et les ordres du Roi après le jugement. Paris, 1786.
Archives de l'Empire. No. X^2 2576. Procès du Collier.
Unpublished autograph letters and documents relative to the Diamond Necklace affair, in the collection of M. Feuillet de Conches.

The Life of Jeanne de Saint-Remy de Valois, heretofore Countess de la Motte, written by herself. 2 vols. London, 1791.
Authentic adventures of the Countess de la Motte. London, 1787.

x AUTHORITIES REFERRED TO IN THIS WORK.

Mémoires Inédits du Comte de la Motte-Valois, publiés d'après le manuscrit autographe, par L. Lacour. Paris, 1858.

Mémoire historique des intrigues de la Cour et de ce qui s'est passé entre la Reine, le Comte d'Artois, le Cardinal de Rohan, Madame de Polignac, Madame de la Motte, Cagliostro, et MM. de Breteuil et de Vergennes, par Rétaux de Villette. Venise, 1790.

Mémoires pour servir à l'histoire des événements de la fin du XVIII° siècle, par l'Abbé Georgel, vol. ii. Paris.

Marie-Antoinette et le procès du Collier d'après la procédure instruite devant le parlement de Paris, par E. Campardon, archiviste des archives de l'Empire. Paris, 1863.

Mémoires sur la vie privée de Marie-Antoinette, par Madame Campan. 2 vols. London, 1823.

Ditto, English translation.

Mémoires concernant Marie-Antoinette, Reine de France, par J. Weber. 2 vols. London, 1805.

Ditto, English translation.

Histoire de Marie-Antoinette, par E. et J. de Goncourt. Paris, 1863.

La Vraie Marie-Antoinette, par M. de Lescure. Paris.

Maria-Theresia und Marie-Antoinette, von A. Ritter von Arneth. Paris und Wien, 1865.

Lettres et documents inédits de Louis XVI., Marie-Antoinette, et Madame Elisabeth, par M. Feuillet de Conches, 3 vols. Paris, 1864.

Correspondance inédite de Marie-Antoinette, par le Comte P. Vogt d'Hunolstein. Paris, 1864.

Procès de Marie-Antoinette, ci-devant Reine des Français. Paris, 1865.

Correspondance secrète inédite sur Louis XVI., Marie-Antoinette, la cour et la ville, de 1777 à 1792, publiée d'après les manuscrits de la Bibliothèque Impériale de Saint-Pétersbourg, par M. de Lescure, 2 vols. Paris, 1866.

Les derniers jours de Trianon, par M. Capefigue. Paris, 1866.

Mémoires du Comte Beugnot, ancien ministre, vol. i. Paris, 1866.

Mémoires de Mademoiselle Bertin. Paris.

Mémoires de M. le Baron de Besenval, écrit par lui-même, vol. iii. Paris, 1805.

Mémoires de la Baronne d'Oberkirche, vol. i. Paris, 1853.

Mémoires posthumes du Feld-Maréchal Comte de Stedingk, par le Comte de Bjornsjerna, vol. iii. Paris, 1844.

Souvenirs de la Marquise de Créqui, par le Comte de Courchamps. Paris, 1834-5.

Mémoires secrets pour servir à l'histoire de la dernière année du règne de Louis XVI., par A. F. Bertrand de Molleville, ministre d'état à cette époch, vol. ii. Londres et Paris, 1797.

Mémoires historiques et politiques du règne de Louis XVI., par l'Abbé Soulavie, vol. vi. Paris, 1801.

Histoire de la décadence de la monarchie Française, par l'Abbé Soulavie, vol. iii. Paris, 1803.

Anecdotes du règne de Louis XVI., contenant tout ce qui concerne ce monarque, sa famille, et la Reine, etc., par M. Nougaret, vol. i. Paris, 1791.

Correspondance secrète de la cour de Louis XVI. Paris.

L'Histoire de France, pendant le XVIII⁰ siècle, par C. Lacretelle, vol. vi. Paris, 1819.

Louis XVI. par M. Alexandre Dumas, vol. iii. Paris, 1851.

Louis XVI. son administration et ses relations diplomatiques avec l'Europe, par M. Capefigue, vol. iii. Paris, 1844.

The Journals and Correspondence of William, Lord Auckland, vol. i. London, 1860-2.

Souvenirs de M. Berryer, doyen des avocats de Paris, de 1774 à 1833, vol. ii. Paris, 1839.

Mémoires sur les prisons de Paris sous Robespierre, vol. ii. Paris.

Les Crimes de Marat et des autres égorgeurs, ou, Ma Résurrection, par P. A. L. Maton de la Varenne. Paris, 1795.

Histoire de la Révolution Française, par M. Louis Blanc, vol. ii. Bruxelles.

The French Revolution, a history; by Thomas Carlyle. 3 vols. (Leipzig edition), 1851.

Histoire monarchique et constitutionnelle de la Révolution Française, par Eugène Labaume, vol. ii. Paris, 1834.

Critical and Miscellaneous Essays, by Thomas Carlyle, vol iv. (Art.—Diamond Necklace). London, 1857.
Biographie Universelle (Articles—De Rohan and Cagliostro).
Le Moniteur, No. 220. Paris, 1792.
Morning Chronicle, Dec. 29, 1786.
Journal de Paris, Nov. 12, 1831.
Gentleman's Magazine, vol. lxi., London, 1791.
Julie philosophe, ou le bon patriote, vol. ii. London.
Histoire de Bar-sur-Aube, par L. Chevalier. Bar-sur-Aube, 1851.
Essais historiques sur la ville de Bar-sur-Aube, publiés d'après un manuscrit inédit portant la date de 1785, par J. F. G. Troyes, 1838.
Letter from the Curé of Bar-sur-Aube, July 17, 1866.
Saverne et ses environs, par C. G. Klein. Strasbourg, 1849.
Histoire anecdotique des Rues de Versailles, par J. A. Le Roi. Versailles, 1854.
Histoire du Bois de Boulogne, par J. Lobet. Paris, 1856.

CONTENTS OF VOL. I.

CHAP.		PAGE
I.	A SCION OF ROYALTY IN TATTERS—"TAKE PITY ON THE ORPHAN DESCENDANTS OF HENRY II. KING OF FRANCE"	1
II.	THE SAINT-REMIS OF VALOIS—A TRAMP UP TO THE CAPITAL	3
III.	MANTUA-MAKER'S APPRENTICE—PENSIONER UNDER THE CROWN—BOARDER IN A CONVENT	10
IV.	THE DIAMOND NECKLACE—ORDERED, BUT NOT SOLD	19
V.	AT BAR-SUR-AUBE—COURTSHIP AND MARRIAGE	28
VI.	COUNTESS DE LA MOTTE—IN BARRACKS AT LUNÉVILLE—ON A FIFTH FLOOR IN PARIS—ENSNARES THE GRAND ALMONER	45
VII.	OSCILLATES BETWEEN PARIS AND VERSAILLES—SENDS OUT BEGGING LETTERS AND PETITIONS—FAINTS IN MADAME'S SALLE D'ATTENTE—DESPAIR	60
VIII.	THE DIAMOND NECKLACE AGAIN—STILL NOT SOLD	78

CONTENTS.

CHAP.		PAGE
IX.	SOI-DISANT CONFIDANT OF THE QUEEN—AT VERSAILLES AND LITTLE TRIANON	84
X.	HIS EMINENCE CARDINAL, COMMENDATOR, GRAND ALMONER, PRINCE-BISHOP LOUIS RÉNÉ EDOUARD DE ROHAN	98
XI.	PRETENDED MEDIATOR BETWEEN THE CARDINAL AND THE QUEEN—A FORGER ON THE PREMISES — BILLETS-DOUX BORDERED WITH "VIGNETTES BLEUES"	109
XII.	THE COUNTERFEIT QUEEN	120
XIII.	THE MIDNIGHT INTERVIEW—"YOU KNOW WHAT THIS MEANS"	129
XIV.	A GOLDEN HARVEST—HISTORY REPEATS ITSELF—BARONESS D'OLIVA IS GIVEN THE COLD SHOULDER	136
XV.	GRAND DOINGS AT BAR-SUR-AUBE	147
XVI.	THE DIAMOND NECKLACE IS SOLD AT LAST	160
XVII.	CHARLATAN COUNT CAGLIOSTRO	176
XVIII.	THE DIAMOND NECKLACE IS DELIVERED	191
XIX.	THE DIAMOND NECKLACE VANISHES!	199
XX.	THE DIAMONDS ARE DISPERSED—COUNT DE LA MOTTE GOES TO ENGLAND ON BUSINESS	211
XXI.	THE GATHERING OF THE STORM	234
XXII.	TWELVE DAYS' STATE AT BAR-SUR-AUBE	248
XXIII.	LETTRES-DE-CACHET IN THE ŒIL-DE-BŒUF—IN THE RUE SAINT-CLAUDE—AND AT BAR-SUR-AUBE	261

CHAP.		PAGE
XXIV.	A DREARY DAY AND NIGHT'S DRIVE—THE BASTILLE — A "VALOIS" SERVED OFF PEWTER	280
XXV.	EFFECT PRODUCED ON THE PUBLIC MIND BY THESE ARRESTS — THE ENEMIES OF THE QUEEN	291
XXVI.	LITTLE TRIANON, AND THE QUEEN'S SOCIETY THERE	300

Erratum.—Böhmer and Bassenge were not crown jewellers during the reign of Louis XV. Böhmer was jeweller to the King of Poland and to Madame Dubarry, and it was owing to the latter circumstance that the order for the Diamond Necklace was confided to him. It was not until early in the year 1785, shortly after the perpetration of the Necklace fraud, that he received through the instrumentality of Marie-Antoinette, who had previously employed him, the appointment of jeweller to the French Crown.—See "Correspondance secrète inédite sur Louis XVI., Marie-Antoinette," etc., vol. i. p. 548.

"Though the descendant of a king, I have been a beggar, a servant, a mantua-maker's apprentice, and the favourite of royalty . . . . . The names of a great queen and of a prince-cardinal unhappily united with mine have spread a blaze around it to attract general notice; and as if I was doomed to be the victim of painful splendour, the ingenuity of my enemies have found means to forge the chains of my dishonour out of a Diamond Necklace."—" Life of the Countess de la Motte, by herself," vol. i. p. 267, and p. 6 of preface.

"Faites attention à ce misérable Collier, je ne serais nullement surpris qu'il renversât le trône."—*Talleyrand to Chamfort.* "Histoire Monarchique et Constitutionnelle de la Révolution Française," par E. Labaume, vol. ii. p. 139.

"I would caution them to despise those who, hacknied in systematic scandal, feast upon the bleeding reputations of their sisters mangled and torn by calumny; let them demand of those who convey such vile insinuations some proof of the circumstances which they relate; let them sift them thoroughly to the bottom; *let them inquire the character of the tale-bearer; let them ask how, where, and when, and whether she knows the woman whom she has so eagerly attempted to disgrace."*—" Life of the Countess de la Motte, by herself," vol. ii. p. 410.

THE

STORY OF THE DIAMOND NECKLACE.

I.

1764.

A SCION OF ROYALTY IN TATTERS.—"TAKE PITY ON THE ORPHAN DESCENDANTS OF HENRY II., KING OF FRANCE."

RATHER more than a century ago, in the year 1764, just as death had closed the career of the once all-powerful Madame de Pompadour, who had long since exhausted all her arts in vain endeavours to revive the jaded passions of her royal lover, and when the star of the notorious Dubarry was gaining the ascendant, as the Marquis and Marchioness de Boulainvilliers, attended by servants and outriders in the gayest of liveries, were returning in a carriage and four from their hôtel at Paris to the château of Passy, of which pleasant village the marquis was *seigneur*, their attention was attracted to a little girl about eight years of age, clad in the beggar's accustomed livery—rags and tatters, who, carrying a younger sister on her back, ran beside the carriage, then proceeding up the hill at a slow pace, and appealed for charity after the following strange fashion:—"Kind lady and gentleman, pray take pity on two poor orphans descended from Henry the Second of Valois, King of France."

The marchioness, struck by the singularity of this appeal, stopped the carriage and commenced questioning the child, much to the annoyance of her husband, who petulantly remarked she ought to know well enough that it was a common trick of poverty to forge lies to excite compassion. The marchioness, however, persisted in her inquiries, and ascertained from the child whereabouts she lived, then, after promising to see into the truth of her statement and telling a servant to give her some few francs, the lady, greatly to the satisfaction of her impatient husband, gave directions for the carriage to proceed.

The next day, in accordance with her promise, the marchioness despatched a trusty servant to the adjacent village of Chaillot, where the children lodged. The people of the house, and the neighbours generally, confirmed, so far as they were able, the truth of the little beggar girl's story, which, as this partakes largely of the romantic and exercised an important influence on her subsequent career, we propose recounting in detail.

II.

1717–1764.

THE SAINT-REMIS OF VALOIS.—A TRAMP UP TO THE CAPITAL.

For a couple of centuries there had resided at Bar-sur-Aube, in Champagne, certain Barons de Saint-Remi, the first of whom was Henri de Saint-Remi, an illegitimate son of Henri II. of Valois, King of France, lover of the beautiful Diana of Poitiers, and who had the ill luck to get killed at a tilting match by a lance thrust in his right eye, accidentally given him by the captain of his Scottish guards, the Count de Montgomerie, ancestor of our Earls of Eglintoun. This son of his, Henri de Saint-Remi, was, in heralds' language, "High and Puissant Lord and Knight, Baron and Seigneur of the Manors of the Chatellier, Fontette, Noez and Beauvoir, Knight of the King's Order, Gentleman of the Bedchamber in ordinary, Colonel of a regiment of horse and a regiment of foot, and Governor of Château-Villain." In the course of a few generations, however, the Saint-Remis appear to have fallen from their high estate, and their broad manors to have become entirely alienated from them, inasmuch as we find that Nicolas de Saint-Remi, the great-grandson of the Henri before mentioned, instead of being styled "High and Puissant Lord and Knight," and Seigneur of various extensive domains, and the holder of numerous offices about the person of the sovereign, was merely one of the king's body-guard in the Duke de Charost's company. He married the daughter of Nicolas-François de Vienne, a great man in the royal bailiwick of Bar-sur-Aube, and who seems at this period to have been the possessor of two of the Saint-Remi manors, namely, Noez and Fontette. The children that sprung from this marriage were two sons, the elder of whom was slain in battle, and the younger, Jacques de Saint-Remi, was father of the little beggar girl whom we found running beside the Boulainvilliers' carriage asking alms.

Jacques de Saint-Remi de Valois, in spite of his illustrious descent, seems to have gradually sunk to the level of the peasant class, and the indigence to which he found himself reduced was aggravated by his imprudently marrying a young girl with a pretty face, but of vulgar manners and somewhat loose morals, the daughter of his *concierge* at the time he had a house to shelter him. The offspring of this union was a son and two daughters, born respectively in the years 1755, 6, and 7, but small as his family was, Jacques de Saint-Remi seems to have been unable to support it. One who knew the family well describes the last of the barons of Saint-Remi as a man of athletic build, who lived partly by poaching and by depredations in the adjoining forest, partly by plundering his neighbours' fields, and partly on the charity of the benevolent.* The vast estates which formerly belonged to the now impoverished family had gradually dwindled away, some having been sold to meet the demands arising from the extravagance of successive owners, while others had passed into the hands of lawyers and money-lenders. At this period there nevertheless remained three domains of considerable extent, deeply encumbered, it is true, with debts, but which left open some real or fancied claim, which, although the beggared heir of the house of Valois had no means of enforcing it, was nevertheless the revery and abstraction of his life. A few sheets of musty parchment, the surviving title deeds of his house, the last wreck, so to speak, of the vast landed property of the Saint-Remis of Valois, these he kept carefully stowed away under the straw thatch of his miserable hut. To pore at times over these old parchments was the one act of worldly vanity in which Jacques de Saint-Remi permitted himself to indulge, but the woman he had married was not so easily satis-

* "Mémoires du Comte Beugnot, ancien Ministre," (Paris, 1866,) vol. i. p. 7.

fied. The continual display of these mysterious documents kindled her ambition, until at length it was raised to such a pitch, that she prevailed on her husband to set out for Paris, there to endeavour to make interest among the great for the restoration of those rights to which as heir of the house of Valois she believed him to be entitled.

After disposing of such few moveables as they possessed, the wretched family set forth and literally tramped up to the capital, a distance of nearly a hundred and fifty miles. That they might not be burthened on the way by their youngest child, then about three years old, the unnatural parents left it behind them, exposed on a window-sill of the house of one Durand, "a wealthy and avaricious farmer," to quote the eldest sister's own words, "who, being in possession of a great part of my father's estate, and having stood sponsor to this unfortunate infant, was therefore deemed the most proper person to be her future protector."[*]

On their arrival in Paris, in a state of extreme destitution, the Saint-Remi family shifted their place of residence from one suburb to another until they eventually settled down at Boulogne, then but a small village on the banks of the Seine, opposite to St. Cloud. Here they lived upon such charity as the gentry of the neigh-

[*] "Life of the Countess de la Motte, by herself," (London, 1791,) vol. i. p. 7.

bourhood, attracted by the singularity of their story, from time to time bestowed upon them. The father at this period had fallen into a state of dotage, and the mother's pet idea of an appeal in high quarters for the restoration of the family estates had to be sacrificed to the powerful struggle which they were forced to undergo for their daily bread. Months thus passed away, until one day Jacques de Saint-Remi, for some cause or other—most likely an unpaid baker's bill—was arrested by an officer of the marshalsea (mounted police) of Boulogne, and locked up in a loathsome cell, where he remained for six weeks. Here the poor man contracted a serious illness, and on his release, which was brought about by the intervention of the *curé* of the parish, the only retreat which the efforts of his neighbours—for friends he had none—were enabled to provide for him —a descendant of the blood-royal of France—was a pallet in one of the wards of the Hôtel Dieu. Here he died on February 16, 1762, a couple of days afterwards.

Within a few days of the death of Jacques de Saint-Remi his wife gave birth to another daughter, and as soon as she was recovered from her confinement, the family removed to Versailles, where the mother made a practice of sending the children into the streets to beg. Jeanne, the eldest daughter, and the heroine of our story, appears to have been treated with great harshness by her mother; for unless the child brought home ten *sous* on ordinary days, and double that amount on Sundays and fête days, as the fruits of her mendicity, she was subjected, she tells us, to the cruellest punishment. The mother had at this time formed a disreputable connection with a discarded common soldier—one Jean-Baptiste Raymond—a native of Sardinia, with whom mendicancy was a positive passion; for, in disregard of the laws, he made it his daily practice to beg in the most public places of Paris, having with him the young Jacques de Saint-Remi, and the family documents, which he boldly exhibited to the passers-by in support of a pretended claim which he himself set up to the honours of the house of Valois. Jean-Baptiste was arrested by the police time after time, for plying his nefarious trade with such marked audacity, and sentenced to various terms of imprisonment. He was, however, incorrigible, and the authorities at last determined upon getting rid of him, so they sent him to prison for a further term of fifteen days, and then ordered him to be exposed for four and twenty hours in the Place de Louis Quinze—subsequently the Place de la Révolution, where for two years the guillotine did its bloody work, and now the handsome Place de la Concorde—with an inscription hung round his neck setting forth the nature of his imposture, together with copies of the titles he had falsely assumed. This public exhibition at an end, Jean-Baptiste Raymond was banished for five years from the capital.

When the day arrived for his departure, the unnatural

mother of the young Saint-Remis set out with her paramour, leaving behind her three children, whom she promised to rejoin in eight days at the very outside, to shift for themselves. Five weeks, however, elapsed without any tidings of her, and it was at this particular moment when the poor children, deserted by their only remaining protector, and reduced almost to a state of starvation, had the good fortune to attract the notice of the kind-hearted Marchioness de Boulainvilliers.

III.

1764–1779.

MANTUA-MAKER'S APPRENTICE.—PENSIONER UNDER THE CROWN.—BOARDER IN A CONVENT.

THE Boulainvilliers' domestic, satisfied with the inquiries he had made, directed the children to take leave of those kind neighbours who had so constantly befriended them, and then to come on to Passy, where they were to inquire for the château, which stood, by the way, on the precise spot where the pleasant "Hameau de Boulainvilliers" now stands. But few preparations being necessary for their departure, they were soon on their road, and reached the château in the course of the afternoon. Their arrival being announced, they were conducted "into a grand hall, in the centre of which rose a magnificent staircase richly ornamented with gold, where a large company of ladies and gentlemen were waiting to view them."* The marchioness descending to the middle of the staircase, asked young Jeanne whether she remembered her again, an inquiry

---

* "Life of the Countess de la Motte, by herself," vol. i. p. 41.

which it is almost needless to say the child promptly answered in the affirmative.

The company having gratified their curiosity at a distance, for no one dared venture into too close proximity with these wretched outcasts, covered as they were with rags and dirt, the marchioness gave orders for them to be cleansed, and for other clothes to be supplied them. A good scrubbing having brought to light indications of various diseases, the usual concomitants of poverty, steps were taken for their speedy eradication; and in the course of a few weeks, thanks to the attention they received, and to the generous food provided them, all traces of their former wretched condition were effaced.

The marchioness's next care was the education of the young orphans, and Jeanne and her sister were sent to a boarding-school in the neighbourhood, where they made rapid progress. In less than two years, however, the youngest girl died of the small-pox, at that time a disease not only very prevalent, but commonly fatal. Jeanne remained at school for several years longer; but during the latter period of her stay, her governess, she tells us, unknown to the marchioness (whom the young Saint-Remi saw but rarely), compelled her to perform the common offices of a domestic servant. "This employment," she observes, "against which it was useless to remonstrate, was but ill-adapted to those elevated notions which reflections on my birth had inspired me with. Was it not," she asks, "painful to feel that, descended as I was from the first family in France, I was yet reduced to be a servant to people of the very lowest rank, nay, even to servants themselves?"*

At length, at her own request, Jeanne was removed from school, and, with the view of placing her in a position to provide for herself (for the marquis, who was half a Jew—his mother being a daughter of Samuel Bernard, the rich Hebrew banker, whom even the "Grand Monarque" would condescend to take by the arm when he was hard up and wanted to coax a loan out of him, and whom the court ladies used to cheat at the queen's card-table—objected to her continuing a pensioner on the Boulainvilliers' establishment), Jeanne was articled to a Parisian mantua-maker for a term of three years. Ill-health, however, compelled her to leave before completing the engagement, and she filled one situation after another, subject during the time to constant attacks of illness, until at length a change in the fortunes of the family made it no longer necessary for her to labour for her daily bread.

The young Jacques de Saint-Remi had received his education under the care of M. le Clerc, the husband of his sister Jeanne's governess, and, on its completion, had been sent to sea. About this time he returned home from his first voyage, and the mar-

---

* " Life of the Countess de la Motte, by herself," vol. i. p. 47.

chioness, having got together various documents in support of the claim of the family to the honours of the house of Valois, consulted with the Marquis de Chabert (the admiral under whom the young Saint-Remi had recently served, and who had interested himself a good deal in the young sailor's history) as to the best course to be adopted to get their claim recognised at court. The marquis at once caused a genealogical memorial of the family to be drawn up, which he transmitted with the necessary confirmatory documents to his cousin, M. d'Hozier de Sérigny, grand genealogist and judge-at-arms of the nobility of France, that the same might receive the sanction of his authority.

When this was returned to the marquis, accompanied by a certificate of M. d'Hozier's attesting its accuracy, the marquis forwarded the various documents to the proper quarter, and in due course obtained the appointment of a day for the reception of young Saint-Remi by Louis XVI., who had only recently ascended the throne. The youth was introduced to the king as the Baron de Valois by the Marquis de Boulainvilliers, the Marquis de Chabert, the Count de Maurepas, and M. Necker. The king was pleased to recognise the title which the friends of the young Jacques de Saint-Remi had persuaded him to assume, but desirous, it was believed, that this should become extinct in the person of its present possessor, recommended the newly-acknowledged Baron de Valois to devote himself to the service of the church.* Jacques respectfully ventured to suggest that his predilections were in favour of the army or the navy. The king thanked the young Saint-Remi for his inclination to serve him, but recommended him again, still more strongly, to dedicate his days to the service of his Maker. "Sire," replied the young man, with a sprinkling of blasphemy which only a Frenchman would have ventured on, "I am serving God when I am serving my king." †

The members of the Saint-Remi family had now their several titles awarded them. Jacques, as we have already seen, was henceforth to be styled Baron de Valois; his sister Jeanne was to be known as Mademoiselle de Valois; and Marianne, the poor child who was left exposed outside Farmer Durand's window-sill, and who was now sent for to Paris, was for the future to be called Mademoiselle de Saint-Remi. But as "fine words butter no parsneps," so empty honours will not suffice to keep the pot boiling. It was, therefore, imperative that the necessary steps should be taken to procure some sort of provision for these destitute off-springs of the blood-royal of France. It is true the national finances were in a most lamentable condition, still everybody agreed that something must be done,

* Roman Catholic ecclesiastics not being permitted to marry, the title of course could not have been transmitted by descent.
† "Life of the Countess de la Motte, by herself," vol. i. p. 87.

which something finally resolved itself into a pension to each member of the family of Valois of eight hundred francs (thirty-two pounds sterling) per annum, commencing from December, 1775. In addition to this, through the intervention of M. Necker, the young Baron de Valois had a commission in the navy given him, with a grant of four thousand francs for his outfit, and shortly afterwards received orders to join his ship at Brest.

We have already mentioned that Jeanne, or, as we must now style her, Mademoiselle de Valois, during the period she was toiling as a mantua-maker's apprentice, was subject to frequent attacks of illness. On these occasions it seems an apartment was set apart for her at the Hôtel de Boulainvilliers, where every care was bestowed upon her until she was completely restored to health. During the period of her convalescence she was constantly persecuted by the marquis with attentions the object of which it was impossible to mistake. These advances, moreover, were subsequently renewed on every occasion that presented itself; in fact, whenever mademoiselle found herself under the Boulainvilliers' roof; and if we can credit her own statement, more than one daring assault was made by the old reprobate upon her virtue. To rid herself of the marquis's importunities she was forced, she tells us, to complain to his wife, who decided upon taking the necessary steps to remove mademoiselle beyond the sphere of her husband's dangerous influence. She and her sister Marianne were accordingly sent as boarders to the abbey of Yéres, in the neighbourhood of Montgeron, some dozen miles or so from Paris, on the road to Lyons. Here, for a time, she pretends that she contemplated taking the veil, a resolution, however, which, if ever seriously entertained, was very soon abandoned.

About this time the Marquis de Boulainvilliers was detected defrauding the excise by means of an extensive secret distillery which he carried on in some vaults beneath his Paris hôtel. The discovery of this fraud caused, as might be supposed, considerable sensation among the *haute noblesse*, and neither the marquis nor the marchioness dared show themselves at court, and hardly even in the vicinity of the capital. They decided, therefore, to retire for a time to their château at Montgeron, no great distance from the abbey of Yéres, and, as a matter of course, the sisters Valois were invited to spend the holidays with them. At the château they would probably have continued to remain had not the marquis renewed his system of persecution. It is, however, tolerably certain that something very like encouragement was given to him by Mademoiselle de Valois, for the pair were surprised one day in a somewhat equivocal situation by the Marquis de Brancas and the Abbé Tacher, and although the lady in her "Memoirs" has the effrontery to speak of "the blush of conscious innocence which coloured her cheek" on this occasion, the result was that she was packed off by the marchioness to the well-known abbey of Longchamp, near Paris—of course, as she says, at her own earnest entreaty. Of this once handsome pile of conventual buildings, all that has survived the fury of the revolutionists of 1793, is a round ivy-mantled tower and an adjacent windmill, both familiar objects at the present time in this favourite locality. In the days of St. Vincent de Paul, the disorders which reigned in the abbey of Longchamp were such as to call forth severe animadversions from this earnest and conscientious priest, and even when the sisters Valois entered it as boarders, the discipline was inclined to be lax; nevertheless the marquis made so many morning calls that the other boarders were scandalized at his constant visits, and the abbess was constrained to give orders that no gentleman should be allowed to visit Mademoiselle de Valois on any pretence whatever. At this abbey the sisters remained for about a year, only quitting it, say they, on the death of the abbess. Other accounts state that they left the convent surreptitiously early one morning, carrying with them a very light bundle, and with thirty-six francs jingling in their pockets, and that their departure was owing to the pertinacity of the abbess pressing them to embrace a religious life, a course to which the young ladies, who were by this time sufficiently partial to worldly vanities, were by no means inclined.* The abbess is supposed to have received her instructions from high quarters, and it is further suggested that the object of them was the gradual extinction of the race of the Valois, together with all their troublesome claims.

* "Mémoires du Comte Beugnot," vol. i. p. 9.

IV.

1773–1778.

THE DIAMOND NECKLACE: ORDERED, BUT NOT SOLD.

WHILE our heroine was being initiated into the mysteries of mantua-making by the most distinguished of Parisian *modistes*, the "chains of her dishonour," as she styles them,* were unknown to her being forged in the form of a Diamond Necklace, such as the world never saw before, and the like of which it can hardly hope to look upon again. Here is a description, penned by a master-hand, of this regal jewel, this unique gem, long an object of desire with queens and women, which caused a nine months' convulsion of the world of Paris, and the remarkable story connected with which was for a time the talk of every city in Europe, and the mystery enveloping which is thought by many to be hardly cleared up even now. "A row of seventeen glorious diamonds, as large almost as filberts, encircle, not too tightly, the neck a first time. Looser, gracefully fastened thrice to these, a three-wreathed festoon and pendants enough (simple pear-shaped multiple star-shaped or clustering amorphous) encircle it, enwreath

---

* See Extracts from the Countess's Life facing page 1 of the present volume.

it a second time. Loosest of all, softly flowing round from behind in priceless catenary, rush down two broad threefold rows; seem to knot themselves, round a very queen of diamonds, on the bosom; then rush on, again separated, as if there were length in plenty; the very tassels of them were a fortune for some men. And now, lastly, two other inexpressible threefold rows, also with their tassels, will, when the Necklace is on and clasped, unite themselves behind into a doubly inexpressible sixfold row; and so stream down, together or asunder, over the hind neck,—we may fancy like lambent zodiacal or Aurora-Borealis fire." *

This matchless jewel had its origin in a freak of Louis XV., the "Well-Beloved," as he was endearingly called at the early part of his reign, whose infatuation in later years for the notorious Countess Dubarry led him into all kinds of extravagance, and caused him to dissipate with more than his accustomed recklessness the already seriously impaired revenues of the State. We learn from the Abbé Soulavie that, during the last sixteen months of the "Well-Beloved's" reign, the sum of two million four hundred and fifty thousand francs, or nearly one hundred thousand pounds sterling—a far larger sum in those days, be it remembered, than at the present time—was paid out of the royal exchequer in hard cash to this one favourite alone. And to satisfy

* Carlyle's "Critical and Miscellaneous Essays," vol. iv. p. 9. See also Appendix to the present work.

us that his statement is accurate, the abbé furnishes us his authority, and gives the details of the eight several instalments of which the grand total is composed.* This, it should be borne in mind, was entirely independent of all manner of royal grants and gifts of places and houses and lands, which had been flung, whenever asked for, into the lap of this frail beauty. Startling as this example of royal prodigality in the days of the decadence of the French monarchy may appear, it is nevertheless indisputable that the infatuated libertine who then controlled the destinies of France, by no means wanted the will to urge him on to still wilder schemes of extravagance. For instance, on one occasion, whilst visiting with his architect the costly pavilion of Louveciennes, lately erected for Madame Dubarry, he expressed his regret that he could not present her with a palace constructed entirely of gold and precious stones. Unable to realize this extravagant whim he resolved to bestow upon his mistress the most costly set of diamonds which could be collected throughout Europe. The result was the world-renowned Diamond Necklace.†

Louis XV. gave the commission to the crown jewellers, Böhmer and Bassenge, who entered heart and soul into

---

* " Histoire de la Décadence de la Monarchie Française," par l'Abbé Soulavie, vol. iii. p. 330.

† " Mémoires Historiques et Politiques du règne de Louis XVI." par l'Abbé Soulavie, vol. iii. p. 71.

the undertaking. The execution of so rare an order was of course an affair of time. Not only had the jewellers to raise funds to enable them to secure the largest and finest diamonds that were in the market, but they had to hunt out and employ the most skilful lapidaries to fashion them to their several shapes. Every important city in Europe, and others far more remote, were ransacked to collect these matchless gems. Some of the finest were met with in Germany, others in Spain, others again in Russia, a few in Brazil, and a very fine one indeed was picked up in the city of Hamburg. "But," says Carlyle, "to tell the various histories of these various diamonds, from the first making of them, or even omitting all the rest, from the first digging of them in far Indian mines.... How they served as eyes of heathen idols, and received worship; how they had then by fortune of war, or theft, been knocked out, and exchanged among camp-suttlers for a little spirituous liquor, and bought by Jews; and worn as signets on the fingers of tawny or white majesties; and again been lost, with the fingers too, and perhaps life (as by Charles the Rash among the mud ditches of Nancy), in old forgotten glorious victories; and so through innumerable varieties of fortune had come at last to the cutting-wheel of Böhmer, to be united in strange fellowship with comrades also blown together from all ends of the earth, each with a history of its own. Could these aged stones—the youngest of them six thousand years of age and upwards—but have spoken, there were an experience for philosophy to teach by. But now, as was said, by little caps of gold and daintiest rings of the same, they are all being, so to speak, enlisted under Böhmer's flag,—made to take rank and file in new order, no jewel asking his neighbour whence he came; and parade there for a season. For a season only, and then to disperse and enlist anew *ad infinitum*." *

For many of their purchases credit was taken by the crown jewellers for a limited period; for others, when they had exhausted their own capital, they were obliged to have recourse to their friends: but they were full of confidence, for two millions of francs—eighty thousand pounds sterling—was the sum fixed to be paid by the king for this jewel beyond price. The work went bravely on at the Böhmer and Bassenge establishment, "*Au Grand Balcon*," Rue Vendôme. The jewellers, their friends, their working lapidaries, their trustful creditors, were all in the highest spirits, when suddenly evil tidings flung dismay into the Böhmer and Bassenge camp. One day comes the intelligence that the king is ill; three days afterwards the news arrives that he is in danger; another week brings the report that he is dead, and the late favourite for whom the rich ornament was destined banished for ever beyond the precincts of the court.

* Carlyle's "Critical and Miscellaneous Essays," vol. iv. p. 8.

Alas! what was to be done now with the magnificent bauble commissioned by one who, at the time, spite of all his low grovelling debauchery, was nevertheless a king, but is now only so much corruption? Böhmer and Bassenge, crown jewellers, find themselves deeply involved; their creditors become clamorous, for their bills as they fall due are returned protested. They have nothing to fall back upon but the Diamond Necklace, which is worth, or at any rate valued at, two million francs. But where is a purchaser to be found for it? Böhmer and Bassenge, crown jewellers though they be, must still pay their debts. Kings, according to a certain fiction of state, never die. "*Le Roi est Mort! Vive le Roi!*" Böhmer and Bassenge, however, learn by sad experience not only that kings do die, but that creditors, alas, do not.

What is to be done? Only one course suggests itself. A young and lovely queen has just ascended the throne. Will it not be possible to induce her to become the purchaser of this unrivalled specimen of *bijouterie?* The office of crown jeweller carries with it the privilege of *entrée* to the presence of royalty at all times and seasons; while "other jewellers, and even innumerable gentlemen and small nobility, languish in the vestibule. With the costliest ornaments in his pockets, or borne after him by assiduous shopboys, the happy Böhmer sees high drawing-rooms and sacred *ruelles* fly open as with talismanic *sesame*, and the brightest eyes of the whole world grow brighter: to him alone of all men the Unapproachable reveals herself in mysterious *négligée*, taking and giving counsel."*

It was to Versailles that Böhmer betook himself, carrying with him the Diamond Necklace in its case of richest velvet, and ere many hours have elapsed he is displaying its matchless variegated brilliancy—its "flashes of star-rainbow colours" to the admiring gaze of the beauteous Marie-Antoinette, then just twenty years of age, of a gay and lively disposition, verging, some say, on to giddiness, yet perfectly innocent; fond of pleasure, and, like other fair young creatures in this world, not indifferent to those personal ornaments which help to enhance the charms which Nature has bestowed upon them with so liberal a hand. Still, pleased as she was with the gem, she nevertheless felt that the times were unpropitious; or else she scorned, may be, to wear an ornament, however beautiful, the original destination of which was, to say the least of it, unfortunate. But be this as it may, one thing is quite certain, the purchase of the Necklace was declined.

Thus in a moment, as it were, were dissipated all those fond hopes with which the crown jewellers had buoyed themselves up for many months past, and they were again constrained to ask each other, "what is now to be done?" Poor men, they were not to blame, for how

* Carlyle's "Critical and Miscellaneous Essays," vol. iv. p. 6.

could they foresee that their royal customer, full of health in November, 1773, when he gave the order, should be dead of small-pox on the 10th of May following? After several days spent in deliberation the partners decided that a drawing of the Necklace should be made and an engraving executed, and that printed copies of this should be sent to all the courts of Europe, to see whether a customer could not be obtained for a jewel which, ransack the entire world through, would be found without its equal.

This scheme, however, clever as it was, proved abortive; for what kind of idea could the cunningest graver and the most liquescent of printing inks possibly give of brilliants of the very finest water? The jewellers next resolved that one of the firm—Bassenge being the younger and more active was eventually fixed upon—should devote himself to travelling over Europe, and to visiting the various courts, where he might personally solicit the different empresses, queens, princesses, landgravines, margravines, electresses, infantas, and grand and arch-duchesses, to purchase this costly jewel, which only a neck flushing with the blood of royalty was worthy to wear. During this time Böhmer was to remain in Paris, to avail himself of any opportunity that might offer for reopening negotiations with Marie-Antoinette. One circumstance, however, rendered the prospect of success doubtful. The queen was already indebted to the crown jewellers in the sum of 348,000 livres, for a pair of diamond earrings, of which amount she had only been able to pay some 48,000.*

In this way several years went by. Shortly after the birth of Madame Royale, the Necklace was again offered to the queen, but although the reduced price of one million eight hundred thousand francs was named for it, there was a more serious obstacle than ever in the way of the purchase. France was at this period engaged in a war with England on behalf of the American Colonists, and her navy was in a most crippled condition. No sooner did the crown jeweller name the subject of the Necklace, than Marie-Antoinette interrupted him with this queen-like remark, " Monsieur, we have more need of men-of-war now than of diamonds."† What reply could a crown jeweller possibly make to so pertinent an observation as this? All he could do was to feel affronted, and affronted he accordingly felt; then hastily making his obeisances, he flung himself into the corner of his carriage, and set off down the long Avenue de Paris on his return to the Rue Vendôme in no very amiable mood.

---

* In the *livre rouge* of Louis XVI. under the date December, 1776, there is an entry, in the king's own hand, "Given to the queen 25,000 livres, the first payment of a sum of 300,000 livres which I have engaged to pay with interest to Böhmer in six years." —See Archives of the Empire.

† Correspondance secrète de la Cour de Louis XVI.

V.

1779–1780.

AT BAR-SUR-AUBE.—COURTSHIP AND MARRIAGE.

WHILE Monsieur Bassenge Calaphibus-like is wandering up and down Europe trying to dispose of the ill-fated Diamond Necklace, let us see what our heroine is doing now that she has freed herself from the restraints of a conventual life to launch forth into the great world with no one to direct, no one to control her. On leaving the abbey of Longchamp the two sisters decided upon making their way to Bar-sur-Aube, and embarked on board one of the Seine barges plying between Paris and Nogent, from which latter place they proceeded up the river Aube to their destination.* The youngest sister, it seems, was possessed with a certain longing to return to the place of her birth. Whether this arose from a feeling of vanity, a desire to show off before the simple rustics of Fontette, or whether love was the actuating principle—for she had left a sweetheart behind her

---

* "Mémoires du Comte Beugnot," vol. i. p. 9.

when she was summoned to Paris—is more than we can tell. Arrived at Bar-sur-Aube, our heroine informs us that she and her sister at once entered a convent, where many visitors called upon them, and invited them to a round of entertainments at which every one present vied with his neighbour as to who should pay them the greatest amount of attention. She even asserts that they received invitations from the different noble families in the neighbourhood, and, in pursuance of these, entered upon a series of visits varying from a few days to a week in extent. These over, we are told that a Madame de Suremont enticed them to board at her house, where they were "very elegantly entertained" for four hundred francs (sixteen pounds) per annum.*

Other accounts, which we believe to be more trustworthy, assert that the sisters arrived at Bar-sur-Aube with merely a few francs in their pockets, and a single change of linen beyond the clothes they had on, and that, instead of entering a convent, they put up at a miserable little inn called "*La Tête Rouge*," where they made good their footing by their high titles and the claims they set up to the manors of Essoyes, Fontette, and Verpilière, in the neighbourhood. The great expectations they announced soon became generally known in a small country town, and the consequence was that

---

* "Life of the Countess de la Motte, by herself," vol. i. p. 146, *et seq.*

the good people round about flocked to see them out of curiosity, and it was then that Madame de Suremont, touched by their distress, offered the fugitives the use of her house for a few days until they could manage to provide some other lodging for themselves.

On retiring for the night their hostess, a very stout lady, kindly lent them two of her own dresses to wear, observing, however, that she was afraid they would be too large to fit them. What was Madame de Suremont's astonishment to see her young guests enter the sitting-room the following morning with the dresses, which they had spent the night in cutting and adapting to their own slim figures, fitting them to perfection! Instead, too, of stopping merely a week at this hospitable house, according to the terms of their invitation, the Mademoiselles de Valois managed to remain in it for twelve months, flirting with all the young fellows who visited there, and exhibiting more levity and freedom than was becoming to their sex.* The ladies, naturally enough, all shrank aghast from this bold behaviour, but the gentlemen were more or less amused at it.

In due course several of these young fellows became smitten with our heroine, and amongst those who contested for the honour of her smiles were two who stood out in advance of the rest. One was M. Beugnot, the writer of the Memoirs we have been quoting, and son of

* " Mémoires du Comte Beugnot," vol. i. p. 10, *et seq.*

a well-to-do citizen of Bar-sur-Aube, who was so alarmed at the mere idea of having Mademoiselle de Valois for a daughter-in-law that he packed off his son to Paris to study law, politics, and human nature, which he did to such good purpose as to escape the guillotine, and get created a councillor of state and a count by Napoleon, by whom he was appointed administrator of one of the Rhine provinces. At the Restoration he was named *ad interim* minister of the interior, then minister of police, next minister of marine, afterwards postmaster-general, and finally director-general of the administration of finances; and was altogether so eager a place-hunter, that a pamphleteer of the time said of him that he would have hired himself out to the plague if the plague only gave pensions. The other was M. de la Motte, a nephew of Madame de Suremont's, and son of a chevalier of St. Louis who was killed at the battle of Minden. This young gentleman, an officer, or as Madame Campan and the Abbé Georgel say, a private in the *gendarmerie*, and destitute of any fortune whatever, had already managed to involve himself deeply in debt. Previous to the Revolution the *gendarmerie*, very different from the force now known by that name, was the first cavalry regiment in France, and the usual refuge for young men of good family but poor estate.

Let us hear what the lady herself has to say respecting this young man (who had only his sword with which to cut his way to fortune), and his pretensions to be considered the accepted suitor of a descendant of the royal house of Valois.

"Amongst many other species of amusement, we frequently performed comedies, in one of which I engaged to take a part. M. de la Motte, an officer in the gendarmes, and nephew of Madame de Suremont, being on a visit to Bar-sur-Aube, acquired great reputation for his performance, and became remarked for his assiduity and attention to please. The part of a valet was assigned to him, and that of a waiting-maid to me. We divided the applause of the company, for having, as they pleased to express, sustained our characters with so much propriety.

"From the moment of our first interview M. de la Motte paid me very pointed attention. He eagerly seized every opportunity of showing me how solicitous he was to please. His compliments were not glaring, but of that delicate nature which could only proceed from the genuine dictates of an honest heart. Elegant in person and manners, insinuating in address, the honourable intention which he manifested could not prove disagreeable to me. I listened, and, what is, I believe, generally the consequence where any of our sex listen to the persuasions of youth, elegance and accomplishments in the other, was not at a great distance from loving him.

"Madame de Suremont perceived the growing attachment of her nephew, and afforded him every opportunity of urging his suit. She frequently left us together when the company were gone, engaging M. de la Motte to remain and write out my parts, and give me instructions in acting them.

"I will ingenuously confess that I loved M. de la Motte. He possessed a sincerity of heart, seldom to be found excepting in the country, blended with those polished manners which mark the *habitué* of the metropolis. He seized every opportunity of rendering himself agreeable, and I had every reason to suppose he entertained favourable sentiments towards me, at least I wished so, and the gradation is so natural that it will not appear strange if I believed it.

"M. de la Motte, I had remarked for some days, appeared thoughtful and melancholy; but as he had never communicated to me the cause, though I was uneasy at the effect of it, I forebore to make inquiry. He advised me to go to Paris to see my brother, and to make known his pretensions to the marchioness, my worthy mother, and endeavour to obtain her consent to our union. Fearful that breaking this matter suddenly to the marchioness, after having carried it on so far without her knowledge, might give her offence, I hesitated some time ere I could form a resolution to acquaint her; but, trusting to her goodness, I at length yielded to his arguments in favour of a determination which was also consonant to the dictates of my own heart.

"When I had resolved on a journey to Paris, which highly gratified M. de la Motte, I at once wrote a letter to Madame de Boulainvilliers, informing her that having heard of my brother's arrival, and being anxious to see him, I should be at Paris the Saturday following by eight o'clock. The interval was occupied by M. de la Motte in giving me directions for my behaviour, and earnestly pressing me to return as soon as possible, and complete his happiness by the celebration of our nuptials. Not a single person in the house, not even my sister, was acquainted with what was in agitation. The attentions of M. de la Motte had long been observed, but our marriage was whispered of only as a conjecture.

"On the Wednesday following, about three in the morning, I set off in the diligence, and after a very tedious and disagreeable journey, over roads which at once prove the neglect of the government and the patience of the people, I arrived near Paris, and found Julia, the marchioness's first woman, waiting with a coach at the Porte Saint-Antoine. I was not a little pleased at being so near the end of my journey, and felt no regret at quitting my disagreeable vehicle for the one which conveyed me to the Hôtel de Boulainvilliers.

"I was impatient to see my brother, but I was disappointed; he had received orders to join his squadron at Brest. Madame de Boulainvilliers received me with that cordiality and affection with which the tenderest of mothers would receive her daughter after a long absence.

She told me that my brother would not have written to inform me of his arrival if it could have been foreseen how soon he was to depart. This information gave me much uneasiness, which Madame de Boulainvilliers used the utmost assiduity to dissipate.

"The evening was occupied by many questions which the marchioness asked me relative to Bar-sur-Aube, concerning our reception and the diversions and entertainments of the place. I took advantage of this opportunity to mention the comedy. I perceived, from a sign she made to Madame de Tonneres, her daughter, that she had some private correspondent in that place, who had informed her of more than I knew, and that the information I had to give was by no means novel. This did not a little surprise me.

"A day or two after they resumed the topic, and Madame de Tonneres asked me what character I played. I told her that of a waiting-maid. She seemed surprised that I should choose a part like that, when there were many others for which I was much better adapted. 'But who,' said Madame de Boulainvilliers, 'was the young man who played the part of Jasmin? Is he a young man? Pray how old is he?' I could not well comprehend the drift of these questions, which, nevertheless, I found myself constrained to answer. 'He is a young gentleman,' I replied, 'who has a commission in the gendarmes,' and I then proceeded to give them information respecting his family. 'And what do you think of him?' 'That he has a pleasing address, is much of a gentleman, and has received a very good education; understands music, and dances to perfection: everybody gives him the credit of being a very accomplished young man, and all admit that he played his character like an experienced actor.' Perceiving me growing warm in my encomiums, the marchioness smiled. Her daughter observed it, and they exchanged some very significant glances with each other, and then, to avoid giving me any suspicions, changed the subject of the conversation.

"On another occasion Madame de Tonneres, with whom I was frequently left alone, examined me yet more closely respecting M. de la Motte. 'What!' inquired she, in a tone of raillery, 'did this presumptuous wretch ever aspire to be your husband?' 'Oh, yes! he proposed demanding me in marriage through his mother, at the same time informing me of his fortune and expectations.' 'And what answer did you make, my dear?' 'That I would beg Madame de Boulainvilliers to give her consent,' replied I. 'But did you give no promise of your own accord, and are you really partial to him?' I answered these questions in the affirmative. 'Well, then, my dear,' replied she, 'from your approbation, I will believe him worthy of your love.' 'Then do me the favour,' replied I, 'to represent my affections to my dear mother, at some convenient opportunity when I am not present; and you may, if you please, inform her, at the same time, that M. de la Luzerne, bishop of Langres, can give her every information of the family, with which he is well acquainted: indeed, he has been requested by the mother of M. de la Motte to demand me in marriage.' The result was that Madame de Tonneres kindly undertook my cause with the marchioness, who, having my happiness at heart, wished me, in a matter which could but once be resolved on, to take time for deliberation.

"Though Madame de Boulainvilliers seemed rather to dissuade me from my purpose than consent to its accomplishment, she nevertheless consented to write to the Bishop of Langres, who the very next evening paid her a visit. As soon as he arrived I made my obedience and retired, leaving him and the marchioness to their private conference.

"I was in no small degree of anxiety to learn the result of a negotiation to me of such importance, yet was at a loss of whom to inquire. The next morning I was relieved from suspense, for I received a letter from the reverend prelate, informing me of their conversation the evening before. He gave me some hopes of obtaining the consent of the marchioness, and this was all; as for the marquis, he positively refused his consent to the match.

"In a few days I departed for Bar-sur-Aube: my regret at parting with the marchioness was increased by my having to return home without obtaining her consent to our marriage, which, though the express object of my journey, I could not consistently with delicacy or duty press any further, lest I should appear too precipitately to reject the prudent advice she had given me.

" My return to Bar-sur-Aube was much more agreeable than my journey to Paris. I had written to my sister and M. de la Motte to apprise them of it, and was met by them about two leagues from Bar-sur-Aube, at a beautiful seat, the residence of M. de la Motte's mother.

" The news of my departure, and the intent of my journey, had transpired and extended to the village; every one spoke of my marriage with M. de la Motte. It was whispered that Mademoiselle de Valois was returned with the consent of her brother and Madame de Boulainvilliers to solemnize this marriage; all welcomed me with as much pleasure as if, instead of a week, I had been absent a year.

" M. de la Motte received me with heartfelt satisfaction, but his countenance seemed to speak a degree of anxiety; he feared that it was the intention of Madame de Boulainvilliers to have married me to some other husband, and trembled for the success of my embassy: he read in my looks that all was not as it should be, while the words which dropped from Madame de Boulainvilliers made me doubtful whether I should be able to obtain her consent. The uneasiness which on this account overspread my countenance was intelligible only to M. de la Motte, by whose advice I was prevailed upon to take the only steps prudence dictated in so delicate and embarrassing a position.

"My pen was the instrument by which I disclosed a secret my timidity could never suffer my tongue to discover; I immediately wrote to Madame de Boulainvilliers three successive letters, entreating her to compassionate my distress, and to let her consent grace our union. I also wrote to the Bishop of Langres, asking that worthy prelate, who before had done me signal service, to intercede with the marchioness in my behalf. The intercession of the bishop I was confident would have its due weight, and indeed it at length produced that consent so essential to my future happiness.

"The approbation of Madame de Boulainvilliers having now given a sanction to our proceedings, an early day was appointed, by the advice of the friends of M. de la Motte, for the celebration of our nuptials, which took place, according to the custom of the province, at midnight on the 6th of June, 1780.

"The day after our marriage a grand dinner was given by Madame de Suremont. The entertainment was profusely elegant. There were two tables, one in the antechamber, and the other in the dining-room. Every apartment was open and very soon crowded; the health of the bride was an apology for drinking wine as though it had been water. When the company quitted the table, all were desirous to salute and wish me joy. The remainder of the day was spent in dancing.

"The banns of marriage had been published at Fontette, which made the peasants of that place curious to know the day. They came in great numbers to Bar-sur-Aube, with the intention of witnessing the ceremony, and remained there some days. Amongst them was a young peasant, a comely young fellow, who came to Madame de Suremont and inquired bluntly for Mademoiselle Filliette, a name by which my sister had formerly been known in the country. 'I know no such person,' replied she: 'who do you mean by Mademoiselle Filliette?' 'Why, madame,' replied the clown, 'the sister of mademoiselle who is just married. Please tell her I am Colas, of Fontette; she will recollect me.'

"Madame de Suremont communicated this to my sister, who, out of compassion for the unfortunate rustic, refused to see him lest such an interview should make him more unhappy. Durand, indeed, to detain my sister in the country, had promised her in marriage to this peasant, whose appearance was greatly in his favour, but the recognition of her birth by the people in the neighbourhood had kindled in the bosom of Marianne hopes of an alliance more consonant to her ideas, more consistent with her present station. Far from despising this poor creature, she wished to avoid giving him pain. She begged me, therefore, to speak to him: I did so.

'Good day, my dear friend,' said I, 'what are your commands for my sister?' 'I wish, madame,' replied he, 'to have the honour of paying my respects to her. She is of the same age, we have stood sponsors together, and M. Durand, her godfather, promised me that I should marry her. But her fortune is changed; she is now Mademoiselle de Valois; and I am not quite such a fool as to think that she will have me for her husband, as she is descended from the blood-royal; but I wish to have the pleasure of seeing her in her fine clothes, for I am sure,' continued he, bursting into tears, 'she is very handsome!'* I could not help shedding a tear of pity for this honest rustic. His grief, however, was not to be alleviated; the presence of my sister would but have increased his misery; at least she thought so, and could not be prevailed upon to see him. Finding himself without hope, he went home again, murmuring at what he termed the false-heartedness of his mistress.

"Some few days after I accompanied my sister to Fontette, where, it being Sunday, we went to mass. All the peasants rose from their seats at our entrance, and desired the curate should do us honour, as the children of the Baron de Saint-Remi their late lord. We received the holy water and the consecrated bread in the seat of honour; the bells were rung, and every one testi-

* M. Beugnot says Mademoiselle de Saint-Remi was a fat, handsome girl, extremely fair, and very dull and stupid, with just sufficient instinct to divine that she was a great lady.

fied their joy on our arrival. They crowded about the house where we were staying; we ordered them six livres a-piece, for which they testified their gratitude by drinking our healths, and the health of the Baron de Saint-Remi de Valois, and his safe return. They then conducted me to the mansion of my ancestors, and round the grounds of the patrimonial estate. This mansion, this noble estate, thought I to myself, might have been possessed by the descendants of those who acquired it by valour,* and enjoyed it with hospitality. I lamented the ravages of luxury: I thought of the credulity and easy temper of my father, who sacrificed everything to the extravagance of his wife. Had it not been for these he might have sustained the dignity of his ancestors, and his miserable offspring have maintained that position to which they were by birth entitled." †

To provide herself with a suitable *trousseau*, Mademoiselle de Valois had been obliged to raise one thousand francs on a mortgage of her pension for two years; while, to defray the expenses incident to the wedding, M. de la Motte, on his part, sold for six hundred francs a horse and cabriolet which he had only bought a

---

* Acquired it rather by the accident of being born bastard offspring of a king.

† "Life of the Countess de la Motte, by herself," vol. i. p. 151, *et seq.* The reader must take this glowing description of the wedding and what transpired subsequently at Fontette, subject to large allowances for Madame de la Motte's habitual exaggeration, to make use of no stronger term.

short time previously on credit at Lunéville, where his corps was doing garrison duty.*

We will close this chapter with a pair of portraits of Monsieur and Madame de la Motte, which their friend Beugnot has sketched for our benefit. "M. de la Motte," observes his rival, "was an ugly man, but well formed and skilled in all bodily exercises, and, despite his ugliness, the expression of his face was amiable and mild. He did not exactly lack talent, still what he possessed was frittered away on trifles. Destitute of all fortune, he was clever enough to get head over ears in debt, and only lived by his wits and the trifling allowance of three hundred francs a year which his uncle, M. de Suremont, was obliged to make him to enable him to retain his position in the gendarmerie."

With regard to Madame de la Motte, Beugnot says: "She was not exactly handsome, was short in stature, slender, and well formed. Her blue eyes were full of expression and over-arched with black eyebrows; her face rather long; her mouth wide, but adorned with fine teeth, and, what is the greatest attraction in such a face as hers, her smile was enchanting. She had a pretty hand, a very small foot, and a complexion of dazzling whiteness. When she spoke her mind exhibited no sign of acquired knowledge, but she had much natural intelligence, and a quick and penetrating under-

* "Mémoires du Comte Beugnot," vol. i. p. 16.

standing. Engaged in a perpetual conflict with society from the time of her birth, she had learned to disdain its laws, and had but little respect for those of morality."

M. Beugnot adds the following anecdote:

"When I returned home that evening my father mentioned to me that fifteen or twenty years previously, whenever he went to collect his rents in the parish of Essoyes, the curé of Fontette never failed to tax his purse for the poor children of Jacques de Saint-Remi, who were huddled together in a dilapidated hovel with a trap-hole in front, through which soup, vegetables, broken victuals, and other charitable doles were passed by the neighbours." *

* "Mémoires du Comte Beugnot," vol. i. pp. 11, 14.

VI.

1780–1782.

COUNTESS DE LA MOTTE.—IN BARRACKS AT LUNÉVILLE.—ON A FIFTH FLOOR IN PARIS.—ENSNARES THE GRAND ALMONER.

FROM the day of her marriage, in the summer of 1780, our heroine assumed the title of Countess de Valois de la Motte, though on ordinary occasions she dropped the former portion of it, retaining only the name of De la Motte, by which she afterwards became so notorious. The wedding did not take place a day too soon, for in the course of the same or following month the countess gave birth to male twins, that died a few days afterwards; upon which occurrence Madame de Suremont, glad of an excuse for getting rid of her new relation—the old lady used to say to Beugnot that "the most unhappy year of her life was the one she spent in the society of this demon"—turned the newly-married couple out of her house.* They took refuge for a time with

* "Mémoires du Comte Beugnot," vol. i. p. 13. Rétaux de Villette, one of the countess's many lovers, and of whom we shall by-and-

Madame de la Tour, a married sister of the count's—the young gendarme, following the example of his wife, had likewise assumed a title—but were finally obliged to rely on their own resources, which, as may be supposed, were of the narrowest. De la Motte himself had nothing but his sword, and the countess had not even her scanty pension to depend upon. Now commenced with them that life of shifts and expedients, which is certain in the long run to disappoint those who are unhappily reduced to enter upon it, which dissolves the principles and destroys the best of habits of even the firmest characters, and too frequently ultimately terminates in crime. By borrowing money from friends and neighbours so long as they were disposed to lend it, by occasional loans from money-lenders at exorbitant rates of interest, by running into debt with the tradespeople, and by certain small bounties received from Paris, to assist the descendants of Henri II., in answer

---

by have occasion to speak, professes to have heard the story of the countess's numerous *liaisons* from her own lips. He says that the reprobate Marquis de Boulainvilliers succeeded in seducing both the countess and her sister, and that the former was moreover *enceinte* by the Bishop of Langres at the time of her marriage with M. de la Motte, which is the reason why this "worthy prelate," as the countess styles him, interested himself in hastening forward the ceremony. This may seem a startling statement, but those who are aware of the extreme immorality which pervaded the upper classes of French society at this period, and especially the clerical section of it, will have no difficulty in believing it.—See "Mémoire Historique des Intrigues de la Cour," etc. par Rétaux de Villette, p. 4, *et seq.*, also *post*, p. 53.

to letters of supplication written by the countess, the newly-married couple dragged on as best they could.

The count's leave of absence having at length expired, he was summoned back to garrison duty at Lunéville, a dull, decaying, fortified town, composed of straight streets and regular buildings, where in subsequent years the treaty of peace between France and Austria was signed, which gave to the former the coveted frontier of the Rhine. The palace built by Philip, duke of Lorraine, grandfather of Marie-Antoinette, was then, as now, a *caserne de cavalerie*, and it was to this barrack that Count de la Motte took his wife to share with him his incommodious quarters. Here madame's "lively complexion" and "excess of vivacity," as she styles them, were not long in exercising their sway over the more susceptible of her husband's comrades. In September of the following year the count and his wife had determined upon proceeding to Paris to urge the Marchioness de Boulainvilliers to interest herself in their behalf, a project which was knocked on the head by the count's commanding officer, the Marquis d'Autichamp, whose too familiar intimacy with Madame de la Motte was the talk not merely of the corps, but of the town,* and who had himself contemplated escorting madame on her journey

---

* "Mémoire Historique des Intrigues de la Cour," etc. par Rétaux de Villette, p. 5. Villette was in the same corps as Count de la Motte, and on duty at Lunéville at the time we are speaking of.

to the capital, peremptorily refusing the count any further leave of absence. Just at this time intelligence reached the De la Mottes that the Marquis and Marchioness de Boulainvilliers were at Strasbourg, only some threescore miles or so away. Commanding-officer d'Autichamp, we suppose, relents; for the count gets a few days' leave, and to Strasbourg the pair hasten as fast as a French diligence of the eighteenth century will carry them, which is, however, not fast enough, for on their arrival they learn from the great charlatan of the age, Count Cagliostro, who just then happens to be showing off in the capital of Alsace, that the Marquis and Marchioness de Boulainvilliers have departed for Cardinal Prince Louis de Rohan's palace at Saverne. There was nothing else but to give chase, so off the De la Mottes start, and on their arrival in the vicinity of the episcopal château, put up at some little inn, whence the countess writes to Madame de Boulainvilliers, apprising her that she is in the neighbourhood, and asking when she may be permitted to call upon her. The next day she is honoured by a visit from the marquis, who escorts her over to his wife. Some few days afterwards, while the marchioness and madame are taking a carriage drive together, they meet the Cardinal de Rohan, Grand Almoner of France, to whom Madame de Boulainvilliers introduces her *protégée*, and strongly recommends her to this powerful prelate's kindly notice.*

* "Premier Interrogatoire du Cardinal de Rohan."

On her return home to barrack quarters, if home indeed they could be called, the countess harped, day by day, upon her fancied claims to the three estates that formerly belonged to her family, and no wonder if she at length came to the conclusion that Paris and Versailles, rather than a dull garrison town like Lunéville, were the proper spheres for her enterprise and ambition. To Paris, therefore, she resolved to go; but, alas! how was she to obtain the means of defraying the expenses of her journey and of her sojourn in the capital? Commanding-officer d'Autichamp would willingly escort her there, and pay all travelling expenses, but her husband cannot be brought to consent. Fortunately for the countess, one of her Bar-sur-Aube friends—the father of the M. Beugnot, of whom we have already spoken—came to the rescue with a loan of one thousand francs, and to her honour it may be recorded, that whenever afterwards she spoke of this service she was always much moved, and, what is perhaps more to her credit, during the period of her dishonest prosperity she paid the money, as she paid all the debts she had contracted at Bar-sur-Aube, her adopted home. However corrupt her general character may have been, she was certainly not wanting in gratitude.

This thousand francs she and her husband divided equally between them, and they then set forth in different directions, it is true, but still with the same object at heart, namely, to procure the restitution of the Saint-Remi estates. The countess went to Paris to press her claims on the attention of those in power. The count resigned his post in the gendarmerie, never to do, from that hour forward, another day of honest work during the remainder of his long life, and betook himself to Fontette to search for evidence on the spot, and to ascertain the exact nature of the steps requisite to be taken to recover possession of this and the adjacent Saint-Remi domains. Arrived at his destination, he caused a *Te Deum* to be chanted in the church, and, as the congregation were leaving, scattered handsful of five-franc pieces among the gaping crowd, who, on experiencing this mark of favour, did not hesitate to hail him as their lord; and lord of Fontette he was by courtesy so long as his money lasted, which, unfortunately for the rustics of the place, was not long. The last franc dissipated, the count was only too glad to get back again to Bar-sur-Aube to such a home as his sister was able to offer him.*

The countess, on her part, so soon as she arrived in Paris, proceeded to set to work. She wrote at once to young Beugnot, who was then prosecuting his legal studies in the capital, informing him that she had a letter for him from his father, and asking him to call upon her. Beugnot lost no time in complying with her request, and found the purport of the letter was to urge

* "Mémoires du Comte Beugnot," vol. i. pp. 17, 19.

him thoroughly to examine the countess's claims to the Fontette, Essoyes, and other estates, and see if there was any real foundation for them. "I took the affair," says Beugnot, "seriously in hand as my father desired me, and readily enough found the letters patent of Henri II. which conferred the domains in question on his natural son, but I could not trace the various acts diverting the possession of them from the Saint-Remis into the hands of those different proprietors who were in nowise connected with the family. One of the latest of these, a M. Orceau de Fontette, superintendent of Caen, had exchanged the lands held by him with the king. This was a favourable circumstance for us in the prosecution of our claim, as the king had only to forego his hold upon the property to restore to the Saint-Remis one of the possessions of their forefathers."*

The young lawyer now proceeded to compose a "Mémoire," wherein, in true French style, he spoke of his client's case as "one more insult of fortune to the Valois, the hard lot of a branch detached from that ancient tree which had so long covered with its royal shade France and other European states. I interspersed my composition," says Beugnot, "with those philosophical reflections then so much in fashion, and asked the Bourbons to pay the natural debt of those from whom they had received so magnificent a heritage.

* "Mémoires du Comte Beugnot," vol. i. p. 18.

I submitted my composition to M. Elie de Beaumont, a celebrated advocate, and also a man of taste. 'It is a pity,' remarked he, 'that we cannot bring this business before the Parliament; it would make your reputation.' Alas! I did not even receive for my labour the honours of print. People said it was entirely a matter for the royal favour, and that to print the 'Mémoire' would be contrary to the respect due to the king."* Beugnot thereupon composed a new "Mémoire," or rather petition to the crown, which was in due course presented, though without producing the result which the sanguine expectations of the countess and her advocate anticipated from it.

Early in November, 1781, either by previous invitation from the marchioness or of her own accord, Madame de la Motte presented herself at the Hôtel de Boulainvilliers, bent upon jogging the marchioness's memory with reference to a commission in the dragoons which she had made a half promise to obtain for the count, her husband, and intending to say a few words respecting her own claim to the Saint-Remi estates, when, to her surprise and grief, she found her benefactress lying dangerously ill. She remained and tended her until her death, which took place in about three weeks; yet, strange to say, she was unable to forego her passion for intrigue even at a time like this, for she admits, while

* " Mémoires du Comte Beugnot," vol. i. p. 20.

the marchioness was lying past hope of recovery, having had a *tête-à-tête* interview with the marquis, on the length of which she was rallied by the gentlemen staying at the hôtel. During this interview the marquis, she tells us, made her "a downright proposal" to the effect that on his wife's death she should reside with him as his mistress, he engaging to procure for her husband a post in some regiment which should "prevent him from troubling them too often." All this she calmly listened to, and when the marchioness was dead still continued to reside under the same roof with the man who had made this disgraceful proposition to her, exposed, as she herself admits, to his daily persecutions. The old reprobate, too, was always upbraiding her, she says, with "loving other men better than him," and openly accused her of carrying on an intrigue beneath his roof with the old Bishop of Langres, who visited her much more frequently than he thought necessary or prudent.

After a while the count, who has been rusticating ever since his Fontette expedition at Bar-sur-Aube, turns up at the Boulainvilliers Hôtel to look after his wife, when the marquis, in revenge, as madame says, for the contempt with which she invariably treated him, endeavoured to arouse the jealousy of her husband by accusing her—falsely, of course—with being too intimate with his son-in-law, and of sundry unbecoming familiarities with the count's cousin, who had pawned his watch to defray the expense of a three-days' frolic with the countess at Versailles; but Count de la Motte, according to his wife, "had too much good sense to give any credit to these insinuations; he listened attentively, but did not believe a single iota." *

While the countess was residing under the Boulainvilliers roof she was constantly on the look-out to push her own or her husband's fortunes, and eventually succeeded in talking over the Baron de Crussol, son-in-law of the Marquis de Boulainvilliers, to procure M. de la Motte a post in the Count d'Artois's bodyguard. This necessitated the count's removal to Versailles; so, turning their backs on the Boulainvilliers Hôtel, where the marquis had for some time past adopted an unpleasant system of retrenchment in order to bring madame to "his way of thinking"—in other words, had placed the descendant of the house of Valois and her tall and hungry spouse on exceedingly short commons—the pair went forth in search of whatever Fortune might please to send them.

From certain hints dropped by the countess it is evident that she had grown disgusted with the avarice and meanness rather than with what she calls the " detested attentions " of the marquis, who, had he only loosened his purse-strings, and dispensed his bounty with a liberal hand, had been looked upon favourably

* "Life of the Countess de la Motte, by herself," vol. i. pp. 189, 191, 204.

enough, and possibly had been the means of saving Cardinal Prince de Rohan from getting entangled in the countess's toils.

It is not to be supposed that at this epoch of her career Madame de la Motte had forgotten her introduction to this prelate, or that she omitted to remind him of it, and of Madame de Boulainvilliers' recommendation of her to his notice and sympathy. Was he not, in fact, Grand Almoner of France, and, by virtue of his office, dispenser of the king's and a nation's bounties? and humiliating though she might pretend it to be for one who had the blood of the Valois in her veins to have to appeal to the servant of the sovereign instead of to the throne itself, the pill, if a trifle bitter, must nevertheless be swallowed.

Cardinal Prince Louis de Rohan, at this time in his eight-and-fortieth year, is described as a tall, portly, handsome-looking man, with a slightly ruddy complexion, bald forehead, and almost white hair. There was a noble and easy bearing about him,[*] and his manners are said to have been singularly agreeable so long as he kept his temper, of late grown exceedingly choleric, under restraint. He was weak and vain, and credulous to a degree; anything but devout, and mad after women.[†] Unrestricted by his priestly office, he led a

---

[*] "Mémoire pour Bette d'Etienville."
[†] "Mémoires de la Baronne d'Oberkirche," vol. i. p. 127.

notoriously dissolute life; still, he was generally regarded as a good-enough sort of man so far as little acts of kindness and generosity were concerned. It is not to be wondered at, therefore, that he responded favourably to the countess's first and second appeals. This gave her hope; and, the better to profit by the grand almoner's liberality, and to secure his influence in support of her claims, she took an apartment in Paris during the summer of 1782 within a short distance of his hôtel. It was a poor sort of a lodging, consisting merely of two ill-furnished rooms on the topmost *étage* at the Hôtel de Reims, in the Rue de la Verrerie, a narrow, ill-paved, irregularly-built street—devoted at the present day, not to glass factories or warehouses, as its name would lead one to imply, but to grocery, and soap and candle and dried fruit stores, and locksmiths' shops, every one of which hangs out its monster red or golden key by way of sign—running from the Rue des Lombards into the Rue de Bercy, which intersects the Rue Vieille-du-Temple, where the Hôtel de Strasbourg, or Palais-Cardinal, as it was sometimes called, was situated, and in which for the moment all the countess's hopes are centred.

This hôtel, built in the year 1712 by Cardinal Constantine de Rohan, uncle of the grand almoner, on a portion of the gardens of the Hôtel de Soubise, is now the Imperial Printing Office, and internally retains no traces of what it was when Prince Louis de Rohan lived here in state befitting the dignity of a prince of the German empire and a cardinal of the Holy Roman Church. The entrance gateway and the buildings forming the external boundaries of the court in front of the hôtel are, with the exception of some evident alterations, much the same as they were in the days when the Countess de la Motte was a frequent visitor at the Palais-Cardinal. The court itself is divided by parallel ranges of buildings at right angles with the principal front, and a gateway on the right-hand side leads to what was evidently the stable-court, where a noble bas-relief by Couston, representing the watering of the horses of the sun, with the animals full life-size, may be seen over one of the arched entrances to the stables—those stables where the horse of one of the cardinal's heyducs dropped down dead on a memorable occasion of which we shall by-and-by have to speak. The façade of the hôtel has undergone only some slight alteration since the cardinal's time, but it is not so with the interior; the grand staircase has been removed, and the magnificent *salons de réception* have been converted into *bureaux* for the officials attached to the imperial printing establishment. In the principal waiting-room are four paintings by Boucher, said to have formed part of the original decorations of the Palais-Cardinal: one represents Mars attiring for the wars, with Venus holding his shield and Cupid handing him his helmet; another shows Mars reposing, with Venus, who looks wonderfully like a French marchioness of the eighteenth century, with even a scantier allowance of drapery than usual, reclining beside him on a cloud; a third represents Juno with her peacock, the immortal Jove facing her, and Boreas and Æolus at his feet, blowing as though they would burst; while in the fourth subject we have Neptune ruling the waves with his trident, and a trio of sea-gods spurting water out of long horn-shaped shells.

The garden front of the Palais-Cardinal is far more elegant than the one which looks upon the court; it is decorated with lofty columns surmounted with enriched capitals, and with sundry emblems and the armorial bearings of the house of Rohan sculptured on the projections of the façade. Only a small portion of the palace garden now remains to it, the chief part having been covered over with long ranges of offices in which the workmen attached to the imperial printing establishment ply their several callings.

The Countess de la Motte was woman of the world enough to know that much may be accomplished by personal solicitation when written applications are of little or no avail. The Cardinal de Rohan too had a reputation for gallantry; and as for the countess herself, she tells us in her "Memoirs" that "her face, if not exactly handsome, had a certain piquancy about it which, combined with her vivacity (Beugnot admits her smile was perfectly enchanting), supplied in her the want of beauty so far as to lay her open to the importunities of designing men." She therefore sought an audience of the grand almoner, and, finding that this would be accorded her, called upon young Beugnot the day before to beg three things of him—his carriage, his servant to follow her, and himself to accompany her. "All these," said she, "are indispensable, since there are only two good ways of asking alms—at the church door, and in a carriage." "I did not," observes Beugnot, "raise any difficulties as to the first two points, but I peremptorily refused my arm, as I could only have presented myself with her before the Cardinal de Rohan in the character of her advocate, after his eminence had been warned of my coming, and had given his permission."* Madame was, therefore, constrained to present herself at the cardinal's hôtel without any other escort beyond the footman lent to her by her friend.

At the first interview Madame de la Motte had with the cardinal, the latter, as might have been expected from his well-known character for gallantry, proved incapable of resisting the countess's artful allurements, and she, bent on completing the conquest which she felt she had made, on the occasion of subsequent visits to the Hôtel de Strasbourg, dressed herself out in the most coquettish style, and made the air of its magnificent saloons redolent with the odour of her perfumes.†

* "Mémoires du Comte Beugnot," vol. i. pp. 21, 22.
† "Mémoire Historique des Intrigues de la Cour," etc., par Rétaux de Villette, p. 10.

VII.

1783.

OSCILLATES BETWEEN PARIS AND VERSAILLES.—SENDS OUT BEGGING LETTERS AND PETITIONS.—FAINTS IN MADAME'S SALLE D'ATTENTE.—DESPAIR.

AT the time the countess was engaged in setting her snares for the Cardinal de Rohan, she dined one day with our young Bar-sur-Aube advocate, who saw that she was in most excellent spirits, which, every now and then, exhaled in malicious remarks respecting their common acquaintances. "I tried in vain," says Beugnot, "to lead her to more serious talk. Irritated at last, I threatened to abandon her entirely to her folly. She answered me gaily that she no longer had need of me. My brow contracted; she saw that she was likely to lose me, and took the trouble to explain to me that I had been exceedingly useful to her in unravelling the particulars of her claim, in composing 'mémoires' and petitions for her—in a word, in all the duties of an advocate—but that she had now arrived at a point where she required counsel of a different kind. She wanted some one who could point out to her the way of getting at the queen and the *contrôleur-général*—who knew equally well what was necessary to be done as to leave undone—in a word, one who was alike capable of concocting a good intrigue, and of carrying it successfully through. It was necessary that I should now hear from her lips, without making an ugly grimace with my own, that in an affair of this kind she looked upon me as the most foolish of men; she had, indeed, already taken several steps without asking my advice. Her husband's condition, she went on to say, was one of ridicule to all the world, and consequently an obstacle to her advancement. She had made him enter as supernumerary into the Count d'Artois' body-guard, which would give him a sort of standing, which the gendarmerie did not. She had found means, moreover, to get him to Versailles to perform his duties there, and where, at least, he would not be so sorry a sight as he was in the country. She observed that she was about to reside at Versailles herself, in order to secure an opportunity of getting at the queen, and of interesting her majesty in her favour. This was the first time," remarks Beugnot, "that she pronounced the name of her sovereign in my presence."[*]

At Versailles, which at this period was crowded with intriguers and adventurers, living for the most part by their wits, the countess resided, first of all with the widow Bourgeois, in the Place Dauphine, whence

---

[*] "Mémoires du Comte Beugnot," vol. i. pp. 25, 26.

she speedily removed to the Hôtel de Jouy, in the Rue des Récollets, a long narrow street leading on to the immense Place d'Armes, in front of the château. Some of its houses—built in strict accordance with the edict promulgated by the *grand monarque* at the time a new Versailles was springing up in the neighbourhood of his vast palace, namely, only a single storey high, with attics, and roofed with slate—evidently date back to the days of Louis XIV. The Hôtel de Jouy, where the countess had her quarters, is now an ordinary dwelling-house, lofty and narrow, with a certain air of respectability about it, situated at the far end of the street (No. 23),* in an opposite direction to the château.

Having next to nothing to live upon, it is not to be wondered at that the De la Mottes were soon deeply in debt. The countess, it is true, converted her apartment into a kind of office, whence she periodically sent forth letters of supplication to the nobility for relief, and petitions to the crown praying for the restoration of the Saint-Remi domains, but, although she urged her suit with audacious pertinacity, the result seems to have fallen far short of her expectations. Fortunately for her there was always the Cardinal de Rohan to fall back upon, and the snares which she laid for him appear to have been set to some purpose, for, ere six months had gone by, Madame de la Motte had so far

---

* " Histoire anecdotique des Rues de Versailles," par J. A. Le Roi.

improved her acquaintance with the grand almoner, who even assisted her in the composition of her petitions and memorials,* as to become convinced, in accordance with the rule she had laid down, that alms could be only effectively asked for at the church-door or from a carriage, that a more respectable lodging was indispensable to enable her to profit by the opportunities which this intercourse seemed to open out to her. There were, moreover, other and most pressing reasons for quitting the Hôtel de Reims. The De la Mottes were fifteen hundred and eighty francs in debt to their landlord, who had latterly not only lodged, but boarded them; in addition to which the countess had quarrelled with the landlady, and had attempted, it was said, to throw her down-stairs.† The result was a police case, and their ejection from the premises. A "spacious *appartement*," the rent of which was twelve hundred francs, was therefore hired by them in the Rue Neuve-Saint-Gilles (No. 13), at that time a quiet and very respectable street leading out of the Rue Saint-Louis, now the Rue Turenne, and consisting entirely of private houses, within sight, too, of the Place Royale, where three centuries ago stood the ancient Palais des Tournelles, at the tournament in front of which Madame de la Motte's royal ancestor, Henri de Valois, lost his life, and almost in a direct line (in an opposite direc-

---

* " Premier Interrogatoire du Cardinal de Rohan."
† " Mémoire pour le Cardinal de Rohan," p. 9.

tion to the Rue de la Verrerie) with the cardinal's hôtel, from which it was distant only a couple of short streets, or some five or six minutes' walk. Owing to their straitened means the De la Mottes were unable to furnish their new *appartement* until the month of May, 1783, and in the meantime madame, when not at Versailles, was obliged to live *au cinquième* with the mother of her *femme de chambre*,* and yet she pretends that at this time she kept five servants, male and female, and a couple of carriages.†

This was mere vain boasting. She was not yet in a position to ask alms from a carriage, but was still obliged to send her begging letters through the post, or be herself the bearer of them. One of these missives, written at this particular epoch, and evidently addressed to some person in an official position—possibly to M. d'Ormesson, the then controller-general, or to M. de Breteuil, minister of the king's household—has been preserved, and furnishes a fair specimen of her style of appeal to persons in power—a little flattery, more·or less hypocrisy, allusions to her high descent and a covert threat or two. We extract its main passages, which we have translated as closely as the bad handwriting and worse spelling of the original document admit of our doing.

* " Mémoire pour le Cardinal de Rohan," p. 10.
† " Premier Interrogatoire de Madame de la Motte."

"You have done me the honour, sir, of informing me that you have caused to be remitted to M. Lenoir several notes which I have sent you; but I believed that you, sir, would have had the goodness to oblige me, who am more sensible than any one of the confidence which the king has in you. You are too just to see any harm in there being granted me so small a sum as has, to my knowledge, just been accorded to a person who is not so much to be pitied as I, nor with so much right. I cannot think who it is that has usurped the place due to my misfortunes. . . . . I know that M. de Forge [intendant of the royal fisheries and forests, of which one or more of the Valois estates was part] is very much opposed to my having the estate which I ask by right; still, I cannot conceive that it matters to him whether I or another am tenant of the king. . . . . I have the honour of assuring you that I had yesterday only a single livre (franc), consequently I may well hope to improve my fortune. . . . . . It is you, sir, and your good faith that console me. I am very sensible that you are not unmindful of my misfortunes. I believe that you told me you would speak to M. de Vergennes. I have inquired if this matter is under his control, and am assured it is on you alone that it depends. I recommend myself, therefore, to your kindness. . . . It is not my intention to offer a menace to any one in declaring that I shall end by throwing myself at the feet of the king, and acquainting him with all my misfortunes. If you, sir, cannot lend me your assistance, I beg you to have the goodness to cause to be returned to me the documents which I have had the honour to send you. I shall see, on the day of the court, whether it will not be possible for me to change my lot, and for my efforts to get me accorded the trifling sum I have asked. M. Lenoir sent me yesterday a safe conduct, which M. Amelon requested of him on my behalf, for a large sum which I have owed these two years past, but which has not yet reduced me to sell my furniture, and thereby cause scandals which would assuredly have been aimed at me. Nevertheless, there is no help for it; I shall be forced to make away with it so that I may live. God has not yet determined my fate, and, if Providence does not show pity on me, people will have to reproach themselves at seeing me come to a most miserable end. I am not ashamed to tell you, sir, that I am going out into the world to beg. I have borrowed from the Baron de Clugny, of the Ministry of Marine, three hundred livres to enable me to live, which, counting on your goodness, I have promised to return him in a week's time. No one, sir, has so much reason to complain as I have—my husband without a post, my sister for a long time on my hands, has, of course, contributed to my debts. People may do as they please with me; still, I say it is frightful to abandon a relation of a king, whom he has himself recognised, and who is in the most frightful position. You will, doubtless, sir, consider me very unreasonable, but I cannot keep myself from complaining, since not even the smallest grace is accorded me. I am no longer surprised that so many people are driven into crime, and I can say, moreover, that it is religion alone that keeps me from doing wrong. . . . . .

" I have the honour to be, with all the attachment of which you are deserving, Sir,

"Your very humble, very obedient Servant,

"COUNTESS DE VALOIS DE LA MOTTE.
" Paris, May 16th, 1783."*

Unless she desired to have a couple of strings to her bow, we can hardly imagine the "safe conduct" referred to in the foregoing letter was required by Madame de la Motte, for in her Memoirs she tells us that the Countess de Provence interested herself to procure for her an *arrêt de surséance,* or writ under the king's sign manual, which not only protected the person named in it from arrest, but saved him or her from being harassed by suits at law as well; she at the same time obtained a "safe conduct" for her husband, the count. Convenient documents, both of

---

* Unpublished Autograph Letter of the Countess de la Motte in the collection of M. Feuillet de Conches. This letter is endorsed "M. Lenoir. The concession asked is impossible. Can they obtain other help? 18th May, 1783." M. Lenoir was lieutenant-general of police at this period.

these, for individuals of the De la Motte stamp. The count's "safe conduct" was not procured until there was pressing need of it, for at this time the ex-gendarme was hiding from his creditors in a little *auberge* at Brie-Comte-Robert,* famous now-a-days for its beautiful roses, and a score or so of miles from Paris on the Lyons road, and close to the Abbey of Jarcy, where his sister-in-law, Mademoiselle de Saint-Remi, afterwards went to reside. The chances are that he had already lost his post in the Count d'Artois' body-guard, although Madame de la Motte pretended that the countess was her protectress, and that the count used to notice her "in a particular manner" whenever she went to church at Versailles—a notice which, by the way, it has been insinuated, subsequently ripened into a too familiar intimacy.†

The furniture which, on the guarantee of a Jew, the De la Mottes eventually succeeded in obtaining for their new *appartement* in the Rue Neuve-Saint-Gilles, was far from splendid, and it was, moreover, every now and then being sent to some neighbour, notably to Burlandeux, the count's barber, to save it from being taken in execution,‡ and not unfrequently to the pawnbrokers to provide the family with meat and

---

* "Confrontations du Cardinal avec Madame de la Motte."
† "Mémoire Historique des Intrigues de la Cour, etc.," par Rétaux de Villette, p. 8, and "Anecdotes du Règne de Louis XVI." vol. i. p. 367.
‡ "Confrontations du Cardinal avec Madame de la Motte."

bread.* The countess of course kept up her intimacy with the cardinal, on whose liberality, or call it charity if you will, she could to a certain extent count. If we believe the cardinal's statement, the donations which he bestowed upon her at this period were far from being of that prodigal character which the countess afterwards asserted them to have been, and were perfectly consistent with his character of priest and grand almoner rather than of lover and man of gallantry, which Madame de la Motte openly insinuated was the nature of the cardinal's then relations towards her. The cardinal asserted that about four or five louis at a time, and at irregular and somewhat distant intervals, was the extent of the benefactions she received from him; but he was forced to admit that he had given her twenty-five louis on one occasion, and it eventually oozed out that he had also made himself personally liable to a Jew money-lender of Nancy for five thousand five hundred livres (francs), a debt contracted by the count when he was stationed at Lunéville, and which amount the cardinal of course eventually had to pay.† These facts would seem to prove that at this period the countess had succeeded in ensnaring her victim, preparatory to making him, as she afterwards did, her dupe and then her instrument.

Madame de la Motte was very much in the habit of

* See *post*, p. 71.
† " Premier Interrogatoire de Madame de la Motte."

exaggerating the amount of the charitable gifts bestowed upon her by members of the royal family and some few of the French nobility, and even claimed to have received certain apocryphal sums from persons of distinction who never once assisted her. The reason for this will be apparent enough in the course of our narrative. In the memorials and reports published in 1786 are various disclaimers on the part of people of rank, among others, the Duke de Chartres (afterwards Orléans Égalité), the Duke de Penthièvre, the Duke de Choiseul, the *contrôleur-général*, &c., showing that these exceedingly liberal benefactors, as the countess had made them out to be, had either given nothing at all, or else that a huge disparity existed between the sum really given and the amount pretended to have been received. Her friend, Beugnot, moreover, speaks at this period of sundry treats of an evening on the Boulevards, consisting of cakes and beer, for which beverage she had a particular liking, while, as regards cakes, she would devour two or three dozen of these at a sitting, making it evident that she had dined but lightly on these occasions, if, indeed, she had dined at all.* She, however, most astonished Beugnot by the voracity of her appetite when she dined with him, as she every now and then did, at the "*Cadran bleu*," a noted tavern in the Champs Elysées, whence on a memorable occa-

---

* "Mémoires du Comte Beugnot," vol. i. p. 21.

sion, some eight years later, five hundred and odd Marseillaise, who had marched up to Paris in defence of their fellow "patriots," and whose march inspired the composition of the world-renowned Marseillaise Hymn, rushed forth on the grenadiers of the Filles Saint-Thomas section, and drove them pell-mell over the drawbridge of the Tuileries. Other friends of the countess's tell, too, of frequent loans of ten, fifteen, or twenty francs at a time, all of which is tolerable evidence of semi-starvation and penury rather than of an abundance or even a sufficiency of means.

Spite, nevertheless, of the limited nature of their resources, there is no doubt but that when the De la Mottes had regularly settled down in the Rue Neuve-Saint-Gilles, they made pretensions to something like display. They borrowed, for instance, a service of silver plate of a friend—a M. de Vieilleville; and according to the countess's own statement, M. de Calonne, at one of the interviews she succeeded in obtaining with him just after his appointment to the office of *contrôleur-général*, plainly told her that she was only "shamming poverty," and commenced twitting her respecting her hôtel at Paris, her cabriolet, her voiture, her travelling-carriage, and her servants in livery. To convince Calonne that whatever might be her style of living, she was nevertheless in great pecuniary difficulties, she took him one day the tickets for numerous articles of furniture pledged by her at the

Mont de Piété, and by this ruse succeeded in securing some small amount of official sympathy, which developed itself in a gift of six hundred livres from the royal treasury, on the express condition, however, that she was to make no further appeals.

Soon after the countess had become regularly resident in the Rue Neuve-Saint-Gilles, she was a frequent attendant at mass at a convent of Minimes, on the opposite side of the way, which has long since been demolished, and barracks for gendarmerie erected on its site, but the remembrance of which is still preserved in the nomenclature of several of the adjacent streets. A certain Father Loth having his eye upon this interesting addition to the common fold, made her an offer of a key by means of which she might let herself into the chapel to the ten o'clock mass, which he explained to her was only attended by persons of her own condition. The countess accepted the offer, and a kind of acquaintanceship sprang up between Father Loth and her, which resulted in the former becoming a constant visitor at the De la Mottes, and insinuating himself into the confidence of the family; and subsequently, when brighter days dawned upon them, officiating as a sort of intendant of their household.

Although the countess went constantly to Versailles, in the hope of obtaining by some lucky chance access to the queen, she seems to have been baffled in all her efforts. She had scraped acquaintance with Desclos, one of the queen's pages, at a man-midwife's at Versailles,* and was on gossiping terms with the gate-keeper of the Little Trianon, but could make no further advance at court, until by a lucky chance she one day succeeded in penetrating into the apartments of one of the princesses. Here, whilst waiting among other visitors for her turn to be introduced, she suddenly fell down like a person fainting from weakness, and otherwise exhibited symptoms of great suffering. Her poverty being known, there was instantly a rumour afoot that common hunger was the cause of this debility. The incident produced considerable excitement in the court circle, and news reaching the ears of the Countess de Provence that a lady of rank had fainted in the *salle d'attente* from lack of sustenance, she flew to her assistance, and after treating her with all the tenderness that humanity dictated, gave her some twelve or fifteen louis to relieve her necessities. The countess, much affected by the occurrence, is said to have mentioned it on the following day to Marie-Antoinette, who was about to yield to the impression it made upon her sensibility; but Louis XVI., who had received so many of the countess's petitions, and had been, one may suppose, sufficiently bored thereby, had conceived a strong prejudice against both the countess and her pretensions, and pronounced her swoon a mere ruse to

* "Memoirs of Marie-Antoinette," by Madame Campan, vol. ii. p. 17.

extort money. The result was that the queen closed her purse-strings, and Madame de la Motte took little or nothing by her move. Most persons in her situation, after this signal failure, would have considered their struggle for court favour as fairly concluded, but it was far from being so with her. She was one of those indomitable spirits gifted with a pertinacity which no mere rebuff could check, no disappointment discourage.

For some time past the countess had made a point of laying siege to one controller-general after another— first to M. Joly de Fleury, then to M. d'Ormesson, and finally to M. de Calonne, in whose antechamber she was a constant attendant, and whom she so pestered with her petitions and memorials and personal appeals for relief, spite of the understanding come to when the six hundred francs were given to her, that she became at length a kind of terror to the minister, who showered gold around him with easy facility from a bankrupt exchequer, when, as a courtier said, "All the world held out its hand, but I held out my hat." To rid himself of the countess's importunities, and urged by Madame Elisabeth and the Countess de Provence (who since the fainting scene had taken some kind of interest in her) to do something towards her relief, M. de Calonne obtained an augmentation of seven hundred francs (twenty-eight pounds) to the De la Motte pension. Instead, however, of feeling in any degree grateful for this act of favour, the countess tells us that when the minister communicated the intelligence to her she indignantly refused this "pitiful addition," as she called it, "to her income." Visions of the restoration of the Essoyes, Fontette and Verpilière estates had been floating before her eyes, and in the heat of her passion she exclaimed, "I will oblige you, sir, to speak of my demands to the king. Tell him, sir, that I will fix myself in this house"—the palace of Versailles—"until he thinks proper to provide me with another home." And the irate countess in accordance with her threat did actually remain for several hours, but at last took her departure, because, as she naïvely remarks, her further continuance there "would have answered no purpose."*

It must have been about this period that the countess, harassed by pecuniary difficulties, and determined to exhaust every chance of relief that suggested itself, ventured upon an appeal to Madame Dubarry, the late king's banished mistress, who living in close upon the skirts of the court at the time, in a pretty in her charming pavilion at Lucienne, within eyeshot of Versailles. Thither Madame de la Motte bent her way (so ostensibly to offer herself as counts de compagnie to the dowager queen as she next annually to pay the visit all-powerful favourite of Louis the Much-loved), and Madame Dubarry, judging from an overt pretensions she put forward with regard to her name and birth,

* Life of the Countess de la Motte, Memoirs, vol. i, 83.

thought her little fitted for the post she sought to fill, and told her that she was not at that moment in want of a companion, adding sarcastically that if she were, she was not great lady enough to engage one of so high a quality as a descendant of the house of Valois. Nothing disconcerted, the countess called a second time a few days afterwards, and made a pitiable appeal to the Dubarry to support her claims at court, shedding floods of tears as she spoke. But as soon as her back was turned, "La Faiblesse," as Marie-Antoinette was accustomed to style the Dubarry, and whose heart was none of the most susceptible, bored by the countess's melting display, and caring not a straw for the house of Valois or any of its bastard descendants, flung both petition and memoir, which the countess had presented to her, into the fire.[*]

The countess now addressed herself to the Duchess de Polignac, the well-known favourite of Marie-Antoinette, and whose influence over her royal mistress, whenever she chose to exercise it, was believed to be supreme. The duchess, however, got rid of her once for all with this freezing reply: "Madame, the duchess is too much engaged for other persons to oblige Madame de la Motte in any claim which she may have to make of the king or the queen, who is already fatigued with numberless applications." The descendant of the house

---

[*] Déposition de la Comtesse du Barry.

of Valois was cut to the quick at the treatment she received at the hands of "this imperious woman, whose haughty demeanour sufficiently characterizes her grovelling extraction. Was this the woman," she exclaims, "whom in my humble station of mantua-maker's apprentice I had so frequently waited upon from Madame Boussel's to obtain payment, and who then instead of money could pay me with courtesy and fair promises? Is this she who before the smile of royal favour no tradesman chose to trust, and even her mantua-maker refused to work for, who had not even a habit to be presented in at court?"*

Sick at heart, weary almost unto death, the wretched woman saw no escape from the pecuniary embarrassments that threatened to overwhelm her, except in suicide. Providing herself, she tells us, with a couple of loaded pistols she bent her steps towards a wood about a league distant from Versailles, and passing through the park, came to a large and deep pit, which had formerly been a stone quarry. Here she prepared to carry her resolution into effect, and had placed one of the pistols to her right ear when thoughts of her husband stayed her hand. Flinging herself on the ground she wept long and bitterly, and then offered up a fervent prayer. On becoming more calm she returned home, still however mourning her unhappy fate.†

* " Life of the Countess de la Motte, by herself," vol. i. p. 265, *et seq.*
† Ibid. vol. i. p. 275.

VIII.

1781–1783.

THE DIAMOND NECKLACE AGAIN—STILL NOT SOLD.

WHILE the events narrated in the last chapter have been transpiring, let us see how it has fared with our friends the crown jewellers and their Diamond Necklace. M. Bassenge, after scouring Europe through, and ascending and descending principal and back staircases innumerable, and dancing wearying attendance in court saloons and antechambers, has returned home without effecting a sale. "Not a crowned head of them can spare the eighty thousand pounds. The age of Chivalry is gone, and that of Bankruptcy is come. A dull deep-presaging movement rocks all thrones: Bankruptcy is beating down the gate, and no chancellor can barricade her out. She will enter, and the shoreless fire-lava of Democracy is at her back. Well may kings a second time 'sit still with awful eye,' and think of far other things than necklaces."*

Bassenge's mission having been without result, let us

---

* Carlyle's "Critical and Miscellaneous Essays," vol. iv. p. 11.

turn to M. Böhmer, and see what kind of luck has attended his efforts. On the 22nd of October, 1781, the Queen of France gave birth to a dauphin. Böhmer, who felt this to be a favourable opportunity for him to renew his application, flew to the palace with his casket under his arm, and saw the king, at that moment the happiest man in the land. Louis XVI. received the jeweller with much condescension, and taking the casket from him, carried it to the queen, telling her, with animated looks, that he had got a present for her. But Marie-Antoinette had no sooner recognised the gorgeous gem which she had formerly rejected than she refused to receive it, even at the king's hands; nor could the most earnest solicitations on his part abate in the smallest degree the feeling of antipathy with which, guided by her prophetic instincts, she seems to have regarded the fatal jewel.

"Is it," asked she, "that Böhmer may take his daughter covered with diamonds to the opera, that you would pay him for his folly in manufacturing this Necklace?"

While uttering these words the queen was greatly excited. Her nurse felt her pulse, and finding it very high begged the king not to insist further. Louis XVI. withdrew completely disconcerted.*

Now Böhmer, the crown jeweller, was a Saxon, and

---

* "Mémoires de Mdlle. Bertin," p. 92.

we all know that the Saxons are a persevering race who do not readily desist from a pursuit. Besides he had gained a step; the king had as good as sanctioned the purchase; he was won over, and in due time the queen might be brought to relent and consent to become the possessor of the most splendid set of brilliants in the world. Moreover she was known at one time to have entertained a woman's partiality for costly jewels. What could be the reason of her present antipathy? Was it natural in one so young and handsome? Was it consistent? Was it, indeed, sincere?

This persecution of Marie-Antoinette, which had begun in 1774, was continued for ten years; and every time the palace guns announced a new *accouchement* the indefatigable Böhmer, his casket under his arm, had been the first to carry his loyal congratulations to the feet of his sovereign. In due time the crown jeweller became noted for this kind of loyalty, so that whenever he was met with in the streets of Versailles, certain wags used to point him out and ask each other, "*Serait ce la Reine qui accouche?*"

Madame Campan, in her well-known work, assures us that this persistent Saxon was for a long time the plague of the queen's life. She relates, among other instances of Böhmer's persecution, that he one day presented himself before her majesty, who had the young princess her daughter with her at the time, in a state of unusual excitement. Throwing himself at the queen's feet, he burst into tears, and exclaimed that he could put off his creditors no longer, that he was a ruined man unless she took compassion on him and became the purchaser of his Necklace, that if she rejected his appeal he would throw himself into the Seine, and so put an end to his misery. The queen reproved him mildly for his rash threat, but at the same time told him that if he were madman enough to put an end to his existence, it would not be she who was responsible for the misfortune. She reminded him that she had not given the order for the jewel, and advised him to extricate himself from his difficulties by taking the Necklace to pieces and disposing of the diamonds piecemeal.*

Mademoiselle Bertin, the queen's milliner, pretends that at the time she was engaged in preparing the wedding trousseau of the bride of the Infant of Portugal, M. de Souza, the Portuguese ambassador, confided to her that he was commissioned by his sovereign to buy for her the most magnificent present which could be met with in all Paris, and that he had decided upon purchasing the crown jewellers' Diamond Necklace. Mdlle. Bertin mentioned the circumstance to Marie-Antoinette the following day, while engaged with her at her toilette.

"I am very glad of it," observed the queen. "I

* "Memoirs of Marie-Antoinette," by Madame Campan, vol. ii. pp. 5, 6.

shall send for Böhmer, and will certainly thank M. de Souza for having relieved me of this hateful Necklace."

When Böhmer entered, the queen took up a book and read for some minutes before speaking, as her habit was when she wished to evince her displeasure, which, on this occasion, must have been the result either of inexplicable caprice or feminine jealousy at a foreign princess becoming the possessor of that jewel to which the negotiations and travels of Böhmer and Bassenge had given a kind of European celebrity, and which had caused such a sensation among queens and women. At length, laying down her book and casting on Böhmer a severe glance, she observed:

"I am very glad to hear, sir, that you have sold your Necklace."

"My Necklace, madame!" replied the astonished Böhmer.

"Yes, your Necklace, that M. de Souza is about to send to Lisbon."

Böhmer having given an emphatic denial to the story, the queen, we are told, cast on Mdlle. Bertin a withering look, as if to reproach her for having needlessly alarmed her.

There was a reception that day, and when M. de Souza appeared, the queen, contrary to all the rules of court etiquette, went straight up to him and said, briskly:

"I have to inform you, M. de Souza, that you will not have the Necklace; it is sold."

M. de Souza appearing astonished,

"You will not have it, sir," continued she, in a tone of triumph. "I am sorry for it." Saying which she returned to her ladies.*

Thus matters stood at the close of 1783, ten years after the order for this ill-fated jewel had been given by the infatuated lover of Madame Dubarry. Although all France was at this time wildly rejoicing over the recently concluded peace between France and England, there was gloom and depression at the Grand Balcony in the Rue Vendôme, for creditors were still urgent and even threatening, and the question again arose: "What is now to be done?"

* "Mémoires de Mdlle. Bertin," p. 99, *et seq*. Certain French bibliographers have pronounced these memoirs to be forged. In quoting from them, however, we are only following in the steps of M. Louis Blanc, who we presume considers them authentic. From the "Mémoire" forwarded to the queen by the crown jewellers on August, 12, 1785, it would appear that negotiations for the sale of the Necklace had been opened with the Court of Spain and not the Court of Portugal, as stated in the Bertin "Mémoires," which circumstance certainly goes a good way to impugn their authenticity.

IX.

1784.

SOI-DISANT CONFIDANT OF THE QUEEN.—AT VERSAILLES AND LITTLE TRIANON.

IN the preceding chapters we have measured the period between the year 1756, when Jeanne de Saint-Remi, now Countess de la Motte of her own creation, was born, and the close of the year 1783, when she had reached the age of twenty-seven years. We have witnessed the destitution of her early days, the dependence of her youth on the kind bounty of a noble benefactress, and the career of adventure and precarious means suddenly plunged into to avoid a life of religious seclusion. We have seen her making her escape from flagrant shame by an improvident marriage; have seen the opening of her conjugal life darkened by a new term of penury and privation, mitigated only by a system of constant appeals for charity. We have also seen that a long and patient probation in the same course had proved barren and abortive in the end, her condition being then precisely the same as it was in the beginning. We can readily conceive that her name and her pretensions had at length come to be regarded as little else than a by-word and a nuisance, and that the time was at hand when the former would have no other influence beyond provoking indignation and contempt.

The family resources proved so far insufficient, that early in the year 1784 household goods and wearing apparel were alike in pawn at the Mont de Piété, which is hardly to be wondered at, as the winter was one of unprecedented severity. Heavy and constant falls of snow rendered any kind of traffic through the streets of Paris impracticable. The Seine, too, was frozen over, so that the transport of provisions—and, worst of all, of fire-wood—to the capital, was entirely stopped.* The times were of the hardest: the winter extended far into the year, and in the month of April the countess solicited and obtained permission to alienate her own and her brother's pension—the sister we presume was obstinate, and would not dispose of hers, hence her being sent adrift to shift for herself, and becoming an inmate of the Abbey of Jarcy—to a goldsmith and money-lender, named Grenier, for the sum of nine thousand francs.† This amount, however, was insufficient to liquidate

* "Louis XVI.," par Alexandre Dumas, vol. iii. p. 1, et seq.
† "Mémoire pour le Cardinal de Rohan," p. 11; and Déposition de Grenier.

the entire of their debts, and at midsummer the countess was forced to borrow three hundred francs from Father Loth to pay her quarter's rent.* The two pensions utterly gone, beggary and open vagrancy loom in the distance, for the cardinal's gifts, however handsome they may have been at this period, go but a small way now that ever-increasing debt is supplemented by habitual extravagance. In a few months more the wretched adventurers will be forced to quit their "spacious *appartement*" in the Rue Neuve-Saint-Gilles, and go forth into the streets and highways, and in the name of Valois again implore charity of the passing stranger. What remedy—what desperate remedy could be devised to prevent this?

The countess's interview with the Countess de Provence, after the fainting scene, had made some little noise, and reports were spread to the effect that Madame Elisabeth, the king's sister, had since received her on several occasions, and had promised to support her claim for the recovery of the Valois estates, and to recommend her case again to the queen. We have no means of judging whether these reports were true, but as Madame Campan admits Madame Elisabeth to have been the countess's "protectress," there was in all probability some real foundation for them. Shortly afterwards, however, other reports got into circulation,

---

* Déposition du Père Loth.

which were undoubted fabrications. The purport of these was, that Madame de la Motte had been honoured by the notice of Marie-Antoinette, that she was received privately at the Petit Trianon, and was rising rapidly in the royal favour. To give an air of probability to this assertion, the countess, who had contrived to scrape acquaintance with the gatekeeper of the Trianon, managed to be seen occasionally stealing out from thence, as though returning from one of these pretended interviews with royalty.

No sooner did it get bruited abroad that the Countess de la Motte had credit at court than she was applied to by that busy and motley group of suitors—some of them in search of places and appointments, others in quest of patronage for new inventions, or on the look-out for opportunities to submit new schemes of taxation and finance, and others again seeking redress of real or fancied grievances—who gather together in the vicinage of royalty. The daring woman saw her chance, and entering boldly on a career of imposture, began to traffic on a credit that had no foundation, and to sell an influence which she could not exercise. This new vocation bid fair to prove a much readier source of emolument than her state petitions for relief. People came to her of their own accord, waited in *her* ante-chamber for an interview, conjured and supplicated *her* to lend them her protection, and in the meantime to permit them to show their gratitude by anticipation, and in a substantial form.

In this new line of business she was assisted by an old acquaintance and former comrade of her husband's in the *gendarmerie*, one Rétaux de Villette, son of a late director-general of excise at Lyons, and at this time about thirty years of age. Villette left Lyons when a lad, and accompanied his mother to Troyes, where he completed his education. His sister having married a captain of artillery, and being himself inclined to a military career, he followed his brother-in-law to the schools of Douai and Bapaume, and when this latter establishment was suppressed, entered the *gendarmerie*, where he formed a sort of intimacy with M. de la Motte—an intimacy which was afterwards renewed at Bar-sur-Aube, whither his mother had removed from the neighbouring town of Troyes. Villette having exhausted the paternal patrimony, had come to Paris to push his fortunes. His ambition was to obtain a sub-lieutenancy in the marshalsea, still he was not averse to turning his hand to anything that offered itself. He was not deficient in talent, and had command of a certain facility, for he wrote sprightly articles in the *Gazette*, could compose pleasing enough verses, and was a very fair musician.[*] Nevertheless he was one of those indolent, careless men, without the slightest forethought, who cannot follow any regular calling, because they are only stirred into activity by sudden caprices, and who too often serve no

---

[*] "Marie-Antoinette et le Procès du Collier," par E. Campardon p. 44.

other purpose beyond replenishing the world's stock of rascaldom, and doing their best to save it from dying out. Finding that he was a suppliant for court favour, Madame de la Motte first of all persuaded him that she could advance his interests, then that she would procure for him some better post than a sub-lieutenancy in the marshalsea, and finally engaged him as her secretary, and by dint of "her piquant face, her bright and piercing eyes, her white and transparent skin, her fine teeth, her enchanting smile, her pretty hand and little foot, her graceful manner, and natural wit," soon enrolled him as one of her lovers.*

We will here let the countess give her own account of her pretended intimacy with Marie-Antoinette, an intimacy which it is impossible to believe in for a single moment, since those who lived in the queen's service and society were unanimous in maintaining that the countess was never once admitted to the queen's presence, nor seen in the company of any lady of her court.

"One day," she observes, "as I was paying my court to Madame (the Countess de Provence), I was attacked with a sudden indisposition (the fainting fit of which we have already spoken), which made some noise at the palace; the queen, having become acquainted with the incident, deigned to evince some interest in me; her majesty even sent for Madame Patri, the principal

* *Vide* "Mémoires du Comte Beugnot" and "Villette's Mémoire Historique."

femme de chambre of Madame, to ascertain the particulars.

"Nothing can escape the eyes of courtiers. They remarked from that hour, that her majesty always distinguished me by a gracious look, whenever I appeared in her presence. The Cardinal (de Rohan) surpassed everybody in giving full rein to his conjectures.

"As I had received his benefits, the most natural gratitude linked me to his fate . . . for him I had no secrets; he had none for me . . . his ambition was to be prime minister, mine to be a lady of influence at Fontette. . . .

"Nothing could equal the astonishment into which I was thrown one day, when having placed myself in the line of the queen's passage, her majesty condescended to honour me with one of those smiles which are so hard to be resisted. I remember that the next moment, having chanced to raise my eyes towards him (the cardinal), I saw his own sparkle with delight. 'Do you know, countess,' said he, 'that my fortune is made, it is in your hands along with your own.' . . . He told me I ought not to hesitate to throw myself at the queen's feet on the 2nd of February, during the procession of the blue ribbons. . . . Accustomed to be guided entirely by him, I promised to do what he enjoined me.

"The important day arrived . . . I went to the palace in full dress, and waited in one of the saloons for the return of the procession. When the queen was passing, I flung myself at her feet, and delivering my petition, said to her, in a few words, that I was descended from the house of Valois; that as such I had been acknowledged by the king; that the fortune of my ancestors not having been transmitted to me along with their title, I had no other resource than the king's munificence; that having found every one of the avenues leading to her majesty unrelentingly closed against me, despair had driven me at last to take the present step.

"The queen raised me up with kindness, took my petition, and, perceiving that I trembled, deigned to bid me be of good cheer. She then passed on, telling me to be at ease, and assured me that due attention should be paid to the object of my request."

In the first private interview she pretends to have had with the queen, the countess relates that Marie-Antoinette said to her:

"'I have read your memorial, the object of which is to urge the minister to act and bestir himself with respect to the property which belonged to your house. Having some private reasons not to second your views . . . I cannot reconcile the desire I may have to serve you publicly, with the inclination I feel to see you in private . . . but I shall still be able to render you indirectly the services you wish to obtain from me.' . . . Her majesty concluded by presenting me with a purse."*

* "Mémoires Justificatifs de la Comtesse de la Motte," pp. 11, 18.

A few days afterwards, she tells us, she was summoned to repair to the Little Trianon, between eleven and twelve o'clock at night! when she received fresh proofs of the queen's generosity. "She presented me at parting," says the countess, "with a pocket-book containing ten thousand livres (francs) on the *caisse d'escompte,* and concluded by saying: 'We shall meet again.'"*
Madame de la Motte then goes on to state that it is needless to tire the reader with a repetition of the frequent interviews she had with the queen, of whose munificence on these occasions she received frequent proofs. "The Cardinal de Rohan," she says, "marked her growing favour, and insisting that his fortune was in her hands, conjured her to let no opportunity slip of mentioning his name to his sovereign."

Let us turn now to the other side of the picture, and see what is said by persons likely to be well informed, as well as by Marie-Antoinette herself, respecting this pretended intimacy.

Lacretelle, whose truth and honesty are beyond question, says "the Countess de Valois never had the least access to this princess," and that "one cannot read this libel (the Countess's Memoirs) without being convinced that the queen never had any kind of communication with these creatures, whose presence would have defiled the throne."†

---

* "Life of the Countess de la Motte, by herself," vol. i. p. 291.

† "L'Histoire de France pendant le XVIIIᵉ siècle," par C. Lacretelle, vol. vi. pp. 114, 120.

The Baron de Besenval speaks of the countess in his Memoirs as "one of those creatures who live by intrigue and the sale of their charms."* Was such a person likely to have been received privately at the Trianon? The Baron de Besenval was a regular visitor there himself, and would have heard of this strange and familiar intercourse if it had ever existed.

What does Madame Campan, first *femme de chambre* to the queen, who enjoyed the confidence of her royal mistress, and was, moreover, constantly in her company, and who, biased though she may seem to be in her favour, invariably speaks what she believes to be the truth—what does she say respecting this tissue of invention?

"Neither the queen herself, nor any lady about her, ever had the slightest connection with the swindler, and during her prosecution she could only point out one of the queen's servants (a man named Declos or Leclos), a page of the queen's chamber, to whom she pretended she had delivered Böhmer's Necklace . . . Declos, on being confronted with the woman La Motte, proved that she had never seen him but once, which was at the house of the wife of a surgeon-accoucher at Versailles, and that she had not given him the Necklace." Madame Campan further states that the countess "had never even been able to make her way into the room appro-

---

* "Mémoires du Baron de Besenval," vol. iii. p. 122.

priated to the queen's women." The same lady also furnishes this additional piece of testimony:

"The queen," she says, "in vain endeavoured to call to mind the features of this person, whom she had often heard spoken of as an intriguing woman, who came frequently on Sundays to the gallery at Versailles; and at the time when all France was taken up with the prosecution against the cardinal, and the portrait of the Countess de la Motte-Valois was publicly sold, her majesty desired me one day when I was going to Paris to buy her the engraving, which was said to be a tolerable likeness, that she might ascertain whether she could recollect in it any person whom she had seen in the gallery." *

Marie-Antoinette herself, when questioned by Louis XVI. on the subject of this intimate acquaintance, assured the king that she had never seen the woman. In a few simple words she repeats her denial when confronted with the Cardinal de Rohan, immediately preceding his arrest. And in a private letter to her sister, written at a time when the affair of the Diamond Necklace was making a great noise throughout Europe, Marie-Antoinette thus denies all previous knowledge of her pretended confidante:

"I have never seen this woman La Motte; it seems she is an adventuress of the lowest class, with a good

* "Memoirs of Marie-Antoinette," by Madame Campan, vol. ii. pp. 17, 19, 291.

address and a bold air; she has been seen two or three times on the back staircase of the Cour des Princes; this is a scheme agreed on to deceive her dupes and to spread the belief that she is received in my closet. The Duke de Nivernois on this occasion has told me that an adventuress from Paris had made her fortune in the days of Madame de Maintenon by seating herself twice a week on the stairs; one day she found the drawing-room of that lady open; she went in, and seeing no one near she walked up to the balcony over the Place d'Armes, thus proclaiming to every one that she was in favour with Madame de Maintenon. We are surrounded in this place by persons of that class." *

Again, at the very last, only a few hours before her head was severed from her body by the guillotine, she still firmly repudiated all knowledge of any such individual. Let us refer to the report in the *Moniteur* of the "*Procès de Marie-Antoinette*," and see what transpired in reference to the matter.

"*The president to the accused*: Was it not at the Little Trianon that you first met with the woman La Motte?

"*The accused*: I never once saw her.

"*The president*: Was she not your victim in the business of the famous Necklace?

"*The accused*: She could not have been, since she was unknown to me.

* "Correspondance Inédite de Marie-Antoinette," par Comte P. Vogt d'Hunolstein, p. 141.

"*The president*: So then you persist in denying that you were acquainted with her?

"*The accused*: Mine is not a system of denial; what I have said is the truth, and that I will persist in."

Of course it was the truth; had it not been, Fouquier Tinville had abundant means of proving the contrary; all France in these days was overrun with spies and informers. The public accuser had really no facts to allege against the prisoner in regard to Madame de la Motte, and confessed he had not when ordered to bring the queen to trial. Had there been the least particle of evidence to prove Marie-Antoinette's intimacy with so abandoned a woman, the attorney-general of the Revolutionary Tribunal would have been only too glad to have brought it forward. He had not far to go, for among the witnesses actually produced were the Count d'Estaing, formerly in command at Versailles, who knew both the queen and the countess, and was a frequent dinner-guest of the latter in the Rue Neuve-Saint-Gilles; and Renée Sévin, for six years under *femme de chambre* to Marie-Antoinette, yet to neither of these did he put a single question upon the subject. Again, there was Reine Millot, another old servant at Versailles, "*bonne citoyenne, excellente patriote*," who did her best to sacrifice her unhappy mistress, deposing that the Count de Coigny had told her that the queen had sent two hundred million francs to her brother, the Emperor Joseph, to enable him to make war upon the Turks, and that she would end by ruining France; and further, that she knew from different people that the queen had conceived the design of assassinating the Duke d'Orléans, which when the king heard of, he ordered her to be immediately searched, and two pistols being found upon her, he commanded her to remain in her own apartment for the space of fifteen days.* A witness such as this would have been only too eager to repeat all the scandal current at Versailles respecting the Countess de la Motte and the queen. Moreover, Count de la Motte himself was known to be living at Bar-sur-Aube at the time of the queen's trial, and could have been readily enough produced, only Fouquier Tinville was perfectly well aware that he could depose to nothing incriminatory in the slightest degree of her whose death, though already determined on, the revolutionary party would have been glad enough to have justified on such a poor pretence even as her complicity in the Necklace fraud.

* " Procès de Marie-Antoinette," Paris, 1865, pp. 40, 64, 65.

X.

1772–1774.

HIS EMINENCE CARDINAL, COMMENDATOR, GRAND ALMONER, PRINCE-BISHOP, LOUIS RÉNÉ ÉDOUARD DE ROHAN.

STRANGE to say, among the tribe of solicitors who put faith in the report of Madame de la Motte's intimacy with Marie-Antoinette, and sought to turn it to their own advantage, and certainly by far the most sanguine of them all, was her "friend" and benefactor, Louis Réné Édouard de Rohan, Cardinal of the Holy Roman Church, Bishop and Prince of Strasbourg, Prince of Hildesheim, Landgrave of Alsace, Grand Almoner of France, Commander of the Order of the Holy Ghost, Commendator of St. Waast d'Arras, Superior-general of the Royal Hospital of the Quinze-Vingts, Abbé of the Chaise-Dieu, Master of the Sorbonne, Member of French Academy, &c., &c. The very man who had been wont to bestow alms upon a descendant of the house of Valois was now almost ready to cringe to the former recipient of his bounty for favour and support. This dissolute and intriguing prelate, who was destined to attain such unenviable notoriety through his connection with the Countess de la Motte, was born on the 27th of September, 1734, and was at this period consequently verging on his fiftieth year. He was, as we have already mentioned, a tall, stout, handsome-looking man, with a fresh coloured complexion, bold forehead, and white grey hair. His manners were amiable; he was fluent in conversation, and though his talents, as the upshot proves, were of a very inferior order, still he was not deficient in that dexterity which goes a long way towards fitting a man for the conduct of public business—he having, by the aid of his shrewd secretary, the Abbé Georgel, rather cleverly filled the post of ambassador at the court of Vienna for between two and three years. He had been sent to that court in January, 1772, to supersede the Baron de Breteuil, thereby making a mortal enemy of that minister, now in high favour with the sovereign. But this was not all. He had also incurred the dislike, and even hatred, of the Queen of France, partly in consequence of having repeated to the Empress Maria Theresa certain scandals current at the French court respecting the unbecoming levity of her daughter, then dauphiness, and partly in consequence of a letter written by him in an unguarded moment, which reflected strongly on the duplicity of the empress with respect to Poland. In this letter he remarked that "Maria Theresa stands, indeed, with the handkerchief in one hand, weeping for the woes of Poland, but with the sword in the other, ready to cut Poland into sections, and take her share,"* an observation in which there was not only point, but far too much truth for it to pass unnoticed. This letter was read and laughed over by Louis XV., and by him repeated to the Countess Dubarry at one of her *petits soupers*, and the countess, in her turn, gossiped about it, until at length the affair became a court joke and reached the ears of the dauphiness, who, repressing her indignation at the time, did not fail to treasure up the circumstance in her memory.

In spite of this aversion on the part of the queen, and which, by the way, was fully shared by Louis XVI., the cardinal, whose ambition led him to covet the office of prime minister, fondly hoped, sooner or later, to recover his ground. When therefore he heard, as very good care was taken he should very quickly hear, that a lady who stood in certain tender relations towards himself, and was under certain pecuniary obligations to him, was in favour with the queen, the credulous dotard suspected neither deception nor exaggeration in the report; which perhaps was hardly surprising, for Nature, we are told, had given the *soi-disant* new favourite a frank and honest face in spite of her proficiency in the arts of deceit. "Without possessing the full splendour of beauty," observes the Abbé Georgel, "the Countess de la Motte

---

* "Mémoires pour servir à l'Histoire des Événements de la fin du XVIII° siècle," par l'Abbé Georgel, vol. ii. p. 220.

was gifted with all the graces of youth, hér countenance was intelligent and attractive, and she expressed herself with fluency; moreover, *the air of truth that pervaded her recitals invariably carried conviction along with it.*" The cardinal, only too ready to be blinded and deluded, counselled his *protégée* how to proceed in order to retain and improve the position which he imagined she had already acquired, intending, without doubt, to avail himself of her interest to recover the good opinion of the queen, whose deep-rooted prejudice against him was the bane of his life.

Madame Campan speaks of the cardinal as a spendthrift, and a man of the most immoral character, whose mission to Vienna opened under the most unfavourable auspices, in consequence of the nature of the reputation which preceded his arrival at that court. " In want of money, and the house of Rohan being unable to make him any considerable advances, he obtained a patent which authorized him to borrow the sum of six hundred thousand livres (twenty-four thousand pounds) upon his benefices; nevertheless he ran into debt for upwards of another million, and thought to dazzle the city and court of Vienna by the most indecent, and, at the same time, the most ill-judged extravagance. He formed a suite of eight or ten gentlemen of names sufficiently high sounding, twelve pages equally well born, a crowd of officers and servants, together with a company of chamber musicians, and various other retainers. But this idle pomp did not last;

embarrassment and distress soon showed themselves; his people, no longer receiving pay, abused the ambassadorial privileges, and smuggled with so much effrontery that Maria Theresa, to put a stop to it without offending the court of France, was compelled to suppress the privileges in this respect of all the diplomatic bodies."*

In these days an ambassador was not only required to be an adept in duplicity, but he was expected, by means of bribery, or other modes of corruption more or less dishonourable, to make himself master of all the secrets of the court to which he was accredited. The cardinal proved himself in this respect equal to the mission with which he was intrusted. At the commencement of the year 1774 he discovered that the Austrian minister, Prince de Kaunitz, had succeeded in purchasing keys of the ciphers in which the despatches that passed between the king and himself and the ambassadors at Constantinople, Stockholm, Dantzic, and St. Petersburg were written. He also discovered that the court of Vienna had obtained copies of and had deciphered all the despatches sent by the Duke d'Aiguillon to the various representatives of the court of Versailles throughout Northern Europe. He learnt, too, that the main offices of interception were Liege, Brussels, Frankfort, and Ratisbon. At these places copies of despatches were taken and forwarded to what

* "Memoirs of Marie-Antoinette," by Madame Campan, vol. ii. p. 42.

was styled the " Cabinet of Decipherers," a department of which Baron Peckler was the head.*

How it was that the cardinal came to make this important discovery and to profit largely by it, as he eventually managed to do, is quite a piece of romance. We will let the Abbé Georgel, at that time secretary to the French embassy at Vienna, tell the story in his own words.

" Returning one evening to the hôtel, the porter gave me a note carefully sealed up, and addressed to me. I read in it as follows :—' Be to-night, between eleven and twelve, at a particular place upon the ramparts, and you will be informed of matters of the very highest importance.' An anonymous note of this tenor, sent so mysteriously, and the unseasonable hour appointed, might have appeared to some persons altogether dangerous and suspicious. But I was not aware that I had any enemies, and, desirous not to have to reproach myself with having missed an opportunity that might never occur again of promoting the king's service, I determined to attend at the appointed place. But I took some prudential precautions, by placing within a certain distance, where they could not be seen, two persons on whom I could rely to come to my assistance upon a signal agreed on. I found at the place of meeting a man wrapped in a cloak, and masked. He put

* " Mémoires Historiques et Politiques du règne de Louis XVI.," par l'Abbé Soulavie, vol. iii. p. 277, *et seq.*

some papers into my hands, and said in a feigned undertone: 'You have my confidence; I will therefore contribute to the success of M. the Prince de Rohan's embassy. These papers will inform you of the very essential services which it is in my power to render you. If you approve of them, come again to-morrow to' another place which he mentioned, 'and bring me a thousand ducats.' On my return to the Hôtel de France, I hastened to examine the papers confided to me. Their contents gave me the most agreeable surprise. I saw that we had it in our power to procure twice a week copies of all the discoveries made by the secret cabinet of Vienna, which was the best served cabinet in Europe. This secret cabinet possessed in the highest degree the art of deciphering quickly the despatches of ambassadors and of the governments with whom they corresponded. I was convinced by the deciphering of our own despatches and the despatches of our court to us—even those written in the most complicated and the newest ciphers—that this cabinet had found means to intercept and obtain copies of the despatches of several European courts, of their envoys and agents, through the treachery and audacity of the frontier directors and postmasters, bribed for that purpose.

"Furnished with these documents and armed with unquestionable proofs of their authenticity, I instantly went post haste to communicate them to the ambassador.

I laid before him the samples of the political magazine, from which we might supply ourselves. The Prince de Rohan felt the value of it, especially to himself personally, inasmuch as this important discovery must necessarily efface the unpleasant impressions which the Duke d'Aiguillon had not failed to make upon the king's mind, by representing to him that Prince Louis, too light, and too much taken up with the pursuits of pleasure, was not so watchful at Vienna as the service of the state required.

"I met the masked man the following night, and gave him the thousand ducats: when he handed to me other papers of increasing interest, and during my whole stay at Vienna he faithfully performed his promise. Our meetings took place twice a week, and always about midnight. The ambassador wisely decided that the occupation arising from this discovery should be confined to him and to myself, with an old secretary whose discretion we knew would stand any trial. The secretary was employed in copying for our court the papers of the masked man, to whom we were obliged to return them.

"A courier extraordinary was at once despatched to Versailles with the first fruits of our newly discovered treasure. He was ordered not to go to bed on his way, and to carry about his person the special packet of secret despatches to the very end of his journey. A separate letter communicated the manner in which this disclosure had been made to us. Our courier returned promptly, the bearer of a despatch from the Duke d'Aiguillon, which contained this acknowledgement of the cardinal's services: 'I sincerely and feelingly share,' said the minister, 'both in the satisfaction with which the king acknowledges your services, and the credit which this discovery throws upon your mission.' From the time of this discovery an extraordinary courier was sent off to Versailles every fortnight with new communications, and always with the same care and precautions as before."*

Soulavie tells us it was through the Austrian ambassador at Versailles, who, like the rest of his fraternity, had a whole host of traitorous officials in his pay, that the court of Vienna got scent of what was going on. The Prince de Kaunitz, suspecting that the treachery was perpetrated in his office, had the locks of his cabinet changed, and made a point of intrusting all the most important despatches to no one except his private secretary. He even went the length of having one of his clerks, of whom he entertained some suspicion, drowned in the Danube; but all was of no avail; the masked man, according to the Abbé Georgel, seemed even to redouble his zeal at each succeeding interview.

Two months after the death of Louis XV. the car-

* " Mémoires pour servir à l'Histoire des Événements de la fin du XVIIIe siècle," par l'Abbé Georgel, vol. i. p. 269, *et seq*.

dinal was superseded in his post. He had hurried off to pay his court to the new king at Compiègne, where he was not long in becoming acquainted with the fact that the queen was his avowed enemy. He obtained an audience of Louis XVI, but it was brief, and by no means satisfactory. The king listened for a few minutes to the cardinal's explanations, and then abruptly said, "I will let you know my pleasure." As for Marie-Antoinette, she positively declined to receive him, although he had a letter from her mother the empress to deliver. The only notice she took of him was to desire that this letter might be sent to her. As a last resource he addressed a written communication to the king, which Louis XVI did not condescend to answer. The cardinal had now no longer any doubt that his disgrace was determined upon.

Although his downfall was really to be ascribed to the joint animosity of Maria Theresa and her daughter, the grounds publicly put forward for it were these. "First, the public gallantries (at Vienna) of Prince Louis with women of the court and others of less distinction; secondly, his surliness and haughtiness towards other foreign ministers, which it was stated would have been attended with more serious consequences if the empress herself had not interfered; thirdly, his contempt for religion in a country where it was particularly necessary to show respect for it (he had been seen frequently to dress himself in clothes of different colours, assuming the hunting uniforms of various noblemen whom he visited, with so much publicity that one day in particular, during the *fête Dieu*, he and all his legation, in green uniforms laced with gold, broke through a religious procession which impeded them, in order to make their way to a hunting party at the Prince de Paar's); and fourthly, the immense debts contracted by him and his people, which were tardily and only in part discharged.*

* " Memoirs of Marie-Antoinette," by Madame Campan, vol. i. p. 65.

XI.

1784.

PRETENDED MEDIATOR BETWEEN THE CARDINAL AND THE QUEEN.—A FORGER ON THE PREMISES.—BILLETS-DOUX BORDERED WITH "VIGNETTES BLEUES."

BEFORE the close of spring in the year 1784, the countess has effectually built up her grand fabrication. Although she neglects no opportunity of giving out that the queen desires this pretended intimacy to be kept a profound secret, yet, like most other profound secrets, it becomes pretty generally known; the imposture is established as a reality, and the Grand Almoner of France has been caught in the net. This singularly credulous individual, weighed down with places and honours, but ambitious of more, is led to believe, quite as much by his own folly as the countess's craft, that a channel has at length been opened for his reinstatement in the queen's favour, and his elevation to the office of prime minister. All the machinery set in motion by the impostor and her confederates to make money by the abuse of the queen's name is now directed with both energy and skill upon the Prince de Rohan, whose paternal hand is employed to diffuse the charities of a kingdom upon those suppliants who best understand how to represent their wants, and whose own annual revenue exceeds a million of francs (£40,000).

Gradually, step by step, the vigilant schemer advances, her dupe's fancy and conceit outstepping the measured tread of the inventor, whose falsehoods are not poured forth fast enough to fill the wide throat of this insatiable gull. First she assures him that she has spoken and interceded for him with the queen, who listened to her with attention but evident suspicion; but after having heard of several instances of his benevolence to herself and other persons, the royal prejudice had given way. The cardinal of course takes heart at this assurance, and waits resignedly for the happy progress of a negotiation which had opened so promisingly. The countess thus describes one of these pretended interviews with Marie-Antoinette in her Memoirs:

"In one of my interviews with her majesty, the queen inquired how I had supported myself before I was introduced to her. This was the moment for naming my benefactor, but it required some caution, lest the queen should discover that I was deeper in his confidence and counsels than it was proper for me to appear. I attempted, if possible, to avoid giving the least cause for suspicion, and expatiated largely, in general terms, on the cardinal's beneficence, charity, and benevolence; enumerated the services he had rendered to almost everyone that applied; that from his generosity he had acquired the esteem he merited; and spoke with a grateful warmth of the favours he had heaped upon me.

"Her majesty regarded me with a curious and penetrating eye: she paused for some minutes, and appeared buried in thought. This was the first moment of my mentioning the cardinal's name, and I had an opportunity of reading in her majesty's face such a degree of aversion that gave me a very unfavourable omen of success: the strength of her antipathy I was then first acquainted with. At length, awakening from her reverie, she expressed her surprise at the information I had given her. She did not think the cardinal capable of such actions."*

In due time the grand almoner is informed that majesty has at last relented, having been of course won over by the countess's continuous praises of him, and by her assurances that he was far less culpable than he was represented to be by his enemies; that he was full of penitence and remorse for any errors he might have committed; that her majesty's aversion to him was his constant affliction; and that his health was yielding to this sorrow.

* "Life of the Countess de la Motte, by herself," vol. i. p. 294.

"I am authorized by the queen," the countess calmly said to him, "to request you to furnish her with a written explanation of the faults imputed to you."

In compliance with this demand, the cardinal delivered to Madame de la Motte a lengthy exculpatory statement, the main purport of which was to accuse his niece, the Princess de Guémenée, of having intrigued to add to his disgrace at court while pretending to act as intercessor on his behalf. From time to time the princess appears to have allured him with specious promises of his ultimate restoration to royal favour, and the kind of return she exacted for her pretended good offices may be judged of from the following passage, which, as will presently appear, Madame de la Motte did not fail to note and profit by: "The princess was sensible of the excessive joy she gave me,* and availed herself of it *to request of me the loan of a pretty considerable sum*. I would have parted with my whole fortune, thinking myself too happy in being useful to a woman to whom I was so greatly beholden. The easy compliance she had met with enticed her to make further demands, which I could not refuse, she always knowing how to accompany them with hopes, with

---

* She had informed the cardinal that the queen had deigned to accept of a white Spanish dog which the cardinal had offered to her through the princess. Of course Marie-Antoinette had done nothing of the kind.

soothing promises, and at the same time with difficulties she would find ways to overcome."* It is inconceivable how, after feeling convinced that he had been the dupe of one designing woman, the cardinal could have been such a dotard as to have been again deluded by an *intriguante* who used precisely the same arts, and who exacted from him precisely the same kind of return. Such, however, was the case.

About three weeks after the delivery of his written justification into the hands of Madame de la Motte, the grand almoner received a note, bordered with "*vignettes bleues*," purporting to be written by Marie-Antoinette, and which stated that she had read with indignation of the manner in which he had been deceived by his niece, assured him that she had forgotten all that had passed, and desired him never again to make the slightest allusion to a matter so unpleasant—a convenient way of tabooing a subject, the discussion of which might have proved extremely embarrassing to the countess, and have sooner or later exposed the fraud which was being practised upon the cardinal. This note wound up with the following passage, the motive of which the reader will be at no loss to divine: "The account which the countess has given me of your behaviour towards her has made a stronger impression on me than all that you have

* "Life of the Countess de la Motte, by herself," vol. ii. p. 12, Appendix

written to me. I hope that you will never forget that it is to her you are indebted for your pardon."*

The plot thickens: all at once we find ourselves in deeper water. Before we had false rumours and reports; now we have forged letters. The cardinal having received the first one as genuine, what is to prevent the success of others? Nothing, it would seem, so long as the countess exercises her customary discretion. Letters and replies thereupon follow each other in quick succession, amounting in course of time to something like a couple of hundred in number. Of these the countess pretended she preserved copies of thirty-one, which she subsequently printed by way of appendix to her autobiography. Judging from these samples, the communications which, according to her assertions, passed between the queen and the cardinal, were not merely tender and familiar, but occasionally touched upon subjects that were positively indelicate.†

It is needless to inform the reader that, so far as the letters attributed to Marie-Antoinette are concerned, they were one and all of them vile fabrications. They were penned, in fact, by the prospective sub-lieutenant of the marshalsea, of whom we have already spoken, Rétaux de Villette, who was attached to the countess in

---

* "Life of the Countess de la Motte, by herself," vol. ii. p. 17, Appendix.

† A few of these letters are given in the Appendix to the present work.

double capacity of "*cavalier servente*" and secretary, and whose chief occupation seems to have consisted in forging letters on gilt-edged paper, or paper bordered with blue flowers (*vignettes bleues*). His *cabinet de travail* was madame's bedchamber, and he worked at a little table by the bedside, on which was a writing-case with a stock of note-paper, such as the queen was known to be in the habit of using.* Monsieur de Villette resided regularly under the De la Motte roof, for Jeanne de Saint-Remi, Countess de Valois de la Motte, having considerable traffic in forgery, found it necessary to keep a forger on the premises, just as other people find it requisite to keep a secretary or a clerk.

If we glance behind the scenes, we cannot help being impressed by this daring woman's strength of mind, which enables her to work so calmly and leisurely while all the time the wolf is at the door. Not only has she her idle husband and herself to support, but there is at times her brother, whose pension she has sold, and her "secretary," and not a single franc of regular income! To add to all this, she is in debt with the landlord, the tax-gatherer, and the tradespeople; duns are calling upon her every hour—duns, too, are waiting in the ante-room while she is dictating forged letters to Villette. Her own pension

---

* "Confrontation du Cardinal avec le Père Loth." The latter described the paper on which Villette wrote as being bordered with "*vignettes bleues*," and in M. Feuillet de Conches' unique collection of autographs of Marie-Antoinette are several notes written by the queen on paper with coloured borders.

and that of her brother being utterly gone, the family have literally no bread to eat but that of charity, and the bread of charity is so scanty and bitter that the descendant of the house of Valois becomes a liar and a forger, and is preparing to become a thief, in order to add to and sweeten it. And all this while, with her thread of life drawn, so to speak, to a single hair, she is the emblem of composure, advancing "stealthily, steadfastly, with Argus eye and ever-ready brain—with nerve of iron, on shoes of felt!" whilst Cardinal Prince de Rohan, her father in years, who lives in palaces surrounded by every luxury, holds one of the highest offices in the state, is superior of numerous important religious establishments and seigneur of countless manors, and has a revenue of a million francs, is feverish with impatience.

According to his usual practice, the cardinal, with Versailles and the Little Trianon closed against him, is spending the sultry summer-time in retirement at his stately palace of Saverne, a huge building of red sandstone in the Italian style of architecture, for the most part newly erected by himself in place of a former edifice consumed by fire a few years previously. At Saverne the Cardinal Prince Louis de Rohan exercises all the authority of a petty sovereign, and keeps up a well-nigh regal state. Gentlemen of high birth do not disdain his service; and such is the prodigality that rules in his establishment, that he has no less than

fourteen *maîtres d'hôtel* and twenty-five *valets de chambre!**
Situated at the foot of the eastern slope of the Vosges
mountains, and almost within sight of the valley of the
Rhine, Saverne has its upper and lower towns, in the
former of which are situated the cathedral, the *chan-
cellerie*, the *hôtel de la régence*, the ancient château, and,
adjoining this last, the palatial residence of the all-
powerful De Rohans. The principal front of this vast
building looked over charming gardens, laid out in the
French style, with handsome terraces and arcades,
geometrically-shaped beds of brilliant flowers, trees
trimmed to pattern, green shady alleys, trellises covered
with vines, arbours, statues, fountains, rivulets, broad
sheets of water, islands, grottos, and kiosques, beyond
all which extended a beautiful park, and at the outskirts
of which again was a pheasantry, bounded by a dense
forest, where in the pleasant autumn months the hunts-
man's horn might be heard incessantly resounding.

The palace, on the garden side, presented one long
façade ornamented with fluted Corinthian pilasters and
richly-carved cornices and mouldings, and having countless windows of a uniform character. Its somewhat
unpleasing regularity was broken by a projecting centre
part with a row of open columns and balustrades, which
formed a kind of gallery, handsomely decorated in its
different stages with ornamental friezes, statues, and

* "Mémoires de la Baronne d'Oberkirche."

bas-reliefs, and having the elaborately-sculptured armorial bearings of the family of De Rohan and its many alliances prominently displayed at either end.*

The principal entrance to the episcopal palace conducted to a handsome vestibule, from whence the grand staircase led to the magnificent suite of reception-rooms where the Prince de Rohan, banished from Versailles, assembled around him a little court of his own, composed of some few members of the old nobility related to his house, discontented courtiers who disliked the young queen, certain too complaisant beauties, and *petits maîtres* from the Paris *salons*, philosophers, prelates, and provincial magnates, military officers from the neighbouring garrison at Strasbourg, and the usual complement of fools and flatterers that invariably dance attendance on the powerful and the wealthy.

The once stately palace of Saverne is now-a-days divested of all its former splendour. It serves alike for the *mairie*, the court of the justice of the peace, and the corn-market; and as barracks, guard-house, forage stores, farriery, and stables, for the troops composing the garrison of the town.

In the summer of the year 1784 couriers bound for Paris would every now and then sally forth from the palace gates with bags of letters, among which there was invariably one elaborately-sealed packet addressed

---

* "Saverne et ses environs," par C. G. Klein.

to the Countess de la Motte. Enclosed in this would be a letter for the queen, begging, entreating, praying for an interview at which the writer might plead his cause and regain possession of his royal mistress's favour. Days and weeks go by while he is waiting and watching for a response. Judge, however, of the cardinal's agitation when one day the countess herself arrives unexpectedly at Saverne—having travelled post all the way from Paris—and announces to him that the long and eagerly-sought interview is at length accorded to him; that the queen has consented to a midnight meeting with him in the Park of Versailles. The countess thought, and thought rightly, that a journey of nearly three hundred miles, undertaken on purpose to be the bearer of this welcome intelligence, would give it all the greater weight, and would effectually dispel any unpleasant doubts that might perchance by this time have taken possession of the cardinal's mind.*

* "Mémoire pour le Cardinal de Rohan," p. 24.

XII.

1784. JUNE—JULY.

THE COUNTERFEIT QUEEN.

COUNTERFEIT *billets doux* having been palmed off on the infatuated cardinal as genuine with such complete success, the countess now ventures on a singularly bold step, nothing less than the personation of majesty itself, and actually succeeds in foisting upon the purblind prelate *une belle courtisane* of the Palais Royal as the beautiful, high-born Marie-Antoinette.

This incident of the nocturnal interview—the most daring of the many daring schemes of which the long intrigue was composed—is so fully and clearly, and, moreover, so artlessly, described by the "*fille du monde,*" who was bribed to perform the character of Marie-Antoinette on the occasion, in her memorial published at the time of the Necklace trial, as to completely exonerate the queen from having been in any way a party to it. Prior, however, to laying this statement before the reader, we have something to say respecting the new character whom we are about to introduce on the scene.

This young person, whose real name was Leguay Designy, was born in Paris in 1761, and was younger than the queen by seven years. Although her reputation was anything but spotless, she was by no means the common creature she is ordinarily represented to have been. M. Leguay Designy, her father, had been a respectable citizen, who at his death was found to have saved money, and when her mother died, a few years before the event which rendered the daughter an object of so much notoriety, Mademoiselle Leguay Designy was left with a competent provision deposited for her in the hands of trustees. These guardians however abused their trust, and after dissipating the bulk of the young woman's property, compromised the matter by the payment of four thousand francs, which money she received in the early part of 1784, only a few months before the day rendered memorable by the midnight meeting in the park of Versailles.

Mademoiselle Leguay Designy, in her memorial, which was drawn up by her advocate, M. Blondel—who, perceiving that the very simplicity of his client was her best defence, had the sagacity to let her tell her story in her own way—thus describes how it was that she first became acquainted with the De la Mottes, husband and wife.

"In the month of June, 1784, I lodged," she says, "in a small apartment in the Rue du Jour, in the Quartier St. Eustache.* I was not very far from the Palais Royal, where I used frequently to go of an afternoon for two or three hours with a neighbour's child, about four years old, of whom I was very fond.

"One afternoon, in the month of July, when I was sitting in the Palais Royal, this child being along with me, I observed a stranger pass by several times; he was a tall young man, and quite alone. He looked at me fixedly, and I noticed as he came near to me that he slackened his pace as if to survey me more attentively. There was a vacant chair two or three feet from mine, in which he seated himself.

"I could not avoid bestowing my attention upon him, for his eyes kept repeatedly wandering over my person. The expression of his countenance becomes grave and earnest, and he appears agitated by a painful and anxious curiosity as he scans my entire figure very narrowly, whilst not a feature of my face escapes him.

"We met in this way in the gardens of the Palais Royal for several successive days, until at last he addressed me, and I committed the error of replying to him.

---

* The Rue du Jour is a narrow street close to the "Halles Centralles," and at the western end of the church of St. Eustache. It contains at the present day several " Hôtels meublés " of a seedy kind, but the "petit hôtel Lambesc," where Mdlle. Leguay Designy had her small apartment on the " premier étage," no longer exists under its original name.

"One evening on leaving him I returned home, when I found that he had followed me without my perceiving it. Suddenly he stood before me in my apartment. He introduced himself with every sign of respectful politeness, and requested me to allow him occasionally to visit me. I could not take upon myself to deny his request, and after obtaining my consent, he was most assiduous in his calls. But I had no reason to complain of these visits, for the young man never passed the limits of propriety. He questioned me, however, with the kindest concern, respecting my income and future prospects, taking a lively interest in my fate. He also spoke of powerful protectors of his own, to whom he could recommend me, and who might be able to serve me.

"Doubtless you are eager to know who this stranger was. It is time to name him; it was M. de la Motte, who represented himself to be an officer of distinguished rank, with great expectations, and supported by illustrious patrons.*

"It was, I think, on the occasion of his ninth visit, one morning at the beginning of August, 1784,† that I observed his countenance overspread with joy and satisfaction, such as he had never shown before. He had,

---

* The count being, according to Rétaux de Villette, a notorious gambler, the Palais Royal, where the salons de jeu most abounded, would naturally have been one of his accustomed haunts.

† More probably towards the end of July.

he said, the most agreeable, the most interesting things to tell me.

"'I have just left,' continued he, 'a person of very great distinction, who spoke a great deal about you. I shall bring the lady to see you this evening.'

"I awaited that evening with eagerness, counting every hour and every moment, for I longed to see this lady of very great distinction.

"M. de la Motte returned at night, telling me that in a few moments I should see the person about whom he had spoken in the morning. Whereupon, and without any further explanation, he withdrew.

"Scarcely had he left me, before I saw a lady enter my chamber; she was all alone—no servant was attending her. She approached me with politeness, and with looks full of affability.

"'Madame,' said she, smiling, 'you must be rather surprised at my visit, unknown to you as I am.'

"I replied that the surprise could not be otherwise than agreeable to me.

"This person was the wife of my pretended patron; she was Madame de la Motte, but she took good care not to say so then. I offered the lady a chair, she drew it herself close to my own, and sat down. Then leaning over towards me, with a look at once cautious and confiding, whilst her eye appeared to gleam with an expression of benevolent regard, she said to me, in a low voice, what I am about to relate.

THE COUNTESS ENGAGES A CONFEDERATE. 125

"'Confide, my dear pet, in what I am going to say; I am a gentlewoman belonging to the court.'

"At the same time she drew out a pocket-book, and having opened it, showed me several letters, which she declared to me were written to her by the queen.

"'But, madame,' answered I, 'all this is a mystery to me; I cannot understand it.'

"'You will soon understand it, my pet. I possess the queen's full confidence; we are like hand and glove together. She has just given me another proof of this trust, by commissioning me to find her a person to do something which will be explained at the proper time. I have made choice of you, and if you like to undertake it, I will make you a present of 15,000 livres (francs); but the present that you will receive from the queen will be much more considerable. I cannot tell you my name just yet, but you shall soon be informed who I am. If, however, you do not think my word sufficient, and desire to have security for the 15,000 livres, we will go directly to a notary's.'"

[In the following paragraph the pen of the advocate has evidently been at work.]

"Ye simple and trustful hearts, pause for a moment after reading this artful speech from the boldest and most audacious intriguer that ever lived. Fancy yourselves in my place, deign to consider what my feelings must have been, what I must have thought and imagined, I, a poor girl of twenty-three, unacquainted with either intrigue or business. What would you have said? What would you have done under similar circumstances?

"From that moment I was no longer myself. I answered Madame de la Motte that I should be proud to be able to do anything that would be agreeable to the queen, without any motive of personal interest to prompt me.

"She replied immediately, 'The Count de la Motte will call for you to-morrow evening in a carriage, and will carry you to Versailles.'"*

The reader will not fail to observe the precision with which the countess enters on her course of action; the quickness with which she manages to come to the point. Her husband takes a fortnight to bring about the introduction of his wife, while she settles everything at a single interview.

The next day the count, who is accompanied by Rétaux de Villette, takes Mademoiselle Leguay to Versailles at the appointed time, and leaves her with his wife in their apartments at the "Hôtel de la Belle Image," kept by the Sieur Gobert, and situated in the Place Dauphine, at that time one of the most aristocratic quarters of the royal town. This "Place" is octagonal in shape, and the houses, which range from four to five storeys high, have all some sort of pretension about them; they have either open balustrades running

---

* "Mémoire pour la Demoiselle Leguay d'Oliva," p. 8, et seq.

along the parapets, or carved cornices with enriched mouldings surmounting the windows, or ornamental iron balconies. Most of them too have large *portes cochères*. The Place, which in Madame de la Motte's days was a large open space, where the public sedan-chairs—the *chaises bleues* and the *brouettes*—used to ply for hire, is now laid out as a flower garden, and has in the centre a bronze statue of General Hoche, after whom the Place is now named. The house where the countess lodged, and formerly known as "La Belle Image," no longer preserves its sign. It is, however, the first house (No. 8)* in the angle on the right hand, on entering the Place from the Rue Hoche. All the apartments, except the attics, must have been of a superior class. Now-a-days the ground floor is appropriated to a "Magasin Anglais," where English cutlery, and needles and pins, and reels and balls of cotton, and patent medicines, and pickles, and old brown Windsor soap, are exposed for sale. To return, however, to Mademoiselle Leguay, whose memorial thus proceeds:

"It was only then I learnt the name and condition of Madame de la Motte, that she was the wife of Count de la Motte, that she went by the title of Countess de Valois at Versailles, and that the queen used to write to her in that name."

The *belle courtisane* of the Palais Royal, whose resem-

* "Histoire anecdotique des Rues de Versailles," par J. A. Le Roi.

blance to Marie-Antoinette is said to have been singularly striking,—she was remarkable for the elegance of her figure, had blue eyes and chestnut coloured hair*— is now dressed and tricked out in coquettish *négligé* —a white robe *en chemise*, bordered and lined with rose colour, and a white lace hood—for the famous interview with the Cardinal de Rohan, who had so earnestly solicited this audience of the queen, with whom the miserable dupe flattered himself he had been all this while corresponding. The memorial proceeds:

"Madame de la Motte delivered to me a small note, folded in the usual way, but without telling me either what it contained or to whom it was addressed, or even by whom it was written. Neither she nor her husband spoke to me on the subject. Madame de la Motte merely said, 'I will take you this evening into the park, and you will deliver this letter to a great nobleman whom you will meet there.'"†

---

* "Deuxième Mémoire, pour le Sieur Bette d'Etienville," p. 17.
† "Mémoire pour la Demoiselle Leguay d'Oliva," p. 16.

XIII.

1784. JULY.

THE MIDNIGHT INTERVIEW.—"YOU KNOW WHAT THIS MEANS."

THE memorial of the Demoiselle Leguay Designy thus proceeds:—

"Between eleven and twelve o'clock I went out with M. and Madame de la Motte. I had on a white mantle and a white lace hood. I do not remember whether I carried a fan in my hand or not; I cannot say for certain. The small note was in my pocket.

"They took me into the park; there a rose was put into my hand by Madame de la Motte, who said to me: 'You will give this rose, along with the letter, to the person who shall present himself to you, and say to him these words: You know what this means? The queen will be there to see how your meeting passes off; she will speak to you. She is there yonder, and will be close behind you. You shall presently speak to her yourself.'

"These last words made such an impression on me, that I trembled from head to foot. I could not help telling them so: I observed to them that I did not know I was to speak to the queen. I asked them, in a stammering voice, what was the proper form of speech. . . M. de la Motte answered me : 'You must always say, Your majesty.'

"I need hardly, I think, break off here to declare that, far from having had the honour of speaking to the queen, or far from her having done me the honour to speak to me, I did not even see her at all. . . .

"We were still walking along when M. de la Motte met a man to whom he said: 'Ah! is that you?' . . . Afterwards, when I dined with the La Mottes, I recognised in Villette, their friend, the same person who was thus addressed by M. de la Motte. . . .

"Madame de la Motte then accompanied me to a hedge of yoke elms, leaving me there whilst she went to fetch the great nobleman to whom I was to speak.

"I remained waiting . . . The noble unknown came up, bowing as he approached me, whilst Madame de la Motte stood aside a few paces off, and appeared to watch the scene.

"I knew not who the great nobleman was, and although the Cardinal de Rohan now acknowledges that he was the person, I am still quite ignorant upon the point.

"It was a dull night, not a speck of moonlight; nor could I distinguish anything but those persons and objects which were familiar to me. It would be quite impossible for me to describe the state I was in. I was so agitated, so excited, so disconcerted, and so tremulous, that I cannot conceive how I was able to accomplish even half of what I had been instructed to do.

"I offered the rose to the great nobleman, and said to him, 'You know what this means,' or something very similar. I cannot affirm whether he took it or let it fall. As for the letter, it remained in my pocket; I had entirely forgotten it.

"As soon as I had spoken, Madame de la Motte came running up to us, saying in a low hurried voice: 'Quick, quick, come away!'

"I left the stranger, and after proceeding a few steps found myself with M. de la Motte, whilst his wife and the unknown went off together and were lost to our view. Count de la Motte conducted me back to the hotel, where we sat talking together until the return of his lady.

"She came home about two in the morning, when I explained to her that I had forgotten to give the note. I was afraid she would have scolded me for this negligence, but instead of doing so she evinced the greatest satisfaction, assuring me she had just left the queen, and that her majesty was in the highest degree delighted with my performance." *

* "Mémoire pour la Demoiselle Leguay d'Oliva," p. 16, et seq.

Such appears to have been the famous scene in the park of Versailles at midnight, when the Prince de Rohan, deluded by an artful woman, was fain to believe that he had been honoured with an interview with the Queen of France, and might soon expect to be openly received at court. The countess knew perfectly well that the cheat would run the risk of being detected if the dialogue were suffered to proceed too far, she therefore frightened away her dupes almost as soon as she had brought them together.

The Countess de la Motte's own account of this interview in the park of Versailles, though at variance with that given by Mademoiselle d'Oliva, nevertheless agrees sufficiently with it to prove that the statement of the latter was perfectly sincere. The countess alleges that the idea of practising this deception upon the cardinal originated with Marie-Antoinette herself — that the choice of the actress who was to personate her, the place appointed for the interview, the young girl's embarrassment before the meeting, were all known at the time to the queen, who was present in an adjoining arbour.

Nay, more. According to the same account, the Cardinal de Rohan was also privy to the trick played upon himself, and connived at the deceit in order to humour her majesty. Madame de la Motte's narrative of the transaction is too long to be transcribed throughout, but it concludes in this manner:—

"The poor girl was dressed and adorned like a shrine.

... Judging from the questions she had put to me since her arrival at Versailles, it was easy to see that she expected some great adventure, and had made her preparations accordingly... Nothing could be more diverting than the embarrassment of this creature, whose real anxiety was about the issue, since she knew she was going to play her part before the queen.

"The scene was the arbour at the lower end of the grass-plot. This arbour is encompassed on its left-hand path by a hedge of hornbeam, supported by a strong lattice-work fence. At a distance of three feet from the inner part of the arbour is a second hedge, and the space between the two quicksets forms a walk which leads round the enclosure without conducting to the arbour itself.

"At the hour appointed I gave the signal by putting into Mademoiselle d'Oliva's hand the rose which Marie-Antoinette had told me to deliver to the cardinal through her means. Having placed her at her post, I withdrew. The queen was not ten paces from me. I was distressed by D'Oliva's timidity, and the queen doubtless experienced the same feeling, for in spite of all her reserve and watchfulness she could not contain herself, but cried out: 'Take courage. Don't be afraid!' D'Oliva admitted this in her examination. The cardinal having come up, the conversation began.

"The cardinal, whose mind was at ease, since he was in the secret, exerted himself to compose the poor girl, by putting none but simple questions to her, and saying courteous things. What chiefly disconcerted her was, that he spoke of former errors forgiven, of his gratitude, and made fine promises for the future. Of all this she understood nothing, answering Yes or No at random. But the cardinal took advantage of these monosyllables to dwell upon his happiness with exaggeration, saying the prettiest things in the world . . . raising her foot at the close of his speech, and respectfully kissing it. It was then Mademoiselle d'Oliva gave him the rose, which he placed against his heart, protesting that he would preserve this token all his life, and calling it the rose of happiness.

"Everything having been said that was to be said, I came forward hurriedly, and announced that Madame and the Countess d'Artois were approaching the spot. Every one vanished with lightning-like rapidity. D'Oliva returned to the seat where my husband was expecting her, the cardinal having rejoined the Baron de Planta, whom he had left at some distance on the watch, came, accompanied by him, to me, and induced me to follow him beyond the avenue, behind which he stopped to see the queen pass. Having caught sight of her as she was stealing out from the corner of the grass-plot and taking the walk leading to the terrace, he urged me to follow her majesty, and try to ascertain whether she was satisfied. Accordingly I did follow her, with light measured steps, and having overtaken her at the entrance to the château, she made me go in along with her, told me in substance that she had been much diverted, paid me a few compliments on my own account, and enjoined me not to tell the cardinal that I had seen her that evening."*

In this account there is much that is false, and but little that is true. A counterfeit queen, and no other, was present at the interview. The cardinal was imposed upon by the trick to which of course he was not privy; and having left the park with the full conviction that he had spoken to his sovereign, was committed to the tender mercies of the countess and her confederates, who pretty quickly proceeded to plunder him of his money.

* "Mémoires Justificatifs de la Comtesse de la Motte," p. 52, *et seq.*

XIV.

1784. JULY—NOV.

A GOLDEN HARVEST.—HISTORY REPEATS ITSELF.—
BARONESS D'OLIVA IS GIVEN THE COLD SHOULDER.

THE evening following that on which the cardinal was so cleverly duped, young Beugnot happening to find himself in the neighbourhood of the Rue Neuve-Saint-Gilles, looked in at the countess's hôtel on the chance of finding her at home. At this period it was no longer a spacious *appartement* that she rented, but the entire house; and yet, with the view of deceiving the cardinal, on whose bounty she was now in a large measure dependent, whenever he called upon her she used invariably to receive him in some mean apartment on one of the upper floors.* "I was told," says Beugnot, "that the master and mistress were absent, and that only Mademoiselle Colson was within. This made me the more inclined to stay. Mademoiselle Colson was a relation of Madame de la Motte's, whom madame had

---

* "Mémoire pour le Cardinal de Rohan."

qualified and raised to the rank of *dame de compagnie*. She was wanting neither in wit nor malice, and whenever I met her we always made a point of laughing together at the foolishness and extravagance of the heads of the house. They used to tell her nothing; nevertheless she managed to find out everything. 'I think,' she remarked to me on this occasion, 'that their royal highnesses are occupied with some grand project. They pass their time in secret counsels, to which the first secretary (Villette) is alone admitted. His reverence the second secretary (Father Loth) is consequently reduced to listening at the door: he makes three journeys a day to the Rue Vieille-du-Temple (to the Palais-Cardinal), without guessing a single treacherous word of the messages they confide to him. The monk is inconsolable at this, since he is as curious as an old devotee.'

"We passed two hours in thus slandering our neighbours and in making guesses and prophesying. When I wished to leave, Mademoiselle Colson pointed to the clock: it was midnight, and there was no chance of finding a *voiture* on the stand. Since I had remained so long, the only thing to do now, she said, was to await the return of Madame de la Motte, who would send me home in her carriage. I consented. Between twelve and one o'clock we heard the sound of a vehicle entering the court, and saw descend from it Monsieur and Madame de la Motte, Villette, and a woman from twenty-five to thirty years of age—a blonde, very pretty, and a remarkably fine figure. The two women were dressed with elegance, but with simplicity; the men wore dress-coats, and had the air of having just returned from a country party. They commenced by joking me on my *tête-à-tête* with Mademoiselle Colson, and spoke of the regret we must both have felt at having been so soon disturbed. They talked any amount of nonsense together, laughed, hummed, and seemed as if they could not keep their legs still. The unknown shared the common mirth, but she restrained herself within due bounds, and displayed a certain timidity. They seated themselves at table, the merriment continued, it increased, and finally became noisy. Mademoiselle Colson and I wore dull and astonished looks, such as one is forced to put on in the presence of very gay people when one is ignorant of what they are laughing at. Meanwhile the party indulging in this excess of hilarity seemed inconvenienced by our presence, as it prevented them from speaking openly of the subject of their mirth. M. de la Motte consulted Villette as to whether there would be any risk in speaking. Villette replied that 'he did not admit the truth of the adage that one is betrayed only by one's own people; in fact anybody and everybody were ready to betray you, and discretion——' Here Madame de la Motte, by whose side the first secretary was sitting at table, suddenly put her hand on his mouth, and said in an imperative tone: 'Hold your tongue; M. Beugnot is too upright a man for your confidence.' I give her own words without changing a syllable. The compliment would have been a flattering one if the countess had not been ordinarily in the habit of using the words 'upright man' and 'fool' as though they were synonymous.

"Madame de la Motte, following her usual practice whenever I was present, turned the conversation upon Bar-sur-Aube and on my family, and inquired when I contemplated returning thither. Every one was wishing the supper to come to an end. I asked Madame de la Motte to lend me her horses to take me home. She raised only a slight difficulty: it was necessary that she should send home the unknown, and eventually decided that the one living farthest off should put down the other on the way. I objected to this arrangement, and asked permission of the lady to conduct her to whatever quarter she lived in, expressing my regret at the same time that however distant this might be, it would still be too near. This woman's countenance had at the first glance caused me that kind of uneasiness which one feels when one is conscious of having seen a person before, but cannot remember when or where. I addressed several questions to her on our way, but was unable to draw anything out of her; either Madame de la Motte, who had spoken to her in private before her departure, had recommended her to be discreet with me, or, what seemed more probable, she had naturally more inclination for holding her tongue than for talking. I set down my silent companion in the Rue de Cléry. The uneasiness which I felt in her presence was, I afterwards called to mind, due to her striking resemblance to the queen. The lady proved to be no other than Mademoiselle d'Oliva, and the mirth of my companions was occasioned by the complete success of the knavish trick which they had played off only the night before in the park of Versailles upon the Cardinal de Rohan."*

This meeting, at which the cardinal was so cleverly fooled, took place, be it remembered, either at the end of July—the countess fixes it on the 28th—or at the commencement of August. His eminence the cardinal was so much elated with his good fortune, in having thus recovered, as he hoped, the favour of the queen, and felt so well assured that he was now in a fair way of becoming prime minister, the great object of his ambition, that the Countess de la Motte resolved at once to reap the first-fruits of his fond hallucination. So great was her decision of character, so thorough her assurance, so precise and prompt her mode of action, that before many days had elapsed she had applied for —by means of a billet bordered with *vignettes bleues*, penned of course by the forger Villette—and obtained

---

* " Mémoires du Comte Beugnot," vol. i. p. 67, *et seq.*

the moderate sum of 50,000 francs in the queen's name, assuring her dupe that the queen required the loan for certain charitable purposes.* Ere another three months had gone by, by the aid of another forged billet purporting to have been penned by the queen, madame succeeded in obtaining another 100,000 francs. Both these amounts she received at the hands of the cardinal's equerry, the Baron de Planta. Thus the Prince de Rohan, who in the month of July had been duped by an interview with a counterfeit queen, ere the year had gone by had been swindled out of no less a sum than 150,000 francs, or £6000 sterling.

This is all the more extraordinary, and only proves the intensity of the infatuation under which the old dotard must have been labouring, for no very long time previously there had been much talk within the purlieus of the court of a daring act of swindling, perpetrated by means of a scandalous misuse of the queen's name, which ought to have put him on his guard. It seems that one Béranger, a *fermier-général*, had been induced to advance a sum of 200,000 francs to a certain Madame Cahouet de Villers, a lady said to be in attendance on the queen, as he believed for the use of her royal mistress. When first the lady applied to him, M. Béranger observed that he should be proud to furnish

---

* In the cardinal's first "Mémoire" he states the sum to have been sixty thousand francs, but at his examination he fixed it at fifty thousand.

the sum required, provided her majesty would condescend to say one word to him—only one little word. But the lady only laughed at his unreasonable demand. If the queen, she said, chose to apply in so open a manner, of course the contents of every strong box in the kingdom would be at her disposal. Then where would be the merit of lending so small a sum on such security?

Poor Béranger was ashamed of himself for having been so unreasonable, and consented to lend the money if the queen would only show him by a look, or even by a nod, that she desired it. This compact was agreed upon.

A few days afterwards, therefore, when the queen with her train of ladies had to pass along the famous looking-glass gallery at Versailles on some occasion of pleasure, the cautious *fermier-général* posted himself in a quiet corner where he could be seen, and by-and-by Marie-Antoinette swept along full of smiles and nods, the whole of which had been cunningly provoked by some smart observations made by the lady above mentioned, and which said smiles and nods the delighted financier applied entirely to himself. A few hours afterwards the two hundred thousand francs were handed to the lady in question. The duped *fermier-général*, who, when the affair came to be commonly known, was toasted as a gallant financier at all parties and in all societies for a month or two afterwards, put the affair into the hands of the police, and my lady was arrested and sent to Sainte-Pélagie, and her husband brought to ruin through having to reimburse the *fermier-général* the amount of which he had been defrauded.

The above transpired in 1777. Five years later another imposture of a somewhat similar character was brought to light, but owing to its having been comparatively harmless in its results, it did not make any particular noise. A female boasted that she was honoured with the confidence of the queen, and exhibited letters sealed with a seal belonging to Marie-Antoinette which had been stolen off a table in the apartment of the Duchess de Polignac, inviting her to Trianon. She gave out that she could influence the favour of the Princess de la Lamballe, and pretended that she had been the means of disarming the resentment of the Princess de Guéménée (the Cardinal de Rohan's niece) and Madame de Chimay against Madame de Roquefeuille. Here we have the same falsehoods, the same sort of dupes, the same farce, and, what is strangest of all, the same name; for the impostor of 1782 was also named De la Motte!—Marie-Josephe-Françoise Waldburg-Frohberg, wife of Stanislas-Henri-Pierre de la Motte, formerly administrator and inspector of the royal college of La Flèche.[*] Thus does

---

[*] "Histoire de Marie-Antoinette," par E. et J. de Goncourt, r. 202.

history, even in its most insignificant byways, repeat itself.

For some time after the incident of the midnight interview, Mademoiselle Leguay was a constant visitor at the De la Mottes, both at Paris and Versailles, and subsequently at their country house at Charonne; for immediately the countess had gathered the first-fruits of her successful fraud a *petite maison de campagne* was added to their other establishments. The demoiselle of the Palais Royal was presented to the somewhat mixed company which she met on these occasions under the title of the Baroness d'Oliva, which the countess had herself conferred upon her, deriving, it is supposed, "Oliva" from "Olisva," anagram of "Valois." She tells us that at the De la Motte table, which was served, by the way, by footmen in elegant liveries, there were to be seen officers of rank, such as the Baron de Villeroy, chevaliers of St. Louis and of Malta, retired notaries and their wives, a relative of madame's, one Valois, a bootmaker, Rétaux de Villette, the countess's secretary, and Father Loth, her *homme d'affaires*,—altogether a tolerably free and-easy-sort of society, we have no manner of doubt.

On one occasion the Baroness d'Oliva accompanied the Countess de la Motte, the Baron de Villeroy, and Rétaux de Villette to the Théâtre Français to see Beaumarchais' comedy, "The Marriage of Figaro," then running its hundred nights; but as time wore on, the countess became less pressing in her invitations, and the intercourse between the two ladies grew gradually less intimate, until some time in the ensuing November, when the Countess de la Motte and the Baroness d'Oliva were no longer on visiting terms. As regards the 15,000 francs which the counterfeit queen was to have received for her single night's performance, and on the strength of which brilliant engagement she had contracted debts which were a source of great future embarrassment to her, this is what she says to the countess in her "Mémoire:"—

"Some days after your return from Versailles, you and your husband came at midnight in a *voiture de place* to the Rue du Jour, and gave me four hundred francs on account.

"On another day you came to me in the evening in your carriage, having only your footman with you, and gave me seven golden louis.

"Another day you drove up to my door in your carriage and sent your footman to inquire for me. I came down and saw Father Loth and the Baron de Villeroy with you in the carriage. I asked you for four hundred francs, which I wanted to pay to Gentil, my upholsterer. Some days afterwards, Father Loth called for me, and we went together to Gentil and paid him the money.

"On another occasion your friend Villette brought me three hundred francs from you.

"Another day I sent my servant to you, according to previous arrangement, when you paid her three thousand francs in notes of one thousand francs each."*

Thus it will be seen that she was only paid 4268 francs of the 15,000 francs promised to her, and that by bit-by-bit instalments. Schemers and sharpers, if they had gold mines at their disposal, would never pay in any other way.

* "Mémoire pour la Demoiselle Leguay d'Oliva," p. 34.

XV.

1784. NOV.

GRAND DOINGS AT BAR-SUR-AUBE.

The sudden possession of a large sum of money produced in the countess an invincible desire to return for a time to Bar-sur-Aube, where a few years previously she had suffered so much poverty, but where she could now display a little pomp. Late in the autumn of 1784, young Beugnot received a very amiable letter from Madame de la Motte, in which she announced to him that having several days to spare, she was about to spend them at Bar-sur-Aube with her friends. "She informed me, in an easy off-hand manner," observes the count, " that she had sent in advance her carriage and saddle-horses, which would be five days on the road, as she had been recommended not to fatigue them, and that she herself would arrive two days afterwards. She apprised her sister-in-law, Madame de la Tour, of her coming in much the same terms, and gave her certain particular directions as to the lodging of herself and suite. Madame de la Tour came to me quite bewildered, and asked me what it all meant, to which I replied that I was as much in the dark as she was. Having compared letters, we agreed that there was a mystification of the worst kind about the affair, but resolved that we would not be duped, and that no preparations should be made for lodging the princess and her suite, and moreover that we would both preserve strict silence with reference to the letters we had received. How great was our astonishment when on the appointed day we beheld a large heavily-laden waggon, drawn by a fine team, and followed by two led horses of great value, drive into the town. A steward who arrived with the waggon instantly gave orders for more provisions than would have sufficed to victual the best house in the town for a period of six months. People stared at each other when they met in the streets, and wondered what this new chapter in the 'Arabian Nights' could possibly mean, and were still wondering when the Count and Countess de la Motte, preceded by two outriders in handsome liveries, drove leisurely through the main street of Bar-sur-Aube in a very elegant *berline*."* Two years before they had left the place with borrowed money and no other clothes but those they had on; now they returned in their own carriage, with their couriers and saddle-horses, and actually required a waggon to convey their wardrobe!

The town of Bar-sur-Aube, on the banks of the river, the name of which it bears, is built partly on the slope

---

* "Mémoires du Comte Beugnot," vol. i. pp. 33, 34.

of a mountain and partly in a valley, and has on its mountain side the remains of some extensive Roman fortifications said to have been constructed by Cæsar during his invasion of Gaul. In by-gone times the town was encompassed by a massive stone wall, and had ditches, and ramparts, and four ancient gateways, with a garrison of arquebusiers and militiamen. Its fortifications however have been long since demolished, and pleasant gardens now occupy their site. At the present day Bar-sur-Aube boasts several ancient churches and chapels containing handsome carved altar-pieces, and many curious antique monuments, and has also its convents, hospitals, college, and theatre. The one object of historical interest that attracts the attention of strangers is the little gothic chapel in the centre of the old stone bridge of seven arches which spans the river Aube, built to mark the spot where, upwards of four centuries since, Charles VII. caused the Bastard de Bourbon, chief of the gang of *écorcheurs* (flayers)—so called because they stripped the unfortunate wretches who chanced to fall into their hands of every particle of clothing, and who had for a long time ravaged Champagne—to be sewn up in a sack and drowned in the river beneath. In the old parts of the town the houses are chiefly of wood, and some of the more picturesque among them have large figures of saints forming their supports. Most of the houses erected during the last eighty or ninety years, however, are built entirely of stone. The outskirts of Bar-sur-Aube are planted with trees, and laid out in public walks, gardens, and orchards; beyond which a chain of small hills, covered with vines or dense plantations of foliage, gives a picturesque aspect to the surrounding country. Owing to the favourable situation of the town and the productive nature of the adjacent districts, Bar-sur-Aube does an extensive trade in various kinds of grain, horses, cattle, wine, brandy, fruit, wool, leather, linen, iron, glass, pottery, and stone and timber for building purposes.

Bar-sur-Aube has something of a history of its own, for it has been the scene of several stirring historical events. It was occupied by the Romans during their invasion of Gaul, was ravaged by Attila, and was pillaged by our own Edward III. in 1360. About four centuries later the inhabitants of Bar-sur-Aube welcomed with great display Louis the Well-Beloved when he passed through the town on his return from the siege of Fribourg. In January, 1814, the Allies, then marching upon Paris, appeared before Bar-sur-Aube, and after a series of hard-fought engagements forced Marshal Mortier, who held the town, to beat a rapid retreat under cover of the night. While in the occupation of the Allies, a conference of the ministers of the different powers was held at Bar-sur-Aube, when Lord Castlereagh resolutely refused all subsidies to the vacillating Bernadotte unless he agreed to support Marshal Blucher with two *corps d'armée*, and so enable the Allies to continue their march upon Paris. At this time there were three crowned heads, the Emperors of Russia and Austria, and the King of Prussia, installed in comparatively humble lodgings in this second-rate provincial town. After the battle of Montmerail, on the 11th of February, the Allies, who were retreating, turned and made a stand, and compelled the French army to retire across the river Aube. On this occasion the town was twice taken and retaken after several severe engagements. In the year following, about three weeks after the battle of Waterloo, the Allies, to the number of 200,000 strong, again appeared before Bar-sur-Aube. This time there was no enemy to face them, so they quietly took possession of the place, levied heavy contributions on the inhabitants, and left a garrison of a couple of thousand men behind them, when they pursued their unopposed march upon Paris.*

The De la Mottes spend several weeks at Bar-sur-Aube, give grand dinner and supper parties to those who consent to visit them, discharge all their debts with the cardinal's money, and assume all the airs of genuine nobility. Most of the inhabitants eat their meat and drink their wine without instituting any curious inquiries as to the source of their strange prosperity; but there was one whose piercing intelligence penetrated every outward vanity, whose keen eye discerned the truth then more distinctly than others

* "Essais Historiques sur la Ville de Bar-sur-Aube," etc., par J. F. G., and "Histoire de Bar-sur-Aube," par L. Chevalier.

have done since, after the exposure of a long trial by the Court of Parliament, and the still more searching investigations of fifty historians. This sagacious man was M. de la Tour, who had married the count's sister. When he dined at the De la Motte table, the countess herself, to whom all others submitted, quailed beneath his cutting sarcasms.

"I chanced to be alone with M. de la Tour," says Beugnot, "on the day of Madame de la Motte's arrival. 'Am I not a thousand times right,' said he to me, 'when I assert that Paris contains the worst persons in the world? In what other place, I ask you, would this little vixen and her big lanky husband have been able to obtain by swindling the things which they are displaying before our astonished eyes? Your good father excepted'—Beugnot's father, it will be remembered, had lent the De la Mottes a thousand francs a few years previously—' who would they have found here willing to lend them a crown? and yet in half an hour they have unpacked more silver plate than there is in the whole town besides, not even excepting the chalices and ornaments of the altar.' . . . 'Do you not know,' remarked I, 'that Madame de la Motte is protected by the queen?' 'I'll say nothing as to the queen's protection,' replied La Tour. 'Between you and me, the wife of our lord the king is not the most prudent person in the world; still she is not such a fool as to have anything to do with people of their stamp, I warrant.'"

The evening after the De la Mottes' arrival they gave a supper to a few intimate friends, which, according to Beugnot, would have been considered magnificent for any kind of guests even in Paris. "Although the town of Bar-sur-Aube," observes he, "is one of the most ancient cities of the Gauls, never perhaps had such luxury been seen in it before, not even when Cæsar did it the honour of stopping there to hang—as they say— the mayor and councillors of that epoch. Faithful to an understanding we had previously come to, La Tour and I ate with good appetites, and without taking particular notice of anything, as though, in fact, we were both accustomed to such festivities. We kept the conversation in our own hands, taking care to confine it to subjects which rendered it difficult for the most expert talker to interpose a remark in praise of any of the things spread before us. M. de la Motte did not like this; he wished to make us admire the dinner-service, which was of a new pattern, and of very fine workmanship. La Tour contended that services of this kind had been known for a very long time, but had gone out on account of their clumsiness. The *nil admirari* was persevered in with respect to everything, and to the very end.

"At last Madame de la Motte thought she had found grace in our eyes in praising a fowl, one of the finest which had just been removed from the table, informing us at the same time that she had ordered the courier to bring her a supply of this kind of poultry so long as she remained at Bar-sur-Aube, because to her taste ordinary country fowls were not eatable. 'I ask your pardon, madam,' interposed La Tour, in a serious tone, 'but I am by no means of your opinion. I consider a country capon such as you have been speaking of, when properly fattened, to be vastly superior to all your Normandy and Mans cocks and pullets, the flesh of which is soft, insipid, and dripping with fat. But after the capon has been fed on a good place, it must be roasted in a proper manner, and for this purpose I care little about the jack. I very much prefer to have the spit turned by a boy of the family, or even by a dog.'

"Madame de la Motte lost patience at the sort of honour paid to her by her husband's relation before four tall footmen who had been brought from Paris clothed in liveries covered with gold lace. 'Sir,' said she to La Tour, in a spiteful manner, 'I feel edified at your preference; it is the result of a country taste which we know you push to its fullest extent.' 'I agree with you there, madam,' replied La Tour; 'country taste or family taste are much the same, and you know, madam, I value one just as much as I do the other.'

"This conversation shortened supper. 'How do you think I have paid my score?' inquired La Tour of me in a low tone of voice. 'You have been almost too liberal,' replied I. 'Not at all; only I was resolved to put down both husband and wife should they have the impertinence to ask me to admire anything. The masquerade which has commenced this evening is a sort of triumph for these people, and I reserve for myself the part of the soldier who on the way tells wholesome truths to the hero of the festival!'"

Madame de la Motte called Beugnot into her room, and began complaining to him of the insolence of her husband's brother-in-law. "She told me," says Beugnot, "that her fortune had changed, that she was now in a good position, both as regarded herself and those belonging to her, and that we were all interested in adopting a different manner towards her. She hinted something of the very high connection she was keeping up at Versailles, and ended by remarking that she did not think she could remain with us the fortnight she had promised herself. I proffered her a first example of the new style of behaviour which she desired by not asking her a single question. I merely undertook to beg her brother-in-law to be more prudent for the future, without, however, anticipating much success from my intervention."

The third day of the countess's sojourn at Bar-sur-Aube was occupied by her in paying visits to people in the neighbourhood. She dressed herself out with all the taste which can result from an excess of magnificence, her robes being of the finest Lyons embroidery, and she herself sparkling with diamonds. She had, moreover, a complete set of topazes, which she also took care to display. "She made herself," says Beugnot, "almost ridiculously engaging and familiar with the neighbouring nobility and gentry. Great and small were alike enchanted with her. They returned her visits, but when she wished to go further, and give some little fêtes, the respectable women of the place excused themselves under various pretexts, and Madame de la Motte found herself reduced to the young men and the women of her husband's family, so thorough was the respect for manners at this time in a little provincial town. 'Madame de la Motte,' said these good ladies to me, 'is a charming woman, and we like her very much; but why do you wish us to give our girls ideas of which they have no need, and which will perhaps awaken in them desires they can never gratify?'

"I was wanting," resumes Beugnot, "neither in respect nor discretion with Madame de la Motte. She seemed to have completely forgotten our old relations, and on this point I was in unison with her. I had become to her simply a well-bred man with whom she could speak on any subject. She told me of the secret vexations she endured through the deplorable position of her husband's family. I consoled her as well as I could, always observing to her that a residence in a little town was in her case quite a mistake—that she ought to have an hôtel at Paris and a château in the country. She replied that she did not wish to buy land, because she was about to obtain the estates belonging to her family, on which she proposed to build. The hôtel in Paris she allowed to pass without notice, but she admitted that she wished to possess one at Bar-sur-Aube, where she could spend the summer months until her projected château was built. I took the liberty of opposing this idea of purchasing a house at Bar-sur-Aube, and maintained that it would be in far better taste to inhabit a cottage while the château was being built by its side; but Madame de la Motte, who had already received many valuable lessons on this subject, did not the less persist in her desire to display her magnificence in those places which had been witnesses of her former misery. She purchased, in spite of my remonstrances, a house at Bar-sur-Aube, for which she paid twice as much as it was worth, and then gave it up to architects, who considered it their duty to commit all the stupidities which the property admitted of, and a few more."*

"As the period of the countess's sojourn at Bar-sur-Aube drew to a close, people grew angry with those who had held aloof from visiting her. M. de la Tour alone underwent no change. I had begged of him to consider the notable alteration which opulence, though sudden, had wrought in the manners and behaviour of both the count and countess. 'I half agree with you,' replied he. 'The wife is a hussy who has gained in penetration; but the husband has lost in every way—he left us a fool and comes back to us a coxcomb. I persist in thinking

---

* "Mémoires du Comte Beugnot," vol. i. p. 35, *et seq.*

badly of them, and even in speaking badly of them, so long as they do not reveal to me by what honest means they have acquired in the short space of six months what we now know them to be possessed of. Whom will they or you persuade that the king, the queen, the Count d'Artois, the *contrôleur-général* — in a word, I know not what powerful persons—have thrown heaps of gold to people who simply asked for bread? The age I know is fertile in extravagance, but not exactly of this kind. Husband and wife have spread a little report around that madame is in favour with the queen. I have noticed them at this for the last fortnight, and if they had mentioned a single word of it in my presence, I had a little story ready for them about the Countess de Gazon and the Queen of Congo with which I should have made all the lookers-on laugh at their expense. My dear friend,' continued La Tour, 'they are altogether far too impertinent, and it is really shameful that people should be duped so cheaply. Believe every word they say if you please, but for my part I adhere to what I know. Now I know, through you, that madame has relations with the Cardinal de Rohan, since she has been conveyed five or six times to his eminence's hôtel at your expense. Possibly she has since been transported there on her own light foot. Of all the acquaintances of this fine lady, the Cardinal de Rohan is the only one to whom prodigality on a grand scale is not impossible. There are then two conclusions—either he has supplied the money for all that we see, or else it has been stolen from him. I ask your pardon for the second horn of my dilemma, but only on condition that you grant me the first; and yet I confess I can only with great difficulty understand how a little village hussy like her can have succeeded in seducing a prince, a prelate, and a scapegrace of such importance." *

A few days before her departure from Bar-sur-Aube the countess placed in the hands of young Beugnot a rouleau of fifty louis in discharge of certain small loans which he had at various times accommodated her with. "I explained to her," remarks Beugnot, "that I could not say exactly what she owed me, but that I was quite certain the amount was below 1200 francs.† 'Nevertheless take it,' replied she; 'and if there is anything over, give it to your mother for her poor pensioners.'" Beugnot, on making up the account, found he had been paid twenty louis too many, which in accordance with the countess's instructions he handed over to his mother. So favourable and lasting an impression did this act of generosity make on Madame Beugnot, that she could never afterwards be brought to believe in the truth of any of the crimes charged against this unhappy woman.

* "Mémoires du Comte Beugnot," vol. i. p. 41, *et seq.*
† There were twenty-four francs or livres in the louis of those days.

XVI.

DEC. 1784—JAN. 1785.

THE DIAMOND NECKLACE IS SOLD AT LAST.

THE countess and her husband, the steward and the four tall footmen, the led horses and the travelling van, the outriders and the elegant *berline*, returned to Paris at the close of November, 1784, when the De la Mottes proceeded, after all their desperate struggles towards this end, to enter at last into the coveted gaieties of the rank and fashion of the most brilliant capital in Europe. At the outset they did not share their good fortune with their sister, who was still passing a dull time of it at the Abbey of Jarcy. All they seem to have done was to resign to her the right of petitioning in the name of Valois, for on the 30th of November in this same year we find her making one of those stereotyped appeals for assistance for which the family had now become notorious to the Abbé Bourbon, natural son of Louis XV.* Irritated no doubt at her having

---

* This letter of Mademoiselle de Saint-Remi's has obtained the honour of being preserved among the historical autographs in the Imperial Archives.

refused to part with her pension, husband and wife determined to leave her to herself to enjoy in retirement its extremely slender benefits.

Suddenly grown rich in the queen's name, after having successfully established a very general belief in her pretended intimacy with royalty, the countess's instinctive tact led her to perceive that a new style of living was indispensable on her part to maintain the delusion, and keep alive that credit which she intended employing as the basis of still larger operations. The very extravagance to which she was naturally inclined became consequently one of the chief elements in her system of deceit. It was no longer "alms" that she contemplated asking from a carriage, since she had made the discovery that credulity was a mine which, properly worked, would furnish a far richer yield than charity was ever likely to do.

Beugnot tells us that on his return to Paris he was confirmed in his opinion that the opulence of Madame de la Motte was due to her intimate connection with the Cardinal de Rohan, and that he regulated his conduct towards her accordingly. "I presented myself," remarks he, "at her door with discretion: I went to eat at her house only when she did me the honour of inviting me; and I took care to place her at her ease by affecting respect towards her. On her part she made me acquainted with her various projects, which she set out before me with that negligence which presupposes the certainty of success. She intended, for instance, to withdraw her brother from the navy—an ungrateful and stupid service in times of peace; a regiment had been promised her for him. As for her husband, she had purchased him a step which would at once give him captain's rank, and she would by-and-by see if she could not get him named second colonel. With regard to her sister, she would not hear of her doing as she herself had done; in other words, contracting some stupid marriage. If agreeable to her, she should be canoness at Douxières or Poulangy, as all the places at Remiremont were kept for ten years. 'If,' remarked she, 'I had espoused a man of name, and who frequented the court, that would have been of some use to me. I should then have got on much quicker; as it is, my husband is to me rather an obstacle than a means. It is necessary that I should do something to make my name pass over his, which is, you know, contrary to all decorum.'

"When I visited Madame de la Motte, she never failed to introduce me to the company as a young magistrate, and always placed me immediately after the titled people. The tone of the house was, at least in those days, that of good company. I met there the Marquis de Saisseval, then a great gambler, rich, and currying favour with the court; the Abbé de Cabres, councillor in the Paris Parliament; Rouillé d'Orfeuil, intendant of Champagne; the Count d'Estaing (one of the heroes of the American war, and subsequently in command of the National Guards of Versailles, when the château was stormed by the mob); the Baron de Villeroy, an officer of the king's body-guard; the receiver-general Dorcy; and Lecoulteux de la Noraye, who, while aspiring to the post of director of the countess's affairs and finances, dreamed of being one day appointed *contrôleur-général* of the finances of the nation, and who considered himself altogether 'a most important personage, though he had only just wit enough to be nothing worse than a fool.'" La Noraye was no favourite with Beugnot, who in after years knocked him down on a particular occasion for playing him some shabby trick when they were fellow-prisoners in La Force in the days of the Terror.*

All the while that madame and her husband were showing off at Bar-sur-Aube, the cardinal was moping at Saverne, fretfully pacing up and down a favourite walk in the episcopal pleasure-grounds, which he had named the "Promenade de la Rose," in honour of the gracious gift of counterfeit royalty at the midnight interview in the park of Versailles. This walk, which led from the palace to the neighbouring woods, formerly went by the name of the "Route de Bonheur" (road of happiness), until the cardinal, to whom happiness still seemed hovering in the future, gave it its new designa-

* "Mémoires du Comte Beugnot," vol. i. pp. 45, *et seq*., 259, 260, 262.

tion.* He had been banished to Saverne in remote Alsace by one of those billets bordered with *vignettes bleues*, penned by the forger Villette, so that he might be out of the way while the De la Mottes were enjoying themselves in their country retreat.

On the countess's return to Paris, the correspondence between the cardinal and the phantom queen is speedily resumed. The letters that are now interchanged are more familiar and are even tender. The amatory prelate, we may be certain, complained that the last meeting was too brief, implored permission to return to the capital, and begged for another interview. Replies were doubtless sent, exhorting him to be discreet, and promising to comply with his request at some future period. One thing, however, is quite certain: it was at this time that madame applied for and obtained in the queen's name the 100,000 francs from the cardinal, of which we have already spoken, for of the 50,000 francs received in August last every sou of course was spent.

All this while the plans are being perfected for the successful carrying out of that grand scheme of fraud, which not only caused the greatest commotion throughout France, but may be said to have startled the entire civilized world by its audacity. The first incidents of the new intrigue appear to have been congenial. Some hanger-on of the countess's would seem to have sought

---

* "Compte rendu de ce qui s'est passé au Parlement," &c. p. 92.

out an emissary of the crown jewellers, employed to find a purchaser for the Necklace with the prospect of a commission for himself, and whispered in his ear that the Countess de la Motte was privately received by the queen, with whom she had both credit and influence, but that unusual reasons existed for not speaking publicly of this intimacy. He thought, however, that the countess, if she could only be induced to undertake the negotiation, was a very likely person to prevail upon the queen to buy the Necklace. This suggestion was duly reported to Böhmer and Bassenge, after which it appears the former waited on Madame de la Motte at her own house, and exhibited the matchless jewel. Everything else followed in due course.

Though evidently interwoven with those strange fabrications in which she delighted to indulge, the countess's own relation of this first stage in the great fraud has a certain air of probability about it, and furnishes us with the ends of some of the threads in this entanglement. After citing the name of a speculator and schemer named Laporte, who was always hatching new projects for making money, and whom she had been the means of introducing to the cardinal with the view of drawing him into some of Laporte's grand undertakings, she observes: "This Laporte was a very active person, and constantly at my house; I had stood godmother to one of his children. Achette, his father-in-law, was an intimate friend of Böhmer's.

One day, when the two latter were at Versailles, Achette said to Böhmer, 'Are you still saddled with your Necklace?' 'Unfortunately I am,' answered Böhmer; 'it is a heavy burden to me—I would gladly give a thousand louis to any one who could find me a purchaser for it.' It is most probable that from the date of this conversation my name was mentioned, Achette explaining to Böhmer how his son-in-law, Laporte, had access to me, and through me to the cardinal.

"One day Laporte having dined at my house, mentioned to me, for the first time, the fatal Necklace, observing that he rested all his hopes on me; that if I would only say a word to the queen, he was convinced her majesty would make the purchase, and that the jewellers were ready to enter into any arrangements that might be agreeable to her."

On this occasion, as well as on a subsequent one, the countess informs us that she declined to interfere, and though urgently pressed, would not listen to the suggestion. A third attempt to induce her to undertake the negotiation is afterwards made, she tells us, when Böhmer came to her house with Achette, bringing the Necklace along with him.

"'Is it not a pity,' said Achette to me, 'that so magnificent a jewel should leave the kingdom whilst we have a queen whom it would so well become, and whom, I am sure, must at heart long to possess it?'

" 'I don't know that,' answered I; 'nor can I understand why you have applied to me to transmit your proposals to her majesty. I protest to you I have no opportunity of submitting them to her, not having the honour of approaching her.'

"' Madame,' replied Achette, with a look full of meaning, 'we are not come hither to pry into your secrets, still less to evince any doubt respecting what you do us the honour to tell us; but believe me I am well acquainted with Versailles; I know what is going on there; and when I took the liberty of introducing my friend to you, it was because I felt convinced that if you would honour him with your support, nobody at court is better able to render him the service we make bold to solicit.'

"Böhmer's mouth was open: I saw he was going to speak to me of his gratitude; so, to get rid of them both, I told them I would see if, by means of my connections, I could contrive indirectly to render them some service."*

These visits took place at the end of December. In January, 1785, the countess contrives to insinuate to the crown jewellers, through some of her high-class connections, that the queen really does desire to have the Necklace. She openly states as much to the cardinal, whom, in the very depth of a bitterly-cold

* "Mémoires Justificatifs de la Comtesse de la Motte," p. 75, *et seq.*

winter, she has summoned to Paris by the aid of a courier armed with one of those well-known and highly-prized billets, gilt-edged, or bordered with *vignettes bleues*, in which the queen is made to say: "The wished-for moment has not yet arrived, but I desire to hasten your return on account of a secret negotiation which interests me personally, and which I am unwilling to confide to any one but yourself. The Countess de la Motte will explain the meaning of this enigma."

After reading this letter the cardinal longed for wings; still he was obliged to content himself with such fleet coursers as the *maîtres de postes* along the line of road to the capital could provide him with. So, well wrapped up in furs, and snugly ensconced in the corner of a comfortable close travelling carriage, he is soon rolling rapidly over the two hundred and eighty miles of frost-bound road that intervene between the episcopal palace of Saverne and the Rue Neuve-Saint-Gilles; and, no sooner has he learned the solution of the enigma, and procured from the countess the address of the crown jewellers—at the sign of the "Grand Balcony," Rue Vendôme—than, puffed up with the importance of the commission intrusted to him, he hies to Böhmer and Bassenge to open negotiations with them for the purchase of the costly gem. The cardinal had not far to go, for the Rue Vendôme (now the Rue Béranger) was only some ten minutes' walk from his hôtel, being situated but a single street from the junction of the Rue

Vieille-du-Temple with the Rue St.-Louis (now the Rue Turenne). At the present day many of the houses have been rebuilt, and of those which were in existence at the time of our narrative only a couple in any way answer to the sign "*Au Grand Balcon*," adopted by the crown jewellers. These are Nos. 11 and 22; the former—which is for the time being the Mairie of the 3rd Arrondissement—a handsome building with an ornamental ironwork balcony in front, before which is an open court, which one has no difficulty in picturing filled with the grand equipages and liveried lacqueys of the customers of our friends Böhmer and Bassenge.

In the excitement of conversation the grand almoner indiscreetly blurted out what he believed to be the fact, but which he had been strictly enjoined to keep secret, namely, that the queen was the actual purchaser of the jewel, though her name was on no account to transpire in the business. The price eventually agreed upon for the Necklace was 1,600,000 francs (£64,000), to be paid in four instalments of equal amount at intervals of six months: the first instalment of 400,000 francs to fall due in August. But the crown jewellers, who had been advised to be cautious in dealing with the cardinal, required that the contract should be authorized by the royal signature. To account for this demand, they explained to the cardinal that they had heavy debts and liabilities which prevented them from parting with an asset of so much value without replacing it with adequate vouchers to satisfy their creditors (and notably M. Baudard de Saint-James, treasurer-general of the navy, to whom they were indebted in no less a sum than 800,000 francs*) who had waited so long.

Strange to say, the person who had cautioned the jewellers to act so guardedly was the great *intriguante* herself, who, accompanied by her husband, had called upon Böhmer and Bassenge at seven o'clock on a raw January morning, a couple of hours or so before the cardinal, to announce his coming, when, after having reminded them that she had been no party to the transaction, she proceeded to recommend them not to come to terms without binding down the cardinal in such a manner as to make themselves secure.† That she took this step, so likely to frustrate her own object, was afterwards proved on the trial. Most persons would have thought that the probability of such a proceeding being fatal to her plans would have prevented her, if she meditated a fraud, acting in the way she did; but does not the reader perceive that this most subtle of impostors had thereby secured, by anticipation, a strong plea in her favour to disprove her guilt?

The obtaining the queen's signature to the contract necessarily gave rise to some delay. The cardinal sent the deed as he believed to Marie-Antoinette through Madame de la Motte, with the intimation that it was

* " Premier Interrogatoire du Cardinal de Rohan."
† Déposition de Bassenge.

THE AGREEMENT ONLY A FORMALITY.

only a form, and would be merely shown to the jewellers, and not delivered up to them. The countess, however, returns with the deed unsigned. Royalty is in dudgeon at its sacred name having been made use of. The grand almoner was greatly distressed at this new obstacle, which he thought her majesty was inclined to aggravate; but what was to be done?

Madame de la Motte returns a second time from Versailles, and pretends to have had a second audience with Marie-Antoinette. The queen, she says, was very angry with the cardinal for having introduced her name into the transaction, but had insinuated:

"If inspiring confidence is all that is requisite, could not the cardinal have devised some other mode? The cardinal is perhaps not aware of it, but I may tell you that I have bound myself by a formal engagement with the king not to sign any deed without his knowledge. So the thing, you see, is impossible. Contrive between you what you can do, or else renounce the purchase altogether. . . . It seems to me that, as this document is only a formality, and as these people do not know my handwriting . . . But you will reflect upon it; still, once for all, I cannot sign it. At all events, tell the cardinal that the first time I shall see him I will communicate to him the arrangements I intend to make with him."*

* "Life of the Countess de la Motte, by herself," vol. i. pp. 340, 341.

The countess then explains that, returning home after this interview, and not reflecting on the serious consequences of using the queen's name in the manner suggested, she resolves to counterfeit the royal signature, and for that purpose applies to Rétaux de Villette, the forger of the letters which to the last the countess always maintained to be genuine.

"I explained to M. de Villette," she says, "the new aspect which this affair had assumed, the cardinal's perplexity, the queen's dissatisfaction, the interview I had had with her majesty, and the meaning I attached to her expression that the jewellers were unacquainted with her handwriting.

"Villette said, if I was certain that the queen had made use of the express words I had just repeated, it would appear to him, as it had appeared to me, that she wished me to understand it did not much signify whose hand inscribed the attestation, since the jewellers did not know her handwriting. 'But,' added he, 'neither the queen nor yourself suspect the risk a person runs by counterfeiting writings. That is an act which the law has included in the list of crimes under the name of forgery. We can however do this. Taking for granted the statement of the queen, that these people do not know her handwriting, it may be fairly supposed that they are equally ignorant of her form of signature. To sign MARIE-ANTOINETTE alone, according to your idea, would be a positive forgery; but the metamorphosis of an Austrian princess into a French one—to say, for instance, MARIE-ANTOINETTE DE FRANCE—would really be unmeaning. If our object was to obtain this Necklace by a swindle, when the imposture came to be exposed such a signature would serve as a proof of it; but as we have no reasonable doubt but that the jewellers will be paid, since they will have the cardinal's guarantee privately supported by that of the queen, I think we may, without much fear of committing ourselves, submit to the necessity; I will therefore do what I now explain to you.

" 'First, I shall not disguise my own writing; and, secondly, I will give the queen the incorrect title of MARIE-ANTOINETTE DE FRANCE. The contract being exhibited by the cardinal to Böhmer and Bassenge, they will not examine it too minutely, I'll be bound; and you must promise me to burn it in my presence when the jewellers have been paid and the matter is at an end.'

"I gave him my word of honour that I would do this, and he signed the deed according to our covenant. I left him directly afterwards, and drove at once to the cardinal. At first I intended to give him the contract approved and signed, without telling him how I had settled matters; but I reflected that Villette and I were not the safest judges; that the affair might be more serious than we imagined, and that if such were the case the cardinal might be placed in an embarrassing position. So I resolved to tell him all."

Thereupon, according to Madame de la Motte's version, the cardinal was informed of the forgery and of the *incorrectness* of the signature, after he had seen the contract without detecting either. He acquiesced, we are told by the countess, in the fraud, merely observing that "since he had been deceived by it, it would be the same with the jewellers."*

Such is the specious explanation given by Madame de la Motte of the forgery of the queen's signature to the contract. But amidst this farrago of falsehood—for there can be no doubt the queen's signature was appended in the absurd form described, owing to the ignorance of this pair of sharpers†—the simple truth remains that the deluded cardinal, hoping thereby to please the queen, had bought the Necklace of the jewellers on his own guarantee for one million six hundred thousand francs, backed with this fraudulent signature of Marie-Antoinette's. The contract had been drawn up with great care by the cardinal himself, and was written with his own hand, since the matter was of course of too secret a nature o be intrusted to a professional engrosser; and after having been exhibited to Böhmer and Bassenge for their private satisfaction, it was left in the cardinal's keeping. The unfortunate

---

* "Mémoires Justificatifs de la Comtesse de la Motte," p. 93, *et seq.*, and "Life of the Countess de la Motte, by herself," vol. i. p. 344, *et seq.*

† Madame Campan states that "*Vu bon.—Marie-Antoinette*" was the form in which the queen certified the accuracy of an account.

dupe of course believed he still held possession of the royal guarantee, the grotesque inventions to the contrary of Madame de la Motte, which we have just laid before the reader, being of no further moment than to expose her own duplicity. The confidence and mental satisfaction of the jewellers when they read the contract, ratified by majesty itself, was equal to that felt by the cardinal. "They read it," says the Rohan memorial, "and appeared full of joy; they then returned it, but the cardinal requested them to take a copy of it, which they had not thought of doing. This copy they made themselves without the slightest doubt being raised in their minds by the strangeness of the signature."

We may instance as another proof of the countess's prompt mode of action, that by the end of January, 1785, the whole affair was settled—in fact within six weeks after she had promised "to see if she could not contrive indirectly to render the jewellers some service;" the famous Diamond Necklace which had been to them a source of grave anxiety for years was off their hands.

XVII.

1781—1785.

CHARLATAN COUNT CAGLIOSTRO.

WHEN, in the autumn of the year 1781, the De la Mottes were chasing the Marchioness de Boulainvilliers, who they had heard was at Strasbourg, the notorious Cagliostro was astonishing the good people of that famous town as much by his singular conduct as by the extraordinary cures he was represented to have performed. "Curious to behold so remarkable a personage, the cardinal," who was then at his episcopal palace of Saverne, "went over to Strasbourg, but found it necessary to use interest to get admitted into the presence of the illustrious charlatan. 'If monseigneur the cardinal is sick,' said he, 'let him come to me and I will cure him. If he is well, he has no business with me nor I with him.' This reply, far from offending the cardinal's vanity, only increased the desire he had to become acquainted with this new Esculapius. Having at length gained admission to his sanctuary, the cardinal fancied he saw impressed on the countenance of this mysterious and taciturn individual, a dignity so imposing that he felt himself penetrated with an almost religious awe, and the very first words he uttered were inspired by reverence. The interview, which was but brief, excited more strongly than ever in the mind of the cardinal the desire of a more intimate acquaintance. This gradually came about, the crafty empiric timing his conduct and his advances so skilfully, that without seeming to desire it, he gained the grand almoner's entire confidence, and obtained the greatest ascendency over him."*

During the next two years or so, Cagliostro seems to have made the episcopal palace at Saverne his home whenever he felt so inclined. When the cardinal happened to be there, the count amused him by performing experiments in the laboratory which had been fitted up in a private part of the palace for his especial use—making, so the cardinal maintained, not only gold, but diamonds, under his very eyes.† But when the cardinal was away the crucibles were no longer in request, and the count would indulge in carousals, prolonged far into the night, with the Baron de Planta, the cardinal's equerry and confidant, and a black sheep of the choicest breed, at which his eminence's matchless Tokay flowed like water.‡

---

* "Mémoires pour servir," etc., par l'Abbé Georgel, vol. ii. p. 47, et seq.
† See post, pp. 183, 184.
‡ "Mémoires pour servir," etc., par l'Abbé Georgel, vol. ii. p. 50.

In the memorial published in his behalf at the time of the Necklace trial, Cagliostro gives a most romantic account of himself. He is ignorant, he says, of the place of his birth, but was brought up while a child in the city of Medina, where he went by the name of Acharat, and lived attended by servants in a style of great splendour in apartments in the palace of the Mufti Salahayn, the chief of the Mussulmans. From Medina, he pretends, he was taken when quite a youth to Mecca, where he remained for three years petted by the scherif. He is next taken to Egypt, visits the chief cities of Africa and Asia, and eventually sails from Rhodes for Malta, where apartments are provided for him in the palace of the grand master. Here, he says, he assumed the name of Cagliostro and the title of count. From Malta he proceeds to Sicily and Naples, thence to Rome, where he makes the acquaintance of several cardinals, and is admitted to frequent audiences of the Pope. He professes to have next visited Spain, Portugal, Holland, Russia, and Poland, and gives a list of the nobles of these countries with whom he had become acquainted. At length, in September, 1780, he goes to Strasbourg, where his fame as a physician had already preceded him. Here, he asserts, with perfect truth, he cured the poor generally, and particularly sick soldiers and prisoners, without fee or reward. Strasbourg was soon crowded with strangers, who came either to see him or to consult him. It is now that he makes the acquaintance of the Cardinal de Rohan, whom he accompanies to Paris to prescribe for the Prince de Soubise, suffering at the time from an accident to his leg. After a short sojourn in the capital he returns to Strasbourg, when being persecuted by a party in the town, it is quite certain that letters are written to the authorities in his behalf by the Count de Vergennes, minister for foreign affairs, the Marquis de Miroménil, keeper of the seals, and the Marquis de Ségur, minister of war, who desire that every protection shall be afforded him.

Cagliostro's story about his residence in Medina, and Mecca and Egypt, and Rhodes and Malta, is a tissue of impudent lies. The truth is, his real name was Joseph Balsamo, and he was the son of a small tradesman of Palermo, in which city he was born. After a career of imposture and adventure—in the course of which he visited many of the chief cities of the Continent, passed over to England, and next went to Paris, where his wife, aged eighteen years, eloped from him, and was only restored to him through the intervention of the French police—he was picked up, while still a young man—being little over thirty years of age—by the sect of Illuminati, who thought, and correctly thought, that they had discovered in him a willing and able instrument for the dissemination of their doctrines. His initiation into the mysteries of Illuminism took place in a cave some little distance from Frankfort-on-the-Maine, when he learnt for the first time that the object of the society of which he was now a member, was to overturn the thrones of Europe, and that the first blow was to be struck in France; that after the fall of the French monarchy it was proposed to attack Rome; that the society had extensive resources, and was in the possession of enormous funds, dispersed among the banks of Amsterdam, Rotterdam, Basle, Lyons, London, Venice, and Genoa, the proceeds of the annual subscriptions of its members. A considerable sum of money, which he afterwards pretended he had acquired by the practice of alchemy, was at once placed at his disposal, to enable him to propagate the doctrines of the sect in France. This was the origin of his first visit to Strasbourg in the autumn of the year 1780, when he adopted for his device the letters L. P. D., signifying *Lilia pedibus destrue* — Trample the lilies under foot.*

Cagliostro was one of those individuals who, for reasons of their own, envelop themselves in a maze of mystery, and are rarely seen through during their lives, because they address themselves to men's imaginations alone. By exciting wonder they disarm reason. He laid claim to many gifts and acquirements; had studied medicine, was an adept at alchemy, and knew something of natural magic. The acts which he performed

* "Louis XVI.," par Alexandre Dumas, vol. iii. p. 154.

were so contrived by his arts and wiles, that all his visitors (and they comprised persons of the highest rank and the most intellectual attainments) considered them to be marvellous, whilst the gaping multitude magnified every feat until it went far beyond this ideal. He set no price on his public exhibitions, and darted looks of wounded honour at those who, he pretended, degraded him by offering him gold; whilst his hand was constantly open to the indigent, whom he waited on in their humble homes with advice, medicine, and money. His widespread acts of benevolence, and the luxurious style in which he lived, proved him to be rich, and yet none were able to discover the sources of his wealth. The houses of the most opulent citizens were thrown open to him, and without seeking the great, but seeming rather to avoid them, he constantly found himself in their company. Among this class he had many proselytes, but none who believed in him so implicitly as the Cardinal Prince de Rohan, who, spite of the count's "perfect quack face," seems to have worshipped him as a being something more than human.

A friend of the grand almoner's, the Baroness d'Oberkirche, who met Cagliostro at Saverne at this epoch, sketches his portrait for us in her "Memoirs," and furnishes us with convincing proofs of the singular influence which the count had succeeded in acquiring over his credulous patron. " Cagliostro was anything but handsome," she observes, "still I have never seen a more remarkable physiognomy; above all, he had a penetrating look which seemed almost supernatural. I know not how to describe the expression of his eyes: it was at once fire and ice; attracted and repelled you at the same time; made you afraid and inspired you with an irrepressible curiosity. One might draw two different portraits of him, both resembling him, and yet totally dissimilar. He wore on his shirt-front, on his watch-chain, and on his fingers, diamonds of large size, and apparently of the purest water. If they were not paste, they were worth a king's ransom. He pretended that he had made them himself. All this frippery showed the charlatan miles off.

"When Cagliostro perceived me he saluted me very respectfully. I returned his salutation without affecting either hauteur or condescension. There were fifteen of us at dinner; nevertheless, the cardinal occupied himself almost exclusively with me, using a sort of refined coquetry to bring me over to his way of thinking with regard to Cagliostro, with whom he was perfectly infatuated. I was placed on the cardinal's right hand, and during dinner he tried by every means to enforce his convictions upon me. I resisted, politely but firmly; he grew impatient, and on leaving table volunteered me his confidence. Had I not heard him with my own ears I could never have believed that a prince of the Roman church, a Rohan, an intelligent and honourable man in so many respects, could have allowed himself to be brought to the point of abjuring both his dignity and free will at the bidding of a *chevalier de l'industrie.*

"'In truth, baroness, you are very hard to convince,' remarked the cardinal; 'what! has not all that he has told you, all that I have just related, satisfied you? I must then avow everything. Understand, at least, that I am about to confide to you a secret of importance.' I was greatly embarrassed. I did not wish to be the depositary of any of the cardinal's secrets, and was about to excuse myself when, divining my intention, the prince exclaimed: 'Do not say no! but listen to me. You see this?'

"The cardinal showed me a large solitaire which he wore on his little finger, engraved with the arms of the house of Rohan; it was a ring worth 20,000 francs at least. 'It is a fine stone, my lord,' observed I; 'I have been already admiring it.' 'Well, it was he who made it; created it out of nothing. I saw him myself. I was present, with eyes fixed upon the crucible, and assisted at the operation. Is this science? What do you think of it, baroness? They tell me that he is only luring me on, that he cheats me; the jeweller and engraver have valued this brilliant at 25,000 francs. You will at least admit that he is a strange sort of sharper to make such presents as this.'

"I acknowledge I was stupefied. The Prince de

Rohan perceived it, and continued, certain of his victory: 'But this is not all: he makes gold; he has made in my presence, in the crucibles of the palace, five or six thousand francs' worth. I shall have more of it—I shall, in fact, have any quantity—he will make me the richest prince in Europe. These are not dreams, madam, these are certainties. Think, too, of his prophecies fulfilled; of the miraculous cures he has performed. I tell you that he is not only a most extraordinary, but a sublime, man, and one whose goodness has never been equalled; the charities he bestows, the benefits he confers, pass all imagination.'

"'Am I to understand your eminence,' inquired I, 'that you have given him nothing for all this—have not made him the smallest advance, have made him no promise, given him no written document which compromises you? Pardon my curiosity, but since you wish to make me a confidant of these mysteries, I——' 'You are right, madam,' replied the prince, 'but I can assure you that he has asked nothing, has received nothing from me.' 'Ah! my lord,' I exclaimed, 'it must be that this man reckons on obtaining from you many dangerous sacrifices since he buys your unbounded confidence so dearly. Were I in your place I should be extremely cautious; one of these days he will lead you too far.' The cardinal only answered by an incredulous smile; but I am certain that later, at the time of the Necklace affair, when Cagliostro and the Countess de la Motte had cast him to the bottom of the abyss, he recalled my words."*

Singularly enough, Cagliostro arrived in Paris just at the time the cardinal was making the final arrangements with the crown jewellers for the purchase of the Necklace. Whether or no he was summoned thither by the cardinal himself we are unable to say, but if the Abbé Georgel's statement is to be relied on, it is quite certain that the grand almoner consulted Cagliostro respecting the business of the Necklace prior to concluding the negotiations. The abbé says: "This Python mounted his tripod; the Egyptian invocations were made at night in the cardinal's own saloon, which was illuminated by an immense number of wax tapers. The oracle, under the inspiration of its familiar demon, pronounced that the negotiation was worthy of the prince, that it would be crowned with success, that it would raise the goodness of the queen to its height, and bring to light that happy day which would unfold the rare talents of the cardinal for the benefit of France and of the human race." †

The Countess de la Motte, who it will be remembered had formerly met Cagliostro at Strasbourg, renewed her acquaintance with him in the *salons* of the Palais-Cardinal, where she was now a constant visitor. For a time it was an affair of diamond cut diamond between

* "Mémoires de la Baronne d'Oberkirche," vol. i. pp. 129, 144.
† "Mémoires pour servir," etc., par l'Abbé Georgel, vol. ii. p. 59.

them. She flattered the arch impostor with the finest art, appeared to be his dupe, and broke out into loud exclamations of surprise when he performed his tricks and practised his delusions in her presence. The crafty cheat was himself cheated. By degrees he became persuaded that she was really a confidant of the French queen, that she had credit at court, and would soon have power. Fully convinced of her influence, and perceiving, as he thought, that his patron the cardinal would by her assistance retrieve his political fortune, he encouraged that sanguine prelate, and worked, as we have seen, upon his imagination, with a view to dispel any lingering doubt he might chance to entertain. So infatuated did Cagliostro become under the influence of his own delusions on the one side, and the spell of this enchantress on the other, that the countess would appear to have controlled the crafty necromancer even in the performance of his own spells.*

Cagliostro, after he was regularly settled in Paris, became a frequent visitor at the countess's house—he and madame, we are told, were like two fingers on one hand—where he was received with an amount of respect verging on to reverence. The De la Mottes and he were close neighbours, for he lived at the Hôtel de Savigny, in the Rue Saint-Claude, only a couple of streets off. "The house which he occupied, and which

* See post, vol. ii. p. 38.

was afterwards the residence of Barras, was one of the most elegant of the quarter. In the *salon*, decorated with an oriental luxury, and bathed in a kind of semi-daylight when it was not resplendent with the blaze of a hundred lights, the pursuits of the philosopher and conspirator might be divined by the side of the projects of the quack. There one saw the bust of Hippocrates, and, in a black frame, inscribed in letters of gold, a literal translation of Pope's Universal Prayer."*
Here Cagliostro lived in state, giving balls, assemblies, and audiences at which he insolently offered his hand to his fair disciples to kiss, while he treated his male visitors, and at times even the cardinal himself, with marked disdain.†

Young Beugnot, who met Cagliostro at one of Madame de la Motte's *petits soupers*, tells us that the countess previously warned him that she would be obliged to disarm the inquietude of Cagliostro, who, for no reason whatever, invariably refused to sup if he thought that any one had been invited to meet him. Moreover, she begged Beugnot to ask him no questions, not to interrupt him when he was speaking, and to answer with readiness any inquiries he had addressed to him. "I subscribed," says Beugnot, " to these conditions, and would have accepted even harder ones to gratify my

* "Histoire de la Révolution Française," par Louis Blanc, vol. ii. p. 82.
† "Réponse pour la Comtesse de la Motte," p. 27.

curiosity. At half-past ten the folding doors were thrown open, and the Count de Cagliostro was announced. Madame de la Motte precipitately quitted her arm-chair, rushed up to him and drew him into a corner of the *salon*, where I presume she begged him to pardon my presence. Cagliostro advanced towards me and bowed, without appearing at all embarrassed at perceiving a stranger. He was of medium height, rather stout, had a very short neck, and a round face ornamented with two large eyes sunken in his head, and a broad turn-up nose; his complexion was of an olive tinge; his *coiffure* was new in France, his hair being divided into several little tresses, which, uniting at the back of the head, were tied up in the form known as the 'club.' He wore a French coat of iron grey embroidered with gold lace, and carried his sword stuck in the skirts, a scarlet vest trimmed with *point d'Espagne*, red breeches, and a hat edged with a white feather. This last article of dress was still necessary to mountebanks, dentists, and other medical *artistes* who made speeches and sold their drugs out of doors. Cagliostro's costume was relieved by lace ruffles, several costly rings, and shoe-buckles of an old pattern but brilliant enough to pass for very fine diamonds.

"There were at supper only the members of the family, among whom I include Father Loth, *minime* of the Place Royale, who reconciled, I know not how, his sacred functions with the place of second secretary to

Madame de la Motte. He used to say mass for her on Sundays, and charged himself during the rest of the week with commissions at the Palais-Cardinal which the first secretary thought beneath his dignity. Neither must I count as a stranger the Chevalier de Montbreul, a veteran of the green rooms, and still a good conversationalist, who was prepared to affirm almost any mortal thing, and was found, as if by chance, wherever Cagliostro appeared, ready to bear witness to the marvels he had performed, and to offer himself as a positive example miraculously cured of I know not how many diseases, of which the names alone were sufficiently startling.

"There were then nine or ten of us at table; Madame de la Motte had on one side of her Cagliostro and Montbreul, and I was on her other side, facing the first, whom I made a point of examining by stealth, and still did not know what to think of him; the face, the style of dressing the hair, the whole of the man, impressed me in spite of myself. I waited for him to open his mouth. He spoke I know not what jargon, half Italian, half French, plentifully interlarded with quotations in an unknown tongue, which passed with the unlearned for Arabic. He had all the talking to himself, and found time to go over at least twenty different subjects in the course of the evening, simply because he gave to them merely that extent of development which seemed good to him. Every moment he was inquiring if he was understood, whereupon everybody bowed in turn to assure him that he was. When starting a subject he seemed like one transported, raised his voice to the highest pitch, and indulged in the most extravagant gesticulations. The subjects of his discourse were the heavens, the stars, the grand *arcanum*, Memphis, transcendental chemistry, giants, and the extinct monsters of the animal kingdom. He spoke, moreover, of a city in the interior of Africa ten times as large as Paris, and where he pretended he had correspondents." Beugnot further mentions, that in between his rhapsodies he would chatter the most frivolous nonsense to the Countess de la Motte, whom he designated his dove, his gazelle, and his white swan. After supper he addressed numerous questions to Beugnot, one following another with extraordinary rapidity. To all the count's catechising the young advocate invariably replied by a respectful avowal of his ignorance, and subsequently was surprised to learn from Madame de la Motte that Cagliostro had conceived a most favourable opinion, not merely of his deportment, but likewise of his knowledge.*

* "Mémoires du Comte Beugnot," vol. i. p. 59, *et seq*.

XVIII.

1785. FEB.

THE DIAMOND NECKLACE IS DELIVERED.

THE Cardinal de Rohan obtained possession of the Necklace early on the morning of the 1st of February, 1785, and had not long to wait ere he was honoured with the queen's commands to deliver it into her royal custody. We shall give two accounts of how this delivery was effected—namely, the story told by the countess, and the statement made by the cardinal in his memorial.

The cardinal of course expected, from having rendered the queen a service for which she could not feel otherwise than grateful, that he would have been permitted to deliver the rich jewel to Marie-Antoinette in person, and when he received from Madame de la Motte the following note, purporting to be written by the queen, he imagined his expectations were on the point of being realized:—

" This evening (Feb. 1), at nine o'clock, you must be

at the countess's house (at Versailles) with the casket and in the usual costume. Do not leave until you hear from me."

The countess lodged, as the reader will remember, at "La Belle Image," in the Place Dauphine, and thither, on this sharp winter's night—it was a hard frost, and the ground was almost like glass—the cardinal proceeded, wrapped up in a long great-coat, and wearing a slouched hat that concealed his features. One can imagine the countess's nervous state on this eventful evening—can see her posted at the window on the watch, peering through the frost on the panes into the dark and almost silent Place, eager for a glimpse of the grand almoner with the coveted treasure. At last two figures are seen crossing the broad square from the Rue de la Pompe, at the end of which is the Hôtel de Rohan—one is the cardinal, the other a man-servant he has brought with him, and who carries the casket, and whom he dismisses a few doors off "La Belle Image."

"At half-past eight o'clock," says Madame de la Motte, "the cardinal called upon me in his disguise, carrying under his arm the casket containing the Necklace, which he set down on a chest of drawers. At half-past nine Lesclos, that faithful messenger of her majesty, whom she so often employed in delicate missions—Lesclos, a man perfectly well known to the cardinal, and the necessary confidant of all the little irregularities mentioned in the correspondence between him and the queen—called upon me with a letter from her majesty which ran thus:—

"' The minister (the king) is at present with me, and I cannot tell how long he will stay. You know the person I send. Deliver the casket to him, and stay where you are. I do not despair of seeing *thee* to-day."

"The cardinal," continues the countess, "having read this note, delivered to the faithful Lesclos, with his own hands, the casket containing the Necklace which he had himself deposited on the chest of drawers. Lesclos went out." *

Such is Madame de la Motte's statement. Let us compare it with the cardinal's, which we extract from one of the memorials produced in his defence at the trial :—

" On his (the cardinal's) arrival at Versailles he called upon Madame de la Motte, who was living in the Place Dauphine; he took with him Schreibert, his *valet de chambre*, who had charge of the casket. The cardinal, when they had reached the house, took it from him and went up-stairs by himself. He found Madame de la Motte alone, and presented to her the rich burden he was carrying.

" Some time after a man, who announced himself as a messenger from the queen, entered the apartment. The cardinal withdrew cautiously into an alcove which

---

* "Mémoires Justificatifs de la Comtesse de la Motte," p .99.

was half open. The man delivered a note. Madame de la Motte sent him for a moment outside the room, then came towards the cardinal and read to him the letter containing the order for delivering up the casket to the bearer. The man was then called in again, the casket was given into his hands, and he took his departure. . . . Who was that man? To the cardinal he seemed to be the same that he had descried in the park of Versailles on the night of the 11th of August, 1784, close to Mademoiselle d'Oliva."*

We will undertake to answer the cardinal's interrogatory. The messenger was an accomplice of the countess's: none other than the forger Rétaux de Villette, made up for the occasion "with large black eyebrows and pale face," and the letter of which he was the bearer was one of his own numerous forgeries. At any rate the countess's *femme de chambre*, Rosalie Briffaut, deposed to having opened the door to him at the precise hour on that particular night, when he immediately entered the countess's apartment.

Success is attained at last! The great fraud is consummated! The woman who when a child we have seen running along the streets with naked feet, the tatters of poverty her only covering, and begging of

---

* "Mémoire pour le Cardinal de Rohan," p. 39. All the persons concerned in the famous nocturnal meeting differed with regard to the date at which it took place. Madame de la Motte, as we have already stated, fixes it on the 28th of July.

lords and ladies to "bestow a few sous on a descendant of Henry II. of Valois, King of France," has at length obtained possession of the famed Diamond Necklace, valued at 160,000 francs, or £64,000 sterling! The jewellers, delighted at having got the troublesome piece of *bijouterie* off their hands, invite the countess to a grand dinner, and madame being pleased to accept the invitation, the affair came off on the 12th of February, when doubtless both the countess and her absent friend the cardinal were toasted in bumpers of the choicest Burgundy, and more than one fine speech was made which, had it been accurately reported, would have read rather curiously a few months afterwards.

It had been arranged, it seems, between the jewellers and Laporte, Achette, some baron—name unknown, but said to be a relative of the cardinal's—and a money-lending goldsmith named Grenier,* the same who had purchased the De la Motte pension, and who, we expect, had got mixed up in the Necklace affair through his connection with the countess, that a commission of 200,000 francs was to be paid to the negotiators, of which amount madame says it was proposed she should receive one-half in articles of jewelry, such as diamond-rings and earrings, a couple of solitaires, a locket set with diamonds, and a watch and chain for herself, with a

* Miswritten "Regnier" in the official records. Regnier was another goldsmith with whom the De la Mottes had considerable dealings, bought their service of plate of, &c.

couple of diamond rings and a watch and chain set with diamonds for her husband. When Laporte sent her a written memorandum of these conditions, and begged her acceptance of them, she declined, and desired him to say no more on the subject, as she had done so little towards effecting the sale of the Necklace, and as, moreover, it was not her habit to receive presents for services rendered!*

When the count, who had not yet been let into the secret of his wife's intention with regard to the Necklace, came to hear of this refusal, he blamed her very much, and it was arranged with Grenier that he should inform the other negotiators of the countess's willingness to accept the proposed presents. It does not appear, however, that she ever received them. The commission was probably dependent on the payment of the purchase-money for the Necklace, and as this was never paid, the arrangement with regard to the commission most probably fell to the ground.

Baudard de Saint-James, treasurer-general of the navy, and the principal creditor of the crown-jewellers, is equally delighted with them at the Necklace being at last sold. He has now before him the pleasant prospect of receiving twenty-four livres in the louis on his large debt, and from a feeling of gratitude presses, through Böhmer and Bassenge, the offer of his services upon the

* "Premier Interrogatoire de Madame de la Motte."

cardinal, to whom, he said, he should be proud to be of use. The cardinal, who, with all his large resources, is continually in want of money, knew, we suppose, what this meant, for he forthwith borrowed 50,000 francs from the treasurer-general of the navy on his simple note of hand.*

This celebrated financier's real name was Baudard; but when he had grown rich he made an addition to it, and called himself Saint-James, after the village from whence he came. This name he in his turn bestowed on a celebrated château and park still existing at the end of the Avenue de Neuilly, the same in which the Duke of Wellington and his staff took up their quarters when the Allies entered Paris after the battle of Waterloo, and which was formerly the residence of the famous Cardinal de Retz, afterwards of Le Normand (uncle of Madame de Maintenon, and the richest *fermier-général* of his time), by whom the château was rebuilt, and subsequently of the treasurer-general of the navy, who dissipated his immense fortune upon it in fancies of the wildest kind. He first enlarged the château, then redecorated and furnished it in the most magnificent style; next extended and relaid out the park, planted miniature woods, constructed artificial grottoes and waterfalls, erected Chinese temples and Turkish kiosques, and formed a superb winter-garden, in which he accu-

* " Premier Interrogatoire du Cardinal de Rohan."

mulated all the rare flora of Asia and America. The feature of the park, however, was its grand rock, the quarrying and transit of which is said to have cost Saint-James the incredible sum of 1,600,000 francs, or £64,000*—exactly the price of the Diamond Necklace—and is known even at the present day by the name of "Saint-James's Folly." What with his reckless expenditure upon this château and park, and his subsequent losses by Böhmer and Bassenge and others, it is not to be wondered at that Baudard de Saint-James came to grief at last—failed, in fact, for a million sterling, got sent to the Bastille, which he only left to die of poverty and grief a short time afterwards.

* "Histoire du Bois de Boulogne," par J. Lobet, p. 141.

XIX.

1785. Feb.—Aug.

THE DIAMOND NECKLACE VANISHES!

THE gigantic swindle it must be confessed had been effected in a masterly manner. Weeks, and even months, passed by, and no one seemed to entertain the slightest suspicion that any fraud had been perpetrated. But this was only the calm that precedes the storm. The crown jewellers, Böhmer and Bassenge, made it no secret that they had succeeded in disposing of their Necklace. They, however, gave out that it had been purchased by the Sultan of Turkey for a favourite sultana. Böhmer afterwards stated that they did this at the request of the cardinal, who had received the queen's commands to that effect. Of course Madame de la Motte was the real person who caused this report to be spread to allay impertinent curiosity. The cardinal flattered himself that he had placed his sovereign under an obligation, and was expecting both favour and power, and was confiding these hopes rather incautiously to his friends. The De la Mottes were openly living in almost Oriental luxury. Nobody would have supposed that any great wrong had been done.

On the 3rd of February, two days after the Necklace had been delivered to the cardinal, he met Böhmer and Bassenge at Versailles. "Well," said he to them, "have you made your very humble acknowledgments to her majesty for having purchased your Necklace?" The jewellers, careless upon this point now the Necklace was fairly off their hands, had not done so; the cardinal upbraided them with their neglect, a fact admitted at the trial.*

Months glide by without the slightest suspicion arising, although the grand almoner is somewhat puzzled at the queen never wearing the Necklace in public. Every time he meets the jewellers he repeats his inquiry whether they have humbly thanked the queen, and renews his very earnest recommendation for them to do so. At length, in the last week of June, after the countess has more than once hinted to him that the queen thinks the Necklace dear, the cardinal receives a letter written in the queen's name by the forger Villette, complaining of the excessive price of the jewel, and demanding a reduction of 200,000 francs, in which case 700,000 instead of 400,000 francs would be paid on the 1st of August, "otherwise," the letter

* " Premier Interrogatoire du Cardinal de Rohan."

went on to say, "the article will be returned."* The crown jewellers murmur, as well they might, at this unexpected demand, but rather than be again burthened with the Necklace, after consulting with Saint-James, give an unwilling consent to the new arrangement. When all is finally settled, by the advice of the cardinal they address to the queen the following letter, the very words of which are dictated by the grand almoner himself:

" Madame,

"We are extremely happy to think that the last arrangements which have been proposed to us, and to which we have submitted with respectful zeal, will be received as a new instance of our submission and devotedness to your majesty's commands, and we feel truly rejoiced to think that the most beautiful set of diamonds in the world will be worn by the best and greatest of queens.

"BÖHMER AND BASSENGE.

"July 12, 1785." †

When the above letter was written, some slight feelings of uneasiness respecting the Necklace had taken possession of the minds of the two partners; for Marie-Antoinette had appeared in public on several occasions

---

* "Life of the Countess de la Motte, by herself," vol. i. p. 350, and " Premier Interrogatoire du Cardinal de Rohan."
† Déposition de Bassenge.

when such an ornament might very properly have been worn, but she did not display it. Böhmer had sought interviews with the queen, who had carefully avoided him, fearing to be again pestered with his importunities, and since his threat of committing suicide, regarding him as partially deranged.

The cardinal, as we have already remarked, was perplexed by the circumstance that the queen did not wear the Necklace, and still more by the freezing aversion she continued to show him whenever they met in public. The fictitious letters too had become more rare, also much briefer than heretofore, and very cold. The apprehension mutually shared by the cardinal and the crown jewellers may be traced in the letter just quoted, in which "the most beautiful set of diamonds in the world" is pointedly alluded to, and something like a hint given that they ought to be "worn by the best and greatest of queens."

This letter was delivered by Böhmer to Marie-Antoinette with a diamond epaulette and buckles which the king had ordered of the crown jewellers as presents to the Duke d'Angoulême on the day of his christening. The queen, who had just returned from mass, went at once into her library, where Madame Campan was present. "She held the note in her hand; she read it to me," says Madame Campan, "observing that as I had in the morning guessed the enigmas in the *Mercure*, I could no doubt discover the meaning of this, which that madman Böhmer had just handed to her. These were her very words. The note contained a request not to forget him,* and expressions of his happiness at seeing her in possession of the most beautiful diamonds that could be found in Europe. As she finished reading the note she twisted it up and burnt it at a taper which was standing lighted in her library for sealing letters, and merely recommended me, when I should see Böhmer, to request an explanation of it. 'Has he assorted some new ornaments?'† added the queen. 'I should be very vexed if he has done so, for I don't intend to make use of his services any longer.'"‡

In the middle of the month of July, but a very short time before the first instalment fell due, the countess, feeling the necessity for gaining time, called upon the Cardinal de Rohan, and told him that the queen would be constrained to devote the 700,000 francs, which she had put aside for the payment of the moiety of the purchase-money due on the 1st of August, to other purposes, and she begged that the cardinal would see the jewellers and obtain a postponement, which the queen thought could not be at all difficult,§ until the

---

* Madame Campan's memory appears to have been at fault here.

† The reader will have observed that specific mention is not made in the jeweller's letter of the Necklace itself, which Marie-Antoinette, in common with everybody else, had no doubt heard had been sold to the Sultan.

‡ "Memoirs of Marie-Antoinette," by Madame Campan, vol. ii. p. 227.

§ "Mémoires pour servir," etc., par l'Abbé Georgel, vol. ii. p. 92.

1st of October. The cardinal received this message with evident consternation, whereupon Madame de la Motte, to reassure him, told him that she had seen in the queen's hands notes to the amount of 700,000 francs, which her majesty had designed for the payment of the instalment in question, and a day or two afterwards she would appear to have brought him a letter from the queen on the subject.* There is no help for it—for needs must when such a charioteer as the countess drives—so the cardinal does as he is bid, somewhat out of temper, it is true, by this time with her majesty's unbusinesslike ways, which bid fair, he tells the jewellers, "to turn his head." Böhmer and Bassenge show such evident signs of dissatisfaction at this new variation of the contract, that to quiet them the prince feels constrained to tell them a fib, namely, that he had *himself* seen in the queen's hands the 700,000 francs in question. This statement he repeats to Baudard de Saint-James, whose interest in the matter we know, and who makes it his business to be kept informed of any hitches that arise in this troublesome Necklace affair. Prompted no doubt by Madame de la Motte, the cardinal seems to have hinted to the financier that it would be a good opportunity for him to secure the queen's favour, and with it the *cordon rouge*, of which Saint-James was particularly ambitious, by lending her majesty this 700,000 francs

---

* See Appendix to vol. ii. of the present work.

for the payment of the first instalment. Saint-James was not unwilling; still he was over cautious, and said that on hearing one word from the queen the amount should be forthcoming.* Georgel says that the reason the affair fell through was because the forger Villette was, as will afterwards appear, away at that particular juncture at Bar-sur-Aube, and the written word consequently was not forthcoming until it was too late,† owing to which lucky accident Saint-James saved his 700,000 francs, which the countess would certainly have spirited away after her usual fashion if the chance had only been afforded her.

After consulting with their most pressing creditors, Böhmer and Bassenge give a reluctant consent to the postponement asked for; but while the affair is still under consideration, the countess, getting alarmed, brings the cardinal 30,000 francs, which she tells him the queen has sent as interest on the retarded payment. Thirty thousand francs as interest on seven hundred thousand francs for two months, or at the rate of nearly twenty-six per cent., and the client, too, a queen! Madame de la Motte had evidently foreseen the famous axiom of Field Marshal the Duke of Wellington, though in an inverted form. With her, bad security implied high interest.

This 30,000 francs, we are told by the Abbé Georgel,

---

* "Premier Interrogatoire du Cardinal de Rohan."
† "Mémoires pour servir," etc., par l'Abbé Georgel, vol. ii. p. 80.

only confirmed the most credulous of mortals in the conviction he entertained of the entire truth of all that Madame de la Motte had asserted. He at once hastened to the jewellers, who accepted the amount, not as interest, but on account of the principal. A few days afterwards, namely, on the 3rd of August, Böhmer, who occasionally visited the father-in-law of Madame Campan, went down to his country house at Crespy— whether or not by invitation from Madame Campan does not appear—when Madame Campan repeated to him all that the queen had desired her to say. Böhmer, she tells us, seemed petrified, and asked how it was that the queen had been unable to understand the meaning of the letter he had presented to her.

"I read it myself," replied Madame Campan, "and I could make nothing of it."

Böhmer observed that he was not surprised at that, as there was a certain mystery in the affair respecting which she was ignorant, but of which he would inform her fully if she would accord him a private interview.

"When I had got rid of the persons who required my presence in the drawing-room," says Madame Campan, "I went with Böhmer down one of the garden-walks." Here the promised explanation was given, on hearing which Madame Campan was "so struck with horror," "so absorbed in grief," that a storm of thunder and rain came on while they were talking together without exciting her attention. During this conversation Böhmer stated that the queen, having changed her mind respecting his "grand Necklace," and having determined to purchase it, had employed the Cardinal de Rohan as her agent in the transaction.

Madame Campan at once told the crown jeweller that he was deceived, for the queen had never spoken to the cardinal since his return from Vienna, and there was not an individual at court less favourably looked upon than the grand almoner.

"You are deceived yourself, madam," replied Böhmer; "the queen must see him in private, for it was to his eminence that she gave 30,000 francs which were paid me on account; she took them in his presence* out of the little *secrétaire* of Sèvres porcelain next the fireplace in her boudoir. This the cardinal told me himself."

Böhmer further stated that he had in his possession all the notes signed by the queen, and that he had even been obliged to show these to various bankers in order to induce them to grant him an extension of time for his payments.

Madame Campan, thunderstruck at what she heard, assured poor Böhmer that he was the victim of a detestable plot; whereupon the jeweller confessed that

---

* This, if true, was a piece of vain boasting on the cardinal's part, for it is quite certain that he received the thirty thousand francs from Madame de la Motte, who professed to have brought them from the queen.

he began to feel alarmed, as the cardinal had declared to him that the queen would be certain to wear the Necklace on Whit Sunday, and he, Böhmer, was greatly astonished when he saw that she did not have it on. On asking Madame Campan what she thought he ought to do, she advised him to go at once to the Baron de Breteuil, and tell him candidly all that had passed, and to be ruled entirely by him. Instead of doing this Böhmer hurried off to the cardinal. What transpired at this interview is not known, but the following memorandum, in the grand almoner's handwriting, was found in a drawer at the Hôtel de Strasbourg at the time a search was made for the cardinal's papers:

" On this day, 3rd August, Böhmer went to Madame Campan's country house, and she told him that the queen had never had the Necklace, and that he had been cheated."

Böhmer must have spoken to the cardinal beforehand of his contemplated visit to Crespy, for the cardinal admitted that, having regard to the queen's injunction to keep her name a perfect secret in the affair of the Necklace, he urged Böhmer not to speak to Madame Campan on the subject, and in the event of any questions being asked him to say the Necklace had been sent abroad.*

* "Deuxième Interrogatoire du Cardinal de Rohan."

The half-crazy jeweller next hastened to Little Trianon, but failed in obtaining an interview with Marie-Antoinette. A day or two afterwards, the queen having sent for Madame Campan to rehearse with her the part of *Rosina*, which she was to play in Beaumarchais' comedy, "The Barber of Seville," at her private theatre at Little Trianon, took an opportunity of asking her why she had sent Böhmer to her (who had been to speak to her, saying that he came at Madame Campan's request), when she did not wish to see him.

"The expression," remarks Madame Campan, "which this man's name produced on my features must have been very marked, for the queen observed it, and commenced questioning me. I begged her to see him; I assured her that it was necessary to her tranquillity; that an intrigue was being carried on of which she was ignorant; that it was a grave one, since agreements signed by her had been shown to people who had lent money to Böhmer. Her surprise and annoyance were great. She made me relate several times the whole of my conversation with him, and complained bitterly of the vexation she felt at the circulation of forged notes signed with her name; but she could not conceive how the cardinal could be involved in the affair. This was a labyrinth to her, and her mind was lost in it. She ordered me to remain at Trianon, while she sent off a courier to Paris, under a pretext which I have now forgotten. He returned the next morning, the very day of the representation of the comedy, which was the last amusement the queen allowed herself in this retreat."*

* "Memoirs of Marie-Antoinette," by Madame Campan, vol. ii. pp. 9, 12, 279.

XX.

1785. FEB.—JUNE.

THE DIAMONDS ARE DISPERSED.—COUNT DE LA MOTTE GOES TO ENGLAND ON BUSINESS.

THE De la Mottes had spirited away the Necklace it is true, but how were they to turn it into hard cash? Every working jeweller in France knew this famed piece of *bijouterie* by repute almost as well as if he had had a hand in its manufacture. The only plan, therefore, was for them, somehow or other, to remove the diamonds from their settings, and to dispose of them piecemeal. The first the De la Mottes contrived to do after a fashion by means of a knife or some such instrument; the last they found a difficult and even dangerous undertaking.

On the 15th of February* the countess's first secretary

---

* It is important that this date should be noted; for the circumstances which transpired on it, and which are chronicled in the police records, effectually dispose of the theory advanced by certain writers —such as M. Alexandre Dumas, in his " Louis XVI." (vol. iii. p. 194, *et seq.*)—who maintain that Marie-Antoinette really purchased the Necklace through the instrumentality of the Cardinal de Rohan, and, after keeping it something like three months, returned it to the jewellers by the hands of Madame de la Motte, on finding that she and the forger of the queen's signature to the contract with the jewellers, Rétaux de Villette, who was of course as deep in the plot as the De la Mottes themselves, was intrusted with about forty of the smaller stones to sell to two Jew diamond-merchants named Adam and Vidal for four hundred francs apiece. Vidal, believing the diamonds to be stolen, gave information to the police, and the consequence was that Villette was arrested and subjected to an examination, in the course of which he was constrained to give up the name of the Countess de la Motte as that of the person who had intrusted him with the diamonds to sell. Madame being well known of old to M. Lenoir, lieutenant-general of police, to whom it will be remembered one of her begging letters was referred,* and her reputation being of the shadiest in her particular "*quartier,*" M. Lenoir gave directions to the inspector who had arrested Villette to make diligent search at the "*Bureau de Sureté*" for information respecting any recent robbery of diamonds. Nothing whatever being discovered to implicate Villette in the least degree, he was discharged, and the diamonds were restored to him.†

---

was unable to raise the money to meet the first instalment. While asserting that Madame de la Motte was really the queen's confidant, the writers referred to are forced to admit that she betrayed her trust, and converted the Necklace to her own use.

* See *ante*, p. 67.

† Déposition de Vidal, and Déposition de Brugnières, inspecteur de police.

This was a narrow squeak for Villette, who naturally enough declined putting his liberty in jeopardy a second time. The consequence was that, burdened though the De la Mottes now were with diamonds, they were unable to turn them to profitable account. If attempting to dispose of a few of the smallest stones excited all this suspicion, whatever would come to pass, thought they, if any quantity of the larger brilliants were publicly offered in the market? The thieves are for the moment at their wits' ends, and do not appear to have been particularly fertile in their expedients, for what next suggests itself to them is to get hold of rather a softish young fellow, calling himself Jean-Charles-Vincent de Bette d'Etienville, whom Rétaux de Villette has met with at some café—singularly enough the Café Valois—and under the assumed characters of the Dame de Courville, personated by Madame de la Motte, the Sieur Augeard, her steward, personated by Villette, and the Councillor Marsilly, personated by Count de la Motte, to make him their pretended confidant in a cock-and-bull story about the lady desiring to get married to some gentleman of title (with a view of legitimatizing a child she has had by some very great nobleman), to whom a bonus of one hundred thousand francs would be given on the day of the wedding. They represented, however, that before this arrangement could be carried into effect, it would be necessary to dispose of the lady's diamonds, which were valued at four hundred and thirty-two thousand francs; and it was proposed to Bette that he should take them to Holland, and sell them to the diamond merchants of Amsterdam—madame of course either accompanying him, or dogging his footsteps to ensure his not giving them the slip. Bette, although he found out a gentleman of title ready and willing to save a lady's reputation at the price of one hundred thousand francs, cash down, seems to have drawn back at this latter suggestion, which foreboded danger he fancied; and all madame's powers of fascination and persuasion proving of no avail, this abortive scheme had to be abandoned.*

All this was of course very disheartening. To have plotted and schemed, and watched and waited, and after doubts and misgivings, and positive fears and dangers, to have at length achieved success, and then for success to prove barren, was something awful. For the moment it seemed as though there was nothing to be done except to barter away as many diamonds as they could, and to have others reset to wear as personal ornaments. It was certainly no use hiding so much brilliancy under a bushel. At the commencement of March we find the Count de la Motte strolling into the shop of Furet, clockmaker to the king, Rue St. Honoré, with whom he had had previous dealings, and buying

* "Mémoire pour Bette d'Etienville," and Déposition de Bette d'Etienville.

from him three clocks, price three thousand seven hundred and twenty francs, and giving him a couple of diamonds, which the jeweller values at two thousand seven hundred francs, on account. A day or two afterwards madame herself calls with a number of diamonds, which she wishes to have mounted encircling a watch; but Furet explains to her that the stones are too large for this purpose, and suggests mounting them as bracelets.* She also exchanges a diamond with a Jew for a couple of china pomade pots, and pays a visit to the goldsmith Regnier, of whom she had bought a pair of diamond bracelets and the handsome service of silver plate with which it will be remembered she astonished her Bar-sur-Aube connections in the preceding year, paying for the same with the cardinal's money, and commissions him to set a couple of large diamonds which she brings with her as rings, one for herself and the other for her husband.†

Transactions of this character, however, did not put them in possession of the one thing needful—namely, ready cash. Diamonds were with them as plentiful as blackberries, but diamonds are not meat and drink, and are at best but an indifferent circulating medium, and the De la Mottes were getting painfully hard up. The countess, however, proved herself as usual equal to the occasion.

By selling, unknown to her husband, a parcel of

* Déposition de Furet. † Déposition de Regnier.

twenty-two diamonds to one Paris, a jeweller, to whom she had been introduced by M. Filleul, a lawyer of Bar-sur-Aube, who occasionally visited them in the Rue Neuve-Saint-Gilles, for the sum of fifteen thousand francs, and subsequently disposing of sixteen more diamonds to the same person for the sum of sixteen thousand francs,* madame found herself in sufficient funds to pack Count de la Motte over to England with a letter of credit for a couple of thousand crowns,† and the bulk of the larger diamonds belonging to the Necklace. These diamonds, which the countess had first declared were sold at the request and on behalf of the Cardinal de Rohan, she afterwards pretended she had received as a gift from the queen, and it will be noticed at the outset of the following narrative that the count takes up this cue, although he stated to the English jewellers that they were a family heirloom. This narrative of the count's is not wanting in circumstantiality, still, like everything else emanating from the De la Motte mint, it has the customary false stamp upon it, more particularly in that portion relating to the amount said to have been received for the diamonds he succeeded in disposing of, as we shall by-and-by show. It should be remembered that this statement was not made public until long after the fact of the

---

* "Premier Interrogatoire de Madame de la Motte." Also *post*, p. 226.

† Déposition de Perregaux, banquier.

sale and purchase of the diamonds in question had been proved beyond a shadow of doubt by the English jewellers concerned in the transaction.

"I arrived in London," says the count, "on the 17th of April, 1785, with the Chevalier O'Neil, who was perfectly acquainted with the object of my journey. As he knew the countess was admitted to the queen, I made no mystery to him *of the present she had received from her majesty,* nor of my motive for parting with the diamonds in London. I had a letter of credit on Messrs. Morland and Co., to whom I went the day after my arrival. On making inquiry for the most noted jewellers, I was directed to Jefferys and to Gray; I first saw Jefferys, who lived in Piccadilly, told him I had some diamonds to dispose of, and left him my address. The next morning he came to my lodgings, where I showed him the eighteen oval stones that belonged to the Necklace, and acquainted him with the price *which the cardinal had fixed.* He requested me to let him take them home in order to examine them, and offered me his acknowledgment, which I accepted. He promised to bring me an answer in four days; the next day I set out with Chevalier O'Nei for Newmarket. During five days that we remained there, I gained by betting nine hundred and sixty guineas, sixty of which I expended in travelling expenses, the purchase of clothes, and various other articles.

"Being returned to London, I went to Jefferys, who

told me that a gentleman had offered four thousand pounds sterling; that he could not pay ready money, but would give notes at six and twelve months' date, and would find ample security. I told him I would consider of it, took back my diamonds, and returned him his acknowledgment. The same day I went to Gray's in New Bond Street,* left with him the largest oval stone, and directed him to come to me the next day, when I would let him see a greater quantity; the same day I purchased of him a self-winding watch. The next day he came, with a Jew named Eliason. I intrusted him with the same stones I had left in Jefferys' hands; he told me he had already examined them, and that a broker whom Jefferys employed had brought them to him. I then let him know the offer that Jefferys had made me, and the terms of payment, adding, that not knowing Jefferys, nor the person he had recommended to me, I did not choose to part with so considerable a property upon credit. That besides, I proposed staying but a few days in London, whither I might probably never again return, and that I did not think proper to leave anything behind me that might create any anxiety.

"He answered that I was perfectly in the right, and that if we agreed on the price he would pay me

---

* Gray's shop was No. 13, and the largest in New Bond Street. The house, which is within two doors of Long's hotel, must have been quite a new building at the time Count de la Motte had dealings with the crack jeweller of that day.

ready money. I told him my price: he took away the diamonds, and promised to bring an answer the following day; which he did, but still accompanied by Gray. He made me an offer of three thousand guineas, which I would not accept. After pointing out stones that had flaws and other defects they left me, with an assurance that the offer they made me for ready money was very adequate; and that I should not meet with a more eligible one. I let them go away, telling them I would keep my diamonds rather than part with them at that price.

"Next morning they returned, and asked to survey the diamonds a second time: I permitted them. O'Neil was present, as well as my *valet de chambre*. Eliason then drew out of his pocket a pearl necklace, consisting of two very beautiful rows, a snuff-box set with brilliants and pearls, with a medallion on the lid, and several parcels of pearl seed. He valued these several articles at about five hundred and sixty pounds sterling. I said that if he would give me four thousand pounds, together with those articles, the bargain was struck. He exclaimed loudly, and then made a motion to go, offering three thousand pounds and the articles I had selected —a proposal which I rejected.

"In the interim Jefferys made a second application; I told him my resolution was to sell them for ready money only. I then delivered to him thirteen stones of the first quality I possessed; the two finest, which belonged to the Necklace, not having been given to the countess; and no doubt but the queen made a present of them to Mademoiselle Dorvat, or some other woman in her intimacy, for there were several which were similar. I had selected two, one intended to be set in a ring for the countess, the other for myself. Regnier, my jeweller at Paris, set them before my departure for London.* Both myself and the countess commonly wore them. The cardinal has seen them both.

"I called the next day at Gray's to purchase several articles in steel; there I found Eliason, who told me I was over-tenacious, that his offer was a very fair one. He showed me some very fine pearls for a pair of bracelets, and a ring forming a neck-button; I went into a separate apartment, where we entered into a bargain. After two hours' difficulty on both sides we at length agreed for the eighteen oval stones, viz. three thousand pounds sterling ready money; the pearl necklace of two rows, valued at two hundred pounds, the snuff-box one hundred and forty, the pearl-seed one hundred and twenty, and a diamond star which I took in Gray's shop, valued at three hundred.

"This was the first bargain. When I had received the money and jewels, he told me that Jefferys' broker had brought him other diamonds which were no doubt my property; that if I chose to sell them, I had better

---

* See *ante*, p. 215.

do business with him than with another: that I should gain by it the commission and some ready money. I went the same day and took out of Jefferys' hands the thirteen stones I had left in his possession. He had come to the knowledge of my dealing with Gray, and being vexed at having missed the opportunity of making the purchase himself, he upon that account pretended, as will be seen hereafter, that he had acted respecting the diamonds with more propriety than Gray, for that he, Jefferys, surmising the diamonds to have been stolen, had given notice at a police office (which in fact was a falsehood*), and had refused to buy them. He afterwards the more readily made a declaration to this purpose before a certain notary named Dubourg, at the request of M. de Carbonnières, agent for the cardinal, as he said he believed me to be in Turkey, and depended upon never seeing me again in England. His behaviour to me when I returned to London will show how *delicate* this Jefferys was in his conduct; since he came to me after judgment was passed to ask me whether I had not any diamonds to dispose of, telling me he would be the purchaser, and allow me a greater advantage than Gray would. It will soon be seen what answer I made him, and the method I took in order to make apparent what the justificatory writings produced by the cardinal consisted in.

* Which in fact was *not* a falsehood. See Jefferys' deposition, given in the " Pièces Justificatives pour le Cardinal de Rohan."

"The thirteen stones taken from Jefferys I carried to Gray, telling him I would come the next day to his shop myself, and that he might appoint Eliason to be there at the same hour. The departure of Chevalier O'Neil prevented my keeping the appointment. He had received a letter from his brother and another from his colonel, requiring his return with all possible speed to join his regiment by the 15th of May. He had not been able to obtain a longer leave of absence as he hoped; the troops the emperor was then marching towards Holland were the occasion of the orders he had received: he was therefore forced to leave me in London. He took charge of several purchases I had made, and of the parcel of pearls I had got in exchange. As he went by the coach, he took his place the day before at Mr. Guyon's office, where he found the Capuchin McDermott, a professed spy, who for the things made known to me by his own confession, (and those certainly are the most harmless,) deserves to be made an example of. The Capuchin knew Chevalier O'Neil, with whom he renewed acquaintance; and finding in the course of conversation he had come over with me, he begged he would introduce him to me, which the chevalier did. He told me that as I did not understand English he would be my interpreter, and do me all the little services in his power. I accepted of his obliging offer, and that day he dined with me. He had been procurator of his order at Vaffy, six leagues distant from Bar-sur-Aube; he knew my family, and had seen me, by his account, a child.

"In this, my first interview, I did not communicate to him anything relative to my having diamonds to dispose of; in short, I acquainted him with no particulars beyond that I had money to remit to Paris. He answered that he knew a merchant in the City named Motteaux, that if I negotiated through his means he would allow me the same advantage as to traders, whereas Mr. Hammersly would deal with me as with a nobleman. He calculated the benefit I should reap by placing that sum with Mr. Motteaux; and as it seemed to me rather considerable, and he persuaded me that Mr. Hammersly would not make me the same allowance, I determined to go to Mr. Motteaux, whither he accompanied me. I delivered to him the three thousand pounds sterling I had already received on the former bargain."

McDermott, it seems, when he and the Count de la Motte were taking a stroll together in Kensington Gardens, questioned the count, in an off-hand Irish way, as to the sources of his wealth, and hinted that he must have made some lucky coups at the gaming-table—one had not to know the count long to discover that he was a practised gambler—whereupon the count replied, in the coolest manner possible, that he was not partial to "play." "The truth is," said he, "I married Madame de la Motte, with her slender income of eight hundred francs, against the wishes of my family, as I had not a single franc of my own; but we came up to Paris, when Madame and the Countess d'Artois recommended us to several of the ministers, who in their turn recommended the countess to lay her case before the queen. She did so, was taken into favour, and hence our present affluence."*

"Let us return now to the thirteen diamonds I had left with Gray. When the Chevalier O'Neil was gone I went to that jeweller, who immediately sent into the City to let Eliason know I waited for him at his house. He came, but we made no bargain; eight or ten days passed away in fruitless meetings and considerations. They often told me they wondered how a gentleman should have such a knowledge of diamonds as to ascertain the exact value of them; but that I certainly was sensible that such articles were difficult to dispose of: that they should perhaps be obliged to keep them two or three years upon their hands, during which time the interest of the money was lost, and other things to the same purport. At length, after much trouble and attendance, we came to a settlement for the thirteen stones, for the sum of two thousand pounds sterling, ready money; a ring, convertible into a neck-button, valued at two hundred pounds sterling, and for which I lately got but one hundred; a parcel of very fine pearls

* Déposition de McDermott.

for the mounting of a pair of bracelets, valued at a hundred and fifty pounds; another parcel of pearls for sixty pounds, and a pair of girandole earrings, valued at five hundred pounds. Such were the two bargains I made with Eliason in presence of Gray. Six diamonds, which formed the rose of two oval ones, I exchanged at Gray's for a medallion set round with brilliants, two steel swords, a shirt-pin, a pair of asparagus tongs, and a wine syphon. Four more diamonds which were between the rose and the four tassels were likewise exchanged at Gray's for a ring, still in my possession, a small hoop of diamond-seeds, a lady's pocket-case, satin and gold, with all its furniture, a pair of steel buckles, and a miniature.

"I had sixty diamonds left, arising from the tassels, twenty-two from the scollops, and the stone which formed the button. Out of the sixty I selected twenty-eight, which I gave to Gray to set in drop earrings; and two-and-twenty of the scollops to make into a necklace of one single row. I then had left only thirty-two stones arising from the tassels, and the stone forming the button. I chose the sixteen finest, which I kept unmounted, and the remaining sixteen I parted with to Gray, at the rate of eighty pounds the carat, out of which I bought in his shop sundry small matters not worth mentioning. Thus terminated all my negotiations for diamonds in London.

"I had still remaining the button stone, which I

showed to Mr. Morland, asking him whether he could not find an opportunity of selling it to my advantage. He said he would let an acquaintance inspect it, and let me know his answer in two or three days. He did so by telling me he had the stone in his bank, and that one thousand guineas had been offered for it, which he believed might be carried to twelve hundred. He proposed my calling in Pall Mall to take the diamond, and from thence go into the City to Mr. Duval's, the person who made the offer; but that he believed it was not for himself. We met with Mr. Duval, who showed me several articles in jewelry. I told him my design was not to purchase any, since I was, on the contrary, come to treat with him about a diamond which Mr. Morland had given him to inspect. After surveying it a second time, he told me that the person to whom he had shown it offered but one thousand pounds, which he (Duval) looked upon to be its full value. I took back the diamond, and resolved to keep it till I found a means to dispose of it more advantageously. The same day I gave it to Gray to set in a ring.

"Let us now proceed to the enumeration of those stones that were sold and exchanged in Paris. Before my departure for England, the countess had delivered to M. Filleul some diamonds, which she had kept privately, that had formed part of the scollops and knots of the tassels; she desired him to sell them for her, and pay her the money, charging him not to make me acquainted with it. He sold the whole parcel to one Paris, a jeweller, for the sum of twenty-eight thousand French livres (francs). Two stones, part of the scollops, were exchanged by me for two pendulum clocks at one Furet's, in the Rue St. Honoré, with twenty-five louis-d'or in addition. One diamond, in like manner from the scollops, was set in a ring by Regnier, my jeweller. I had a chain in small brilliants which Franks the Jew had sold me; that I gave to Regnier, adding a few small diamonds which belonged to the knots of the tassels, the whole of which he made into a chain, which the cardinal's counsel valued at forty thousand livres. I with much difficulty parted with it for *sixty pounds sterling* in London. It was nearly the same with every particular; they were, in order to obtain their ends, obliged to multiply the price for which every article sold in a like proportion; and thus, from this false estimation, endeavour to prove that the *whole* of the Necklace had been in my possession.

" I had now left in all sixteen diamonds which I had brought back from London, four-and-twenty very small ones, which were on the sides of each oval stone at the bottom of the tassels, twenty-eight encircling the two large oval stones, two small ones on each side of the button, eighteen of the small size, six of which held the two oval stones between the scollop, and the twelve others which were immediately adjoining to the ribbon at top. The roses and what held the tassels were not yet taken to pieces. I delivered the whole to Regnier, out of all which he selected the best diamonds, and nearly of an equality, to encircle the top of a bonbonnière and mount a small pair of drop earrings which the countess wanted to make a present of. The remainder I directed him to sell, for which he got thirteen or fourteen thousand livres. These made up the number of what I sold, as well at Paris as at London. Let us now recapitulate.

" I received in ready money in London *five thousand pounds* sterling from Mr. Eliason, and fifty or sixty pounds from Mr. Gray.

" In exchange I received a medallion, a pair of girandole earrings, a ring, a shirt-pin, a hoop, two steel swords, a pair of steel buckles, one pound of pearl-seed, two rows of pearls forming a necklace, a mount for bracelets, a small parcel of pearls, a neck-button convertible into a ring, a snuff-box, a pair of asparagus tongs, a wine syphon, a lady's pocket-case, satin and gold with appurtenances, a miniature, and a pen-case of roses valued at sixty pounds sterling. Some few other small articles I had from Gray's shop, as needles, knives, steel forks, spring-pincers, scissors, a pair of silver buckles, an opera-glass, a small steel watch-chain.

" I sold at Paris to M. Paris several diamonds to the amount of twenty-eight thousand livres, and I received nearly fifty louis-d'or for a part of the pearl-seed carried from London by Chevalier O'Neil. The remainder of the pearl-seed was sold to Mordecai, a Jew residing in the Rue aux Ours.

"I have already said I had delivered to Gray twenty-two stones to set in a necklace, and twenty-six for drop earrings. I had acquainted him with the day of my departure, and he had promised the work should be completed; yet the day previous thereto he showed me all the pieces, only sketched, assuring me there was a great deal more work than he had at first imagined, and that if I would leave them with him he had an opportunity of conveying them to Paris within a fortnight. I left him the diamonds with my address, and set out upon my journey on a Sunday morning with the Capuchin McDermott, who attended me as far as Dover. At parting with him I made him a present of a snuff-box with a very handsome painting on the lid, and defrayed his journey back to London.

"When I left Paris I had taken credit for two thousand crowns; I won at Newmarket near a thousand pounds sterling; out of both which sums I expended a hundred guineas in saddlery, harness, and race-horse body-cloths, a hundred guineas more for a phaeton, a hundred and fifty guineas in English stuffs and clothes for myself and servants; the rest was spent in travelling, and during my six weeks' stay in London, which will not appear extraordinary when it is known I had taken up my residence at one of the principal hotels in that town, that I kept two servants, a hired coach, and two saddle horses, that I often gave entertainments, and that, keeping the most fashionable company, I was obliged to play and enter into expensive pleasures.

"All I now had left of the famous Necklace were two rings—one for myself, the other belonging to the countess—a small diamond mounted on a plum-coloured stone, a pair of drop earrings, and a circle on a black tortoiseshell-box, and what I had left with Gray—namely, the necklace of twenty-two stones and the earrings.

"Thus I have given a minute detail of the diamonds I possessed, and of the manner in which I had disposed of them.

"From the account I have kept and have just set forth of all the diamonds I had in my possession or that of the countess belonging to the Necklace, and by comparing it with an exact representation thereof engraved on a scale of the size of the diamonds, it appears that the queen had kept *two hundred and fifty-six diamonds* of the same magnitude, *ninety-eight* smaller ones of the same form, and the *two finest diamonds* of the first size. The two hundred and fifty-six diamonds were what composed the most beautiful part of the Necklace, on account of the assemblage and the regularity of so great a number of stones." *

Unfortunately for the count's reputation for accuracy,

* "Mémoires Justificatifs de la Comtesse de la Motte," p. 194, *et seq.*

a sworn affidavit of Gray's, setting forth a true extract from his ledger, and produced at the time of the trial, gives the following version of his dealings with the count. This not only shows a considerable variation of price in respect to several articles received in exchange, but yields in round numbers a total of nearly three thousand pounds in excess of the amount admitted by the count to have been received :—

Monsieur le Comte de Valois, of London,
Dr. to Robert Gray.

May 20th, 1785.

	£	s.	d.	Prices quoted by Count de la Motte.
A medallion set with diamonds	230	0	0	
A diamond ring	94	10	0	
A pearl knot for a lady	52	10	0	
A hand fire-screen	1	4	0	
A funnel and glass	0	6	0	
A purse	4	14	6	
A handsome steel sword	100	0	0	
Ditto ditto	45	0	0	
Two toothpick-cases	12	12	0	
A carving-knife and fork	1	4	0	
A pair of blue steel buckles	0	18	0	
2000 needles	1	10	0	
A strong casket	5	5	0	
A diamond hoop ring	13	13	0	
Four razors	1	0	0	
Setting a diamond ring	1	8	0	
A ring-case	0	8	0	
A silk pocket-case, with fittings complete	12	12	0	
A corkscrew	0	12	0	
A handsome star-shaped diamond brooch	400	0	0	300 0 0

THE STORY OF THE DIAMOND NECKLACE.

	£	s.	d.			
A pair of asparagus tongs	2	12	6	Prices quoted by Count de la Motte.		
A gold watch	38	0	0			
A purse	4	14	6			
A cord for a cane	1	1	0			
A pair of scales for diamonds	1	1	0			
A wine syphon	5	5	0			
A pair of spring pincers	0	10	6			
A pearl necklace	170	0	0	200	0	0
1800 pearls	270	0	0	120	0	0
A diamond aigrette in the form of a rose	60	0	0			
A pair of steel buckles	18	18	0			
A watch-chain	6	16	6			
A handsome pair of diamond girandole earrings	600	0	0	500	0	0
A brilliant ring	100	0	0	200	0	0
A diamond snuff-box	120	0	0	140	0	0
A diamond shirt-button	28	0	0			
A pair of buckles	7	7	0			
Ditto ditto	3	13	6			
A parcel of pearl-seed and other pearls, for embroidery	1890	0	0	210	0	0
Paid in cash	6090	0	0	5060	0	0
Total	£10,371	6	0			
Credit by value received in various diamonds	£10,371	6	0*			

While the count was away leading a life of ease and pleasure—bargaining, it is true, about diamonds to-day, but "betting at Newmarket" on the morrow, riding about town in his "hired coach" or on his "saddle

* "Pièces Justificatives pour le Cardinal de Rohan."

horse," with his groom behind, giving "occasional entertainments at the principal hotels," "keeping the most fashionable company," and "playing deeply," and "entering into the most expensive pleasures,"—while all this was going on, madame the countess was putting off troublesome inquiries respecting her husband's whereabout as best she could, saying one day that he was in Berry looking after a legacy, at another time that he was in Poictou, and finally that he was in England, where he had won £1000 on a horse-race.* Still she managed to enjoy herself after her own fashion. Cardinal Prince de Rohan reluctantly admitted that she visited him at the episcopal palace at Saverne at the end of May, dressed in man's clothes, and moreover, that he had sent one of the episcopal carriages to fetch her— from Strasbourg, we imagine.† One can fancy the high jinks between the countess and Cagliostro, and blacksheep Baron de Planta, and the Prince de Rohan, and "*la petite comtesse,*" as Cagliostro's wife was called, over the cardinal's matchless Tokay on this notable occasion.

* "Confrontation du Cardinal de Rohan avec le Père Loth."
† "Premier Interrogatoire du Cardinal de Rohan."

XXI.

1785. June 22—Aug. 6.

THE GATHERING OF THE STORM.

On the 22nd of June, Count de la Motte finds himself in Paris again, with a letter of credit for the sum of 122,896 francs in his pocket-book on Perregaux the banker—the same shrewd Perregaux who, according to the popular story, after refusing the services of young Jacques Lafitte, engaged him the instant afterwards from observing him pick up and carefully preserve a common pin as in dejected mood he crossed the court-yard of the banker's hôtel, and who subsequently took him into partnership and gave him his daughter in marriage, and so enabled him to found the great house of Lafitte and Co., of which he was so many years the distinguished head.

The count turns his letter of credit into hard cash on the following day,* and then calls upon Regnier with some of the stones he had failed to get rid of in Eng-

---

* Déposition de Perregaux.

land, commissions him to mount the best of them round the lid of a circular box, to set others for a small pair of drop earrings which the countess intends making a present of,* and sells him the remainder — namely, twenty brilliants, weighing in the aggregate forty-two carats, one weighing four and a quarter carats, and thirty-nine weighing fifty-nine and a half carats—for 27,000 francs, discharging at the same time Regnier's claim for setting the two diamond rings for himself and madame, and also an old debt due for either jewellery or plate.†

The De la Mottes now make no secret of the affluence which, after years of watching and waiting, is theirs at last. Madame, they confidentially admit, is in high favour with the queen, who, they insinuate, showers gifts upon her confidant with no niggard hand. The countess's ambition was to be lady of the manor of Fontette. She has the means of gratifying it now; nevertheless, it is not to Fontette that she goes, but to Bar-sur-Aube, which, with its somewhat free and pleasant society, has greater charms for her. On retirement for a time to Bar-sur-Aube her heart is fixed. She and the count had been long looking forward to spend the present autumn in their new abode, which by the aid of the Parisian decorator, who for months past had been exercising his talents upon the principal apartments, was rapidly

---

* See *ante*, p. 228. † Déposition de Regnier.

becoming a model of elegance and taste. One little thing, however, was troubling them at this moment and casting its shadow across their anticipated enjoyment—namely, the affair of the Necklace, the first instalment in respect of which would soon be falling due. Still the countess, having accomplished what she had, would surely find it no very difficult task to arrange a postponement which would leave her husband and herself at liberty to enjoy their autumn holiday in peace and quietude. It is with this view that the countess calls upon the cardinal, as we have already stated, while the count, looking upon the affair as good as settled, hies down to Bar-sur-Aube to await the arrival of several waggon-loads of furniture which were on their way from Paris. Among these we may be certain there were some handsome suites of the very latest fashion, ordered, we know, of Héricourt, Fournier, and Gervais, the crack upholsterers of the period, at a cost of 50,000 francs. There was no lack of clocks too from Furet, of marble groups from Adams and Chevalier, nor of mirrors, and chandeliers, and table-glass, and Wedgwood ware, then getting into fashion in Paris, from Sikes.* A little automaton bird too, that flew about the room all alone, and for which madame had given 1500 francs,† would certainly not be forgotten.

* "Marie-Antoinette et la Procès du Collier," par E. Campardon. Paris, 1858, p. 98.
† "Mémoire pour le Cardinal de Rohan," p. 49.

It must have been at this particular juncture that the cardinal chanced to see some two or three letters actually written by Marie-Antoinette, and that, struck by the dissimilarity of the handwriting of these letters and those received from Madame de la Motte, he communicated his doubts upon the subject to the countess.* She, with her active brain and ever ready tongue, had of course a hundred reasons to prove to the credulous cardinal that he was mistaken, and so set his mind at rest. Not so as regarded her own; she felt none of that confidence with which she could so readily inspire her dupe. She feared the mine was on the point of being sprung, and that the explosion would take place before she could make good her retreat. To reassure alike the cardinal and the jewellers she goes with her casket of jewels, —which Regnier tells her are worth 100,000 francs— to her notary, one Mainguet, with whom she pawns them for a loan of 35,000 francs, 30,000 of which she takes to the Prince de Rohan to give to Böhmer and Bassenge. Then she packs off Rétaux de Villette posthaste to Bar-sur-Aube, and so much was she taken up with these urgent matters that she neither dines nor sups nor sleeps at home on that day.†

One can imagine the consternation of the Count de la Motte as, while superintending the arrangement of the new furniture and chatting with the decorator

* "Premier Interrogatoire du Cardinal de Rohan."
† "Mémoire pour le Cardinal de Rohan," p. 72.

respecting the extremely satisfactory effect of the *tout ensemble* of madame's boudoir, he catches sight of Villette driving up to the house in hot haste, and looking far more grave than is the fellow's wont. The count rushes down the steps to meet him—they turn aside for a few minutes' conversation, and after a hurried lunch, and some hasty instructions to the workpeople, the order is given to put fresh horses to the carriage, and the pair are rattling over the road to Paris. By dint of handsome "*pour boires*" to postillions, and considerable wear and tear of horseflesh, the hundred and forty miles that intervene between them and the Rue Neuve-Saint-Gilles are got over in less than the four-and-twenty hours. At noon on the following day (August 3) a council is held, at which it is decided that madame shall send a message to Bassenge, requesting him to favour her with a call. The jeweller, in the belief that the summons can only refer to the Necklace, takes the Hôtel de Strasbourg in his way, sees the cardinal, speaks to him of his own and his partner's inquietude at the queen having taken no notice whatever of the firm's letter of July 12, and informs him of the message he has received from Madame de la Motte, to whom he now hastens. Bassenge finds the countess alone, with no other furniture in the apartment beyond a bedstead and a couch, and everything about the house betokening a sudden "flitting." The jeweller simply thought he was dreaming when, after the ordinary compliments had passed between them, madame, with the calmest of countenances and the firmest of voices, said to him: "I have sent for you to let you know that you have been deceived—the word '*approuvé*' and the signature attached to the paper containing the conditions of sale of the Necklace are forgeries—the queen's handwriting has been counterfeited. As for the rest, the cardinal, you know, is very rich; you had better look to him, and insist upon his rendering himself personally liable."*

Bassenge, as soon as he recovered his self-possession, hurried home to communicate to his partner the astounding intelligence he had just received, but Böhmer, it will be remembered, was at Crespy with Madame Campan on this very day.† The jeweller therefore resolves to look in again on the cardinal, and ask an explanation from him. The Prince de Rohan, on being apprised of what the countess had said, shared in the fears of the jeweller, though he dared not avow as much. He hesitated for some time ere he made a reply; then he strove to reassure Bassenge by affirming that he had in his own possession a written agreement of the queen's, and he bade the jeweller go home and make himself perfectly easy; and home, and somewhat easier in his mind, Bassenge went. Great stress was laid at the trial on this mis-statement of the cardinal's,

---

* Déposition de Bassenge. † See *ante*, p. 206.

still we can very well understand it to have been nothing more than an exaggeration of the fact that he was in possession of letters which he believed to be written by the queen, authorizing the purchase of the Necklace on her behalf.

When Böhmer returns home from Crespy on the following day, the two partners compare notes, and decide that the queen ought to be seen without a moment's delay. To Versailles, therefore, Böhmer hastens, but, as we have already stated, is refused an audience by Marie-Antoinette. A day or two afterwards, however, he finds himself summoned by courier to wait upon the queen, who has' by this time learnt from Madame Campan the result of her conversation at Crespy with the crown jeweller, and is anxious to hear the astounding recital from his own lips. Böhmer, disregarding all that Madame Campan has told him, and in the full belief that the cardinal holds the queen's written agreement for the purchase of the Necklace, proceeds to Versailles in all confidence, determined to be no longer trifled with even by royalty itself. On his arrival he is ushered into the queen's private cabinet, when Marie-Antoinette at once inquires of him: "By what fatality it is that she is still doomed to hear of his foolish pretensions about selling her an article which she had steadily refused for several years?" Böhmer, reassured by what the cardinal had told Bassenge, no longer felt any doubt as to the queen being really a party to the purchase of the Necklace, and replied, "that he was compelled, being unable to pacify his creditors any longer." "What are your creditors to me?" inquired the queen. Böhmer then regularly related to her all that, according to his deluded imagination, had passed between them through the intervention of the Cardinal de Rohan. She was equally thunderstruck, incensed, and surprised at everything she heard. In vain did she speak; the jeweller, alike importunate and dangerous, repeated incessantly: "Madame, this is no time for feigning; condescend to confess that you have my Necklace, and order me some assistance, or else a bankruptcy will soon bring the whole to light."*

Marie-Antoinette, driven almost frantic by this flagrant imposture and the wanton manner in which her name had been abused and trifled with, immediately sent for the Abbé de Vermond, "her private secretary, her confidant, and her counsellor;"† and subsequently

* "Memoirs of Marie-Antoinette," by Madame Campan, vol. ii. pp. 283-4. Madame Campan is the single authority for this reputed interview between Böhmer and the queen. Other accounts agree in stating that the queen invariably refused to see the crown jeweller, under the pretence that his threats of suicide alarmed her. Still, as Madame Campan was so intimately mixed up with the affair at this particular juncture, she could hardly be mistaken on so important a point as this interview. If it really did take place, Böhmer must have kept the cardinal in ignorance of it, for had he known of it he would hardly have counselled the jeweller to attempt to throw dust in the eyes of the acute De Breteuil. See next page.
† Ibid.

for the Baron de Breteuil—the cardinal's two bitterest enemies. Delighted at the prospect they saw of crushing the grand almoner, not merely by effecting his utter ruin at court, but by disgracing him in the eyes of all Europe, they never for a moment thought of the consequences of permitting the name of the second personage in the kingdom to be mixed up in a swindling transaction and associated with those of a profligate ecclesiastic, a wholesale forger, a Palais Royal courtesan, a sharper, and an abandoned woman and thief.

Hardly had Böhmer made his partner acquainted with what transpired at his interview with the queen, ere another courier in the royal livery dashes up to the door of the jewellers' establishment—"Au Grand Balcon," in the Rue Vendôme—this time with a letter from the Baron de Breteuil, minister of justice and of the king's household, and the Prince de Rohan's declared enemy, again requiring Böhmer's attendance at Versailles. On the receipt of this new summons, Böhmer hurries off to the cardinal for instructions, finds his eminence by this time pretty well crazed with this same Necklace business. Nevertheless he enjoins the jeweller not to breathe a word about the queen, for should the minister discover that her majesty had purchased the detested jewel, he would certainly inform the king, and they would all be involved in one common disgrace. Should the Baron de Breteuil question him as to the meaning of the letter which the firm had sent to the queen, he had better reply that it referred to some new set of diamonds which they desired to sell to her majesty. Primed with these instructions, Böhmer goes to his interview with the minister; but whether he was as reticent as the cardinal bade him be on the subject of the sale of the Necklace we have our doubts. Böhmer's object was to get his money; but then he dared not go in face of the instructions he received from the minister. He therefore played fast and loose with the cardinal, not daring to break with him for fear he should lose his 1,400,000 francs, but betraying him so far as he thought he might safely venture to do to his acknowledged enemy. The result was that a few days afterwards, on the recommendation of the Baron de Breteuil, who assured the jewellers they should be paid for the Necklace, a memorial was drawn up and forwarded to the queen by the crown jewellers, wherein was set forth a complete history of the negotiations which had been entered into with the cardinal, and which had resulted in the sale to him of the Necklace, as they believed, on her majesty's account.

At this point the arch *intriguante* seems to have lost her head, for on the morning of the 4th, the day after she had made her damaging admission to Bassenge respecting the signature to the contract, she sends her maid to the Hôtel de Strasbourg to beg the cardinal to call upon her. He does so, when she receives him seemingly all in tears, and tells him that she is a victim to the malevolence of the courtiers of Versailles, who are jealous of the favour shown her by the queen; that she is obliged to fly to avoid their attacks, and entreats of him to afford her an asylum until she can provide herself with some safe retreat. The stupid cardinal, not even yet convinced that he has been duped, or, if so, fearing to admit as much, hesitates at first, but eventually consents to receive her, her husband, and her maid at his hôtel.* The countess afterwards pretended that it was the cardinal who sent for her and the count; that he kept them almost prisoners, and used every argument to induce them to cross the frontier into Germany with all speed, so as to be out of the way when the storm burst forth. She even went so far as to say that the count was obliged to threaten to use force ere he could get released.†

Only one motive can be suggested for the countess taking refuge at the Palais-Cardinal. She knew, or she suspected, that the police were watching her house and tracking her footsteps, and she did not know how soon the outstretched hand of justice might be upraised to strike, and she thought from the cardinal's high position, and the power and influence of his friends and connections, that it would not dare to violate the sanctity of

* " Mémoire pour le Cardinal de Rohan," p. 74.
† " Life of the Countess de la Motte, by herself," vol. i. p. 375, et seq., and " Premier Interrogatoire de Madame de la Motte."

the episcopal domicile. For two entire days the De la Mottes remained in close seclusion at the Hôtel de Strasbourg, when finding the confinement irksome, or thinking possibly that the affair would be certain to be hushed up, or that the law if put in force would not trouble itself about a couple of fugitives hidden in some far-away country town in Champagne, they left the cardinal's on the evening of the 5th of August for their own house in the Rue Neuve-Saint-Gilles. Without a moment's loss of time arrangements appear to have been made for sending the forger Villette out of the way. Madame, calling him aside, confides to him what he is already well aware of, namely, that her affairs are somewhat embarrassed, and that she and the count propose retiring to Bar-sur-Aube until the storm has blown over and the atmosphere is a trifle clearer. Placing 4000 francs in bank-notes in her faithful secretary's hand, "Go you," said she, "to Italy for a time;" and then to console the lover, whom hard necessity forced her to abandon, she added, "I will soon recall you near me again." The docile Villette promised to do as he was bid. A cabriolet seems to have been in waiting for him in the court-yard of the countess's house, and into it Villette got, and a little after two o'clock in the morning he was presumed to be on the road to exile.*

* "Mémoire pour le Cardinal de Rohan," p. 83. Villette evidently lingered for some time on French soil, for his passport for Italy was not dated until August 20, two days after the countess's arrest.

The following morning, while the count was giving some directions respecting the last van-load of furniture, which was then being packed in the court-yard of the hôtel, Bassenge looked in, and in answer to his inquiries after madame's health, was informed by the count that she had been at Versailles for the last three days pleading for the cardinal. De la Motte added that he had only returned from Bar-sur-Aube three days ago, when he heard about the Necklace business for the first time. "If," remarked he, in a jocular way, "the queen should ask you the meaning of the letter of thanks which I hear you have addressed to her, why not say it merely meant that the Necklace had always been at her disposition, and that it was only a renewal of the offers of it which had been previously made?" *

No sooner had the count seen the last van-load of furniture safely off than he went with Father Loth to Mainguet the notary, paid him his 35,000 francs, and took away the jewels which madame had deposited with him a few days previously.† These were necessary to the coming display which the De la Mottes were bent upon making at Bar-sur-Aube. Determined to lose no further time, the count and countess set out the same evening for their country retreat; and it is said that at the moment the countess stepped into the

* Déposition de Bassenge. † Déposition du Père Loth.

carriage she consoled the cardinal by promising to return the very instant he should have need of her.*

* "Mémoire Historique des Intrigues de la Cour," etc. par Rétaux de Villette, p. 59.

XXII.

1785. AUGUST 8–17.

TWELVE DAYS' STATE AT BAR-SUR-AUBE.

THE countess had informed Beugnot, who had called upon her a short time previously to know if she had any commands for Bar-sur-Aube, whither he was about returning to spend his holidays, that it would not be until about the commencement of October that she would again have the pleasure of seeing him. "I was therefore very much surprised," observes he, "to see Madame de la Motte arrive at Bar-sur-Aube in the early part of August, bringing with her her entire establishment, husband included. Villette alone remained in Paris as a forlorn sentinel, and, what appeared most strange, every day there arrived waggons loaded with furniture—a far larger quantity in fact than the house would hold—and magnificent furniture too." There were numerous handsome mirrors and looking-glasses with which the walls of the *salon*, already resplendent with a profusion of gilding, were decorated;

the chairs and couches, covered with beautiful tapestry, were also gilt.* Furet's clocks, and Adams and Chevalier's marble groups and bronzes ornamented the mantelpieces, and scattered about the *salon* were some of those costly fancies with which the arts contrive to tempt the extremest opulence, such as a pair of automatic canaries that sang a duet together, and another automaton bird, which flew about the room of itself. There were likewise two gold musical boxes—things which have become common enough since, but were still rare at that time; clocks which by means of certain mechanical arrangements displayed different scenes every hour they struck. On seeing these things, one divined that they could only have been bought by people tired of their money and anxious for the first opportunity to fling it out of window. In the dining-room were two magnificent buffets on which were displayed a profusion of valuable porcelain and two complete services of silver plate."† The hangings of the countess's bed were of crimson velvet trimmed with gold lace and fringe and embroidered with gold and spangles, while the counterpane was worked

---

* "Some of the De la Mottes' fine furniture may still be seen at Bar-sur-Aube, in the *salon* of the son of a former postmaster of the place, who subsequently bought the house itself of the count. To-day, improvements in the town of Bar-sur-Aube have necessitated the partial destruction of the De la Motte abode, fragments of which exist in no less than three separate streets."—*Letter from the Curé of Bar-sur-Aube to the author.*

† "Mémoires du Comte Beugnot," vol. i. pp. 70, 71.

all over with pearls * brought, it will be remembered, by the count from England, and for which Gray had charged him over two thousand two hundred pounds, and which, according to the countess, were reported in the neighbourhood to be of the value of one hundred and fifty thousand francs. "As a consummation of imprudence," remarks Beugnot, "the De la Mottes exhibited a casket containing more than two hundred thousand francs worth of diamonds. The count himself being supplied with a far larger quantity than seemed proper for an honest man."

"In the De la Mottes' stables were twelve splendid horses, and in their coach-house no fewer than five or six handsome carriages, made in England," says Beugnot, "with a care and intelligence which showed that expense was the last thing these people troubled themselves about." Among these vehicles was a light and beautiful cabriolet in the form of a balloon, and upwards of ten feet high. In this singular vehicle Count de la Motte used to drive about the neighbourhood, stared at by the gaping peasants and townspeople.† The countess when paying visits of cere-

---

* "Authentic Adventures of the Countess de la Motte," p. 119.

† Ibid, p. 120. The author of this work states that he was at Bar-sur-Aube at this particular period, and saw the count riding about in the balloon-shaped carriage above mentioned. Balloons, it should be remembered, were then a recent invention, Montgolfier having made his first ascent in December, 1783, some twenty months previously.

mony rode in a carriage drawn by six horses with
little silver bells jingling at their collars and foxes'
brushes flopping at their ears. She was invariably
preceded by a couple of outriders, and one day greatly
astonished the Abbé of Clairvaux—who, though a little
king in these parts, only sported four horses himself—
by driving up to the abbey gateway in this unwonted
state. The number of servants on the De la Motte
establishment was considerable, and their liveries were
as a matter of course extremely rich. Among them
was one of those little negro pages called "Jokeis,"
then much in fashion, engaged for madame's special
service. In short, the count and countess at this period
of their career displayed in all their appointments a
magnificence and a profusion more than rivalling that
of the wealthiest families in France.

Madame's superb embroidered robes and her valuable
point lace were only in keeping with the splendour of
her household display. As for her jewels, she no longer
depended on a pair of diamond bracelets to attract attention, for had she not now the magnificent pair of
girandole earrings for which Gray the jeweller had
charged the count six hundred pounds sterling, and
the diamond star-shaped brooch which had cost another four hundred pounds, and one of the handsomest diamonds in the whole Necklace set as a ring
by Regnier, besides other diamond rings innumerable?
The necklace, formed of "twenty-two of the very finest

diamonds from the scollops," which Gray had mounted in accordance with the count's instructions, was flashing at this moment in the jeweller's shop window, 13 New Bond Street, dazzling the eyes of Piccadilly and Bond Street loungers, and exciting the envy of high-born English beauties; for Gray, hard man as he was, would not part with the handsome jewel to the Capuchin McDermott—whom the count had commissioned to procure it, and who had made application for it to Gray on the count's behalf—until he had been paid the expense of setting.

"We used to think," remarks Beugnot, "that the Cardinal de Rohan paid for all this brilliant extravagance, and we admired the good use which his eminence made of the funds of the grand almonry. The first representation we had witnessed of the magnificence of the De la Motte household had astonished us; at this fresh display we felt uneasy and well nigh indignant. Neither husband nor wife showed the least sign of inquietude. Their dinners were excellent; and fête followed upon fête. They endeavoured to attract the neighbourhood to their house and get invited out in return, and to a certain extent they succeeded."*

Within about ten miles or so of Bar-sur-Aube is Brienne, famous for its military school, where the young

---

* "Mémoires du Comte Beugnot," vol. i. p. 71.

Buonaparte it will be remembered studied mathematics and the art of war; and where, in the neighbouring château, lived Louis Lomenie de Brienne, last Count of Brienne, brother of the Archbishop of Sens, prime minister of France just before the outbreak of the Revolution, and who was himself war minister for a time under Louis XVI. The ends of both brothers were alike untimely. One, the archbishop, died from a midnight carouse in which he was forced to join by the Jacobin emissaries who came to carry him off from his palace at Sens to the guillotine; the other by the guillotine itself; going thither in the same set of tumbrils as Madame Elisabeth, the king's sister. At the Château de Brienne—a splendid edifice built by the count with the large fortune he had received with his wife, the daughter of a rich *fermier-général*—as at almost every other château of any importance at this period, private theatricals appear to have been in vogue.

"M. de la Motte one day mentioned to me," remarks Beugnot, "that he had received an invitation to one of these entertainments at the Château de Brienne, and would be pleased if I would accompany him and accept of a seat in his carriage. Being well known to M. de Brienne, I acceded to the count's request without hesitation, and on the appointed day we set forth in a gorgeous equipage drawn by four splendidly-caparisoned horses, and with three footmen behind us. Prior to our starting I felt strongly inclined to recede, as I foresaw that I should have to undergo my share of ridicule for this ostentatious display. On our arrival at the château we alighted to the great scandal of those who saw us arrive. Happily for us the preparations for the play absorbed almost everybody's attention, and among others that of the master and mistress of the house. We entered the *salon* so that we might be seen, and passed from thence into the *salle de spectacle*. I was seated by the side of M. de la Motte, and soon perceived that he was the object of malevolent glasses, which were passed from hand to hand with shruggings of shoulders and mocking smiles. He certainly furnished a good subject for them, for he was dressed in a most singular style, and, what was in the worst of taste, diamonds were displayed in every part of his toilette at a period when the greatest simplicity already reigned in male attire."

One can picture the count with one side of his three-cornered hat looped up with the magnificent diamond aigrette which he had bought of Gray, and with the medallion set with diamonds for which he had given two hundred and thirty pounds attached to a ribbon round his neck; with his diamond watch-chain, his various diamond rings, and his diamond snuff-box, value one hundred and twenty pounds; and with one or other of the very handsome steel swords which he had brought over with him from England swinging at his side.

"The count wore a dress coat of sky-blue cloth, a white waistcoat embroidered all over, and breeches of canary-colour taffeta. Still this only indicated the somewhat faded elegant; but here is what completed the absurdity. Madame de la Motte had taken it into her head to have the left facing of her husband's coat embroidered over with a fine bouquet of lilies and roses intermixed. Nothing of the kind had been worn by any one up to that time, and most certainly not since. Everybody was asking what it could possibly mean: there were some who professed to see in it a sort of parody upon the united escutcheons of monsieur and madame, one of which contained *fleurs-de-lis*, the other roses. Stupidity and self-conceit could hardly have gone farther.

"When the play was over we returned to the *salon*. The assembly was composed of the distinguished families of the neighbourhood and of men of letters from Paris —of the Abbé Morellet, La Harpe, Masson de Morvilliers, &c. I saluted Madame de Brienne, who scarcely condescended to nod to me in return, and then turned her back upon me. My reception by the master of the house was reduced to a " Good evening, sir," uttered in a dry tone. One feels ill at ease in the midst of a numerous circle after having been coldly received by the host and hostess. I continued standing, not knowing whither to bend my steps in the midst of this hostile camp, when my good star brought to the *salon* the Count de Dampierre, a great bore, who relieved me of my difficulty by at once seizing hold of me. He profited by the opportunity to speak to me of innovations of every kind which were already fermenting in his brain; and under the circumstances it was quite a treat to me to listen to him. In order that we might not be separated during supper, he dragged me at once to table, and seated me by his side, when he offered me in his own person the example of an individual capable of speaking with warmth and eating with avidity at one and the same moment. I was occasionally a trifle inattentive, owing to my desire to observe how my travelling-companion was faring; but M. de Dampierre always brought me back to the subject of his discourse. 'Never mind him,' he would say, 'he's only some poor devil of a swell at whose expense people have been amusing themselves for the last two hours. Do you know him?'

"'Yes, a little.'

"'Well, what is he? Is he one of us? Does he know where we are?'

"'Not the least in the world.'

"'Well, then, let them do what they please with him;' and M. de Dampierre forthwith resumed his dissertation.

"I only knew from the tales told by some of the guests of the tricks which had been played upon M. de la Motte at the supper-table. It seems that in spite of the splendid repast spread before his eyes he had been debarred from partaking of the slightest nourishment, and that he rose from the table as badly ballasted as Sancho Panza at the conclusion of the first feast served to him under his own government. This could only have been brought about by a concert of 'good turns,' the success of which enraptured the originators who came to relate the affair to us. The Count de Dampierre inveighed against this interruption:

"'Ah! well, well! but leave us alone; we have neither diamonds nor canary-colour breeches, nor bouquets embroidered at our button-holes. There is your man cowering in a corner of the chimney; go and laugh at his expense, since he is in the humour to submit to it, and permit us to talk sense!'

"After a time M. de la Motte grew bold, and came to me to propose that we should leave. I consented with all my heart; but there still remained a dreg at the bottom of the cup for me to swallow.

"When I went in all humility to salute M. de Brienne, and to ask him almost tremblingly if he had any commands to give me for Bar-sur-Aube, he signalled to me to advance, so that in getting clear of the hands of M. de Dampierre I fell into those of M. de Brienne, who was quite M. de Dampierre's equal in holding fast to a good listener. M. de Brienne had not been at table, and had had of course nothing to do with the practical jokes of which M. de la Motte had been the victim. Indeed he had listened with suppressed anger to the account which had been given him of the tricks played off upon the count, still he did not approve of my having presented myself at his house in such company. I excused myself as well as I could, assuring him M. de la Motte had informed me that he was invited for that particular day. M. de Brienne proved to me that whether M. de la Motte was invited or not, I did very wrong to accompany him. I agreed with him, and asked his pardon, as the shortest way of terminating the discussion, whereupon he immediately opened a conversation upon another subject. There were scarcely any affairs in the commune in which M. de Brienne did not take a lively interest, and he did me the honour to consult me upon many of them, consequently there were plenty of materials for a lengthened conversation.

"Poor M. de la Motte remained at a distance, watching our gestures, and awaiting the moment when I should be at liberty. During all this time people passed and repassed him with expressions of contempt or pity. I did not dare utter his name, though I had observed he had been waiting for me fully an hour. I risked a first salute to M. de Brienne, as if about to take my leave, but he paid no attention whatever to it, and continued speaking. A few minutes afterwards I made a new attempt to release myself, whereupon my host proposed to me to sleep at Brienne. As our discussion continued I could see that my travelling-companion was on live coals. At last, by a courageous effort, I succeeded in disengaging myself, and left with M. de la Motte. We stepped into his magnificent carriage, having behind us two footmen with lighted torches, and a negro covered from head to foot with silver lace. The windows of the *salon* looked out upon the court of honour of the château; Madame de Brienne and every one present were at the windows to observe the magnificence of our departure, and saluted us by clapping their hands, laughing, and indulging in mocking remarks which distinctly reached our ears. The carriage only rolled on the faster." *

A day or two afterwards Madame de la Motte proposed to Beugnot to accompany her on a visit she was about to pay to the Duke de Penthièvre, but Beugnot, not wishing to place himself in a ridiculous position a second time, very decidedly declined the honour. He however accepted the countess's offer to set him down at Clairvaux, where he had been invited, and which was on the road from Bar-sur-Aube to Château-Villain, and to call and fetch him on her return in the evening.

" In accordance with this arrangement," says Beugnot, " we left Bar-sur-Aube at eight o'clock in the morning of the 17th of August, 1785, a day I shall never forget. Madame de la Motte having set me down at Clairvaux, as had been agreed, went on to Château-Villain, where

---

* " Mémoires du Comte Beugnot," vol. i. p. 71, *et seq.*

she dined and met with a reception which astonished those who composed the Penthièvre court. The duke himself reconducted the countess at her departure to the door of the *salon* opening on to the grand staircase, an honour which he did not pay even to duchesses, but reserved exclusively for princesses of the blood-royal, so strongly were the lessons of Madame de Maintenon on the honours to be paid to illegitimacy impressed upon his mind." *

* "Mémoires du Comte Beugnot," vol. i. pp. 76–77.

XXIII.

1785. August 15-23.

LETTRES-DE-CACHET IN THE ŒIL-DE-BŒUF—IN THE
RUE SAINT-CLAUDE—AND AT BAR-SUR-AUBE.

At noon on the 15th of August, 1785, on the festival of the Assumption, and the fête-day of Marie-Antoinette, the Cardinal de Rohan, attired in his sacerdotal robes, was waiting in the "Salle de l'Œil-de-Bœuf" the arrival of the king and queen, before whom he was about to perform high mass in the chapel of the Château of Versailles. Conspicuous among the cardinal's vestments is his gorgeously-embroidered alb, worn by him only upon grand occasions, and valued at upwards of one hundred thousand francs, and which has his arms and device, in the form of medallions, crowning the larger and more brilliant flowers of which the rich and elaborate design is composed.* The handsome "Salle de l'Œil-de-Bœuf," which takes its name

* "Mémoires de le Baronne d'Oberkirche," vol. i. p. 127.

from the two bull's-eye windows level with the ceiling, was thronged, according to custom, with noblemen of every degree of rank, grand court ladies, great officers of State, soldiers and dignitaries of the Church, all watching for the doors communicating with the royal apartments to be thrown open, and for the king and queen to make their appearance. As it was in the days of the "Grand Monarque"—as it was in Louis XVI.'s time—as it was on that eventful morning of October 7, 1789, when the château was stormed and the terror-stricken Marie-Antoinette fled across it for life, when the loud cry arose of "Save the queen"—so the "Salle de l'Œil-de-Bœuf" is now. Round the ceiling, from which hang suspended three magnificent chandeliers of rock-crystal, runs a handsome deep-gilt frieze of cupids, some with hunting-horns, and dogs engaged in the chase; others either reaping or binding sheaves of corn, or snaring birds or playing at see-saw. At the sides of the doorway leading into the grand looking-glass gallery, where those not having the *entrée* of the "Œil-de-Bœuf" were accustomed to congregate to see the royal procession pass, are two equestrian portraits, the one of Louis XIV. in the costume of a Roman warrior, wearing, however, his customary full-bottomed wig, with Fame crowning him with a wreath of laurel; the other of the king's brother, the Duke d'Orléans. Facing the same doorway is an elaborate mythological picture representing the "Grand Monarque" surrounded by his family, all of whom are robed in exceedingly scanty draperies, the wigs of the men being their principal article of attire, and all of whom have that unpleasant leer in the eyes which the painters of the seventeenth century seemed to have considered most bewitching, if not becoming.

Suddenly the doors are flung open, but, instead of the tall *suisse* shouting out the customary announcement, "*Messieurs, le Roi!*" the Cardinal Prince de Rohan is summoned to attend the king in his private cabinet.

On proceeding thither, the grand almoner found the king and queen together. Louis XVI., without any preliminary observations, thus abruptly addressed him:

"I hear you have purchased some diamonds of Böhmer?"

"Yes, sire," replied the cardinal.

"Pray, what have you done with them?" inquired the king.

"I thought they had been delivered to her majesty."

"Who commissioned you to make the purchase?"

"A lady called the Countess de la Motte-Valois, who handed me a letter from the queen, and I thought I was performing my duty to her majesty when I undertook this negotiation."

"How, sir," exclaimed the queen, "could you believe that I should select you, to whom I have not spoken these eight years, to negotiate anything for me, and especially through the mediation of such a woman— a woman, too, whom I do not even know?"

"I see plainly that I have been cruelly duped," replied the grand almoner, darting upon the queen as he said so a look of indignation and disdain.* "I will pay for the Necklace: my desire to be of service to your majesty blinded me. I suspected no trick in the affair, and I am sorry for it."

The cardinal then took from his pocket-book a letter purporting to be written by the queen to Madame de la Motte, and intrusting her with the commission. This letter he handed to the king, who after looking at it held it towards the cardinal, saying: "This is neither written nor signed by the queen. How could a prince of the house of Rohan, and a grand almoner of France, ever think that the queen would sign herself MARIE-ANTOINETTE DE FRANCE? Everybody knows that queens sign their baptismal names only."

Louis XVI. then produced the copy of a letter sent by the cardinal to Böhmer, and inquired whether he had ever written such a letter. After glancing over it, the grand almoner replied that he had no recollection of having done so; but when the king asked him what he would say if the original letter, signed by himself,

---

* See Georgel, who attributed this movement of the cardinal's to his firm belief at the time that the queen had really employed Madame de la Motte as her intermediary in the Necklace affair.

were shown to him, the cardinal could not but confess that the letter was genuine.

"'If this be the case,' observed the king, 'explain to me the whole of this enigma. I do not wish to believe you guilty; I had rather you would justify your conduct. Account, therefore, for these manœuvres with Böhmer, these securities, and these notes.'

"In reply to the king's remarks, the grand almoner, who was extremely confused, kept continually repeating: 'I have been deceived, sire. I will pay for the Necklace. I ask pardon of your majesties.' Then turning pale, and leaning against the table, he said: 'Sire, I am too much agitated to answer your majesty in a way——'

"'Compose yourself,' interposed the king, 'and retire into the adjoining closet. You will there find pens, ink, and paper; write down what you have to say to me.'

"The grand almoner retired as directed, and returned in about a quarter of an hour with a written statement of a somewhat incoherent character. After receiving it, Louis XVI. commanded him to withdraw."*

De Besenval says that at this moment the king warned the cardinal he was about to be arrested. "Oh,

---

* "Memoirs of Marie-Antoinette," by Madame Campan, vol. ii. pp. 13, 14, 15, 286-7. Madame Campan has extracted the foregoing narrative, nearly word for word, from a newspaper of the time—the *Journal des Débats*. See the Abbé Soulavie's "Mémoires Historiques et Politiques du règne de Louis XVI.," vol. vi. p. 81, *et seq.*, where the same account will be found quoted.

sire!" exclaimed the prince, "I shall always obey the orders of your majesty, but deign to spare me the shame of being arrested in my pontifical habit before the eyes of the entire court." "It is necessary it should be so," replied the king. The cardinal wished to insist, but the king abruptly quitted him.* On leaving the royal cabinet the grand almoner encountered his deadly enemy, the Baron de Breteuil, who had been lying in wait for him, and who at once called out to a sub-lieutenant of his majesty's body-guard, "In the king's name, follow me! Arrest the Cardinal de Rohan!" The officer proceeded to take charge of his prisoner, who, precipitated as it were in a moment from his high pinnacle of fortune, was conducted on foot in his rich pontifical vestments, guarded on all sides, and pressed upon by an amazed crowd of court idlers and hangers-on, to his hôtel looking upon the north wing of the château. The distance he had to go was not great, through the long looking-glass gallery—every eye in the immense throng with which it was lined turned inquisitively upon him—through a few apartments and down the marble staircase, and across the marble court and the broad "Cour Royale," with the noonday sun shedding its burning rays upon his head, and gilding as it were his gorgeous vestments; past the gaudy,

---

* "Mémoires du Baron de Besenval," vol. iii. p. 127. The baron adds that he heard the whole of this detail told to the queen, but nothing was said of the contents of the paper written by the cardinal.

gilded, and over-decorated chapel in which he, Grand Almoner of France, was never more to officiate with a king and queen and a brilliant court appearing to give ear to his ministrations; thence through the iron gate leading into the Rue des Réservoirs, where the Hôtel de Rohan—a singularly plain-looking building, with rather a pretty garden approached from a balustraded terrace in the rear, and which may be easily identified at the present day as the residence of the receiver-general of the district—was situated.* So soon as the necessary preparations could be made, the cardinal, guarded like a common criminal, was whisked off to Paris to the Hôtel de Strasbourg, from whence he was speedily transferred to the Bastille.

Ere, however, he quitted the palace of Versailles, "notwithstanding the escort that surrounded him, and favoured by the attendant crowd, the grand almoner stopped for a few moments, and stooping down with his face towards the wall, as if to fasten his buckle or his garter, snatched out his pencil and hastily wrote a few words on a scrap of paper placed under his hand in his square red cap. He rose again and proceeded. On entering his hôtel he contrived to slip this paper unperceived into the hand of a confidential 'heyduc' who waited for him at the door of his apartment." The

* It is No. 6 in the Rue des Réservoirs. *Vide* "Histoire Anecdotique des Rues de Versailles," par J. A. Le Roi.

"heyduc" posts off to Paris, and arrives at the Palais-Cardinal early in the afternoon. His horse falls dead in the stable, and he himself swoons in the apartment of the Abbé Georgel after exclaiming wildly, "All is lost; the prince is arrested." The slip of paper which drops from his hand is caught up and read with eagerness by the abbé, and in accordance with the instructions contained in it, the scarlet portfolio which held all the cardinal's secret correspondence, including the letters—gilt-edged or bordered with *vignettes bleues*—penned by the phantom queen, and on which the Prince de Rohan set such store, is forthwith committed to the flames.*

While the foregoing events were transpiring the Count and Countess de la Motte were receiving and returning visits in tranquil security at Bar-sur-Aube. It was two days after the arrest of the cardinal that the countess set out on her visit to the Duke de Penthièvre at Château-Villain, and Beugnot was awaiting her

---

* There are other versions of this incident: we have, however, preferred to follow the Abbé Georgel's. See "Mémoires pour servir," etc., vol. ii. pp. 103-4. Madame Campan says that the cardinal borrowed the pencil which he used from the sub-lieutenant into whose custody he was given, and who, when reprimanded for having permitted the cardinal to write, excused himself by saying that the orders he received did not forbid his doing so; and that, moreover, being himself in great pecuniary difficulties, he thought the unaccustomed summons, "In the king's name, follow me," addressed to him by the Baron de Breteuil, concerned him personally, which for the moment so unnerved him that he hardly knew what he was doing. See "Madame Campan's Memoirs," vol. ii. pp. 15, 16, 284.

arrival at Clairvaux in the evening. The abbé had pressed the young lawyer to pass three days there if the ensuing fête of Saint-Bernard would not frighten him, and had promised him as a reward that he should hear the famous Abbé Maury from Paris preach the saint's panegyric. "I agreed," says Beugnot, "with all my heart. The day of Saint-Bernard was a grand affair at Clairvaux. The poor who presented themselves at the door of the abbey received charity, and the *bourgeoisie* of Bar-sur-Aube and its environs were entertained at dinner in the refectory, at which the abbé presided. I desired to be present at this banquet to laugh at the abbé, who had spoken to me of this old custom as a piece of tomfoolery he was about to suppress, and had mentioned with contempt the guests who would be present at it.

"The Abbé of Clairvaux was above the middle height, and of a fine and graceful figure. When after his election he had the honour of being presented to the king at Versailles, the queen, struck with his handsome person and the dignity with which he wore the costume of his order, could not refrain exclaiming, 'What a handsome monk!' Dom Rocourt was polite with men and gallant with women, and with all this, or in spite of it, very stupid. I was never able," says Beugnot, "to make him comprehend when the revolution arrived that the age had done with him, his abbey, and his monks, who would have been only too happy to abandon him."* The Abbey of Clairvaux, founded in the year 1114, was one of the richest and most magnificent abbeys in France. Its annual revenue was between three and four hundred thousand francs. Situated in a picturesque glen, the conventual buildings comprised the abbé's residence, a handsome church, said not to have been inferior to Nôtre Dame de Paris, and where several early French kings and princes lay buried, with a treasury for its ornaments and relics, an infirmary, a refectory and dormitories: besides which there were a valuable library and beautiful gardens.† Lastly, one must not forget its gigantic wine-vat, which held upwards of 200,000 gallons. To-day the abbey is a house of detention for criminals; the site of its magnificent church—demolished during the first year of the Restoration—being now a prison-yard. The abbé usually drove out with four horses to his carriage, and had an outrider to precede him. He caused himself to be addressed as "my lord" by his monks and dependents, and by all those numerous persons who had need of his assistance. He governed despotically numerous convents of monks and nuns that were dependent on his abbey, and it is said that he took especial pleasure in visiting the nunneries subject to his sway.‡

We left Beugnot at Clairvaux waiting Madame de la

* "Mémoires du Comte Beugnot," vol. i. p. 79.
† "Essais Historiques sur la ville de Bar-sur-Aube," par J. G. F.
‡ "Mémoires du Comte Beugnot," vol. i. pp. 79, 80.

Motte's return. Soon after eight o'clock she made her appearance, when he at once acquainted her with the engagement he had entered into. She wished to share it and remain for the fête of Saint Bernard, but the abbé excused himself, explaining to her that the fête was altogether a religious one, and that the ladies who commonly inhabited Clairvaux fled from it on that day, abandoning it to the religion of Saint-Bernard and to their children. They returned, however, on the following day, and the abbé, who was lost in reverence and adoration of Madame de la Motte, pressed her to augment their number. He was no doubt aware of the intimate connection which existed between the countess and the Cardinal de Rohan, and he treated her accordingly like a princess of the church.

A large company was assembled at the abbey on this particular evening in anticipation of meeting the Abbé Maury, whose arrival from Paris was now momentarily expected. The clock having struck nine without the looked-for guest making his appearance, the company sat down to the supper-table. Scarcely had they taken their seats, however, before the sound of carriage-wheels announced some new arrival. This proved to be the Abbé Maury, with " his Jesuistic eyes, his impassive brass face, image of all the cardinal sins," who, after being welcomed by his brother ecclesiastic, and introduced to the guests in the supper-room, without being allowed time to change his travelling-dress, took his seat at table, when, as a matter of course, he was at once assailed by the inquiry as to whether there was anything stirring in Paris—in fact, any news.

"'What mean you?—any news?' replied the Abbé Maury; 'why, where do you all come from? There is a piece of news which none can understand, which has astonished and bewildered all Paris. The Cardinal de Rohan, Grand Almoner of France, was arrested last Tuesday, the festival of the Assumption, in his pontifical vestments, as he was leaving the king's cabinet. They talk of a Diamond Necklace which he was to have bought for the queen, but which he did not buy at all. Is it not inconceivable that for such a bauble as this a grand almoner of France should have been arrested in his pontifical vestments—do you understand, in his pontifical vestments?—and on leaving the king's cabinet?'

"As soon as this intelligence reached my ear," says Count Beugnot, whose narrative we are quoting, "I glanced at Madame de la Motte, whose napkin had fallen from her hand, and whose pale and rigid face seemed as it were immovably fixed above her plate. After the first shock was over she made an effort and rushed out of the room, followed by one of the chief attendants. In the course of a few minutes I left the table and joined her. The horses were already put to her carriage, so we at once set forth."

"'I have perhaps done wrong in leaving so suddenly,

above all in the presence of the Abbé Maury,' remarked Madame de la Motte. 'Not at all,' replied I; 'your relations with the cardinal are known, and almost avowed. He may have to forfeit his life perhaps; your plan is to run away in advance of couriers, letters, or news. You would have done wrong in losing time by supping at Clairvaux—but can you explain this arrest to yourself?' 'No,—at least only through some trick of Cagliostro's: the cardinal is infatuated with him: it is not my fault, I have warned him a hundred times.' 'So much the better,' remarked I; 'but what is this story about a Necklace which the cardinal has been buying for the queen? How is it that a cardinal is charged with such a purchase? and how comes it about that the queen should choose for such a commission Prince Louis, whom she openly detests?' 'I repeat to you, it is all Cagliostro.' 'But you have received this charlatan at your house. Are you not compromised in any way with him?' 'Absolutely not in the least, and I am perfectly tranquil; I did very wrong to leave the supper-table.' 'It was not wrong. If you are tranquil on your own account, you ought not to be so on account of an unfortunate friend.' 'Ah! bah! you do not know him; only see him in a difficulty; he is capable of abusing a hundred persons, of saying a hundred foolish things to get himself out of it.' 'Madame de la Motte,' replied I, 'you have just said more than I wished to hear; I have a last service to propose to you; it is now ten o'clock at night, we are approaching Bayet. I am going to leave you there in care of a friend for whom you know I can answer. I will return with your carriage to Bar-sur-Aube, and will warn M. de la Motte, who in an hour's time can come and fetch you in a post-chaise drawn by your best pair of horses. He will take charge of your most valuable effects, and you will together take, this very night, the road to Châlons, since that to Troyes would not be safe for you. Do not go to Boulogne, Calais, or Dieppe, at which places instructions perhaps have been already given to stop you; between these ports there are twenty places where for ten louis they will land you in England.' 'Sir,' replied Madame de la Motte, 'you are wearying me; I have allowed you to go on to the end because I was thinking of something else. Is it necessary to repeat to you ten times running that I have nothing to do with this affair? I repeat it, I am very sorry at having left the table, as though I were an accomplice in your cardinal's fooleries.' 'Madame,' observed I, 'let us say no more on the subject. Still I should like to add once more—after your avowal—that you will repent not having followed my advice. May heaven grant in this case that your repentance may not be more poignant than usual.'

"We drove along in silence for half an hour. As we entered the town I entreated her to at least burn any papers which might compromise her or the cardinal. 'It is,' said I, 'a measure dictated by honour on the one side and by prudence on the other.' She consented: I offered to assist her, and as she did not refuse, on leaving the carriage I accompanied her to her room. Her husband, who had left home early in the morning to join a hunting party, had not yet returned. We opened a large chest of sandal-wood filled with papers of all colours and dimensions. Being nervously anxious to make quick work of the matter, I inquired if there were amongst them any bills of exchange, bonds, bank-notes, or drafts, and on receiving an answer in the negative I proposed to throw the entire heap into the fire. She insisted on at least a cursory examination being made of them. We proceeded with it, very slowly on her part, very precipitately on mine. It was whilst casting furtive glances upon some of the hundreds of letters from the Cardinal de Rohan, that I saw with pity the ravages which the delirium of love, aided by that of ambition, had wrought in the mind of this unhappy man. It is fortunate for the cardinal's memory that these letters were destroyed, but it is a loss for the history of human passions. What must have been the state of society when a prince of the church did not hesitate to write, to sign, and to address to a woman letters which in our days a man who respects himself the least in the world might commence reading, but would certainly never finish?

"Among these motley papers there were invoices, offers of estates for sale, prospectuses and advertisements of new inventions, &c. Some of the letters were from Böhmer and Bassenge, and made mention of the Necklace, spoke of terms expired, acknowledged the receipt of certain sums, and asked for larger ones. I consulted Madame de la Motte as to what should be done with them. Finding her hesitate, I took the shortest course, and threw them all into the fire. The affair occupied a considerable time. When it was over I took my leave of Madame de la Motte, urging her to depart more strongly than ever. She only answered me by promising to go to bed immediately. I then quitted her apartments, the atmosphere of which was poisoned by the odour arising from burning paper and wax impregnated with twenty different perfumes. It was three o'clock in the morning; at four o'clock she was arrested, and at half-past four was on her way to the Bastille. The examination which I had made of her papers, although a superficial one, had settled my doubts. I had observed so much extravagance in the letters of the cardinal, that I believed both he and the countess lost, and the one through the other."*

The countess was sound asleep when the officers of justice arrived. An inspector of police drew aside the bed curtains, and arousing her, showed her the *lettre-de-*

---

* "Mémoires du Comte Beugnot," vol. i. p. 80, *et seq.*

cachet for her arrest.* From this moment until her departure from Bar-sur-Aube the countess was closely guarded by *exempts* and cavalry of the marshalsea, while other *exempts* compelled her husband, who had returned home in the meantime, to accompany them while they made a strict search throughout the house."†

"M. de la Motte," observes Beugnot, "was very little affected at the arrest of his wife. He had been hunting the day before, and contemplated devoting several more days to this amusement. He called on me at six o'clock in the morning, and told me in a quiet, confidential sort of way, of the countess's arrest. He assumed a calmness in my presence that surprised me. 'Madame,' said he, 'will only be away for three or four days at the utmost. She is going to give the minister some explanations which he requires of her. I reckon that she will return on Wednesday or Thursday, when we will go and meet her, and bring her home in triumph.' 'Sir,' I replied to him, 'you are I dare say unaware that last night I advised your wife to start at once for England, and by the quickest route. Had she followed my counsel, she would not be as she now is, on the high road to the Bastille. I now advise you to follow the course I suggested to her, which will be much safer for you than losing precious time and deceiving yourself by vain illusions.' The count shrugged his shoulders and

* "Anecdotes du règne de Louis XVI.," vol. i. p. 385.
† "Premier Interrogatoire de Madame de la Motte."

left me, humming a tune. On the same day he took his place in the diligence, and gained England without delay. It was on the 18th of August that he left. Four days afterwards the police came to arrest him,"* but found their bird had flown.

Neither the forger Villette nor the counterfeit queen D'Oliva were objects of suspicion even until several weeks had elapsed; but eight days after the arrest of the cardinal, Count Cagliostro and his wife were arrested and sent to join the grand almoner and the Countess de la Motte in the Bastille. In a memorial prepared by Cagliostro, wherein he puts forward a claim for damages on account of the losses sustained by him in consequence of this arrest, he says: "On August 23, 1785, the Commissary Chénon came to my house, attended by a bailiff and eight police-officers. He told me that he had orders to escort me to the lieutenant of police. He asked me for my keys, and obliged me to open my escritoire, which contained various medicines, amongst others six bottles of precious balsam. The bailiff in my presence seized upon the articles he chose to take, and particularly four bottles of the balsam. The sbirri that accompanied him followed their chief's example, and the pillage began."

The count then proceeds to estimate the amount of this pillage item by item, and ends by bringing it up to

* " Mémoires du Comte Beugnot," vol. i. pp. 85, 86.

the considerable sum of 100,000 francs (£4000 sterling). Amongst these items he cites a green pocket-book containing forty-seven bank notes of 1000 francs each, besides which he asserts there were gold and silver coin—double-louis, sequins, and Spanish quadruples—plate, jewels, diamonds, &c., taken away.*

The cardinal's equerry and particular confidant, the Baron de Planta—a man of shady character, who had held a commission in a Swiss regiment in France, had been broke for some misconduct, and had been for years under a cloud at the time he was picked up by the Prince de Rohan during his Vienna embassy—was likewise arrested, but had the luck to get released after undergoing a brief examination.†

* " Mémoire pour le Comte de Cagliostro contre Maître Chesnon fils et le Sieur de Launay," p. 4, *et seq.*
† " Mémoires pour servir," etc., par l'Abbé Georgel, vol. ii. pp. 49, 108.

XXIV.

1785. AUG. 19—SEPT. 13.

A DREARY DAY AND NIGHT'S DRIVE.—THE BASTILLE.—
A "VALOIS" SERVED OFF PEWTER.

As we have already mentioned, the Cardinal de Rohan immediately after his arrest was conducted, closely guarded, to his hotel at Versailles. In the afternoon of the same day he was removed to Paris, to the Palais-Cardinal, where he remained during the night; the officer commanding the escort of royal body-guards, having been solemnly cautioned to that effect, slept in the same apartment as his prisoner, whom he never trusted out of his sight for a single instant.

The day following the Marquis de Launay, governor of the Bastille, came to receive the grand almoner into his custody, and to transfer him to the iron grip of that mysterious state prison which rarely rendered up its victims until they were snatched away by the icy hand of death. The cardinal wished to go thither on foot under cover of the night, so as to be free from observation. This favour was granted him, but, what is far more remarkable, he was allowed to take with him a couple of *valets de chambre* and a secretary, and was informed that he would be permitted to see his friends at stated periods in the hall of this gloomy fortress.*

The Countess de la Motte was arrested it will be remembered at four o'clock on the morning of the 18th of August, and was at once hurried off to Paris, distant about one hundred and forty miles from Bar-sur-Aube, "entirely ignorant," she remarks, "whither I was intended to be conveyed, and so little anticipating the event that I was dozing in the carriage. In the course of our journey the *voiture* was stopped, and questions asked by some person without, to whom the person within said: 'Don't you know this *voiture*?' 'Oh yes,' replied the other. 'Don't stop us then; we have nothing but a state prisoner;' upon which the *voiture* proceeded. Hearing this conversation I awoke; the termination of it roused all my faculties. 'What do you say?' exclaimed I in a tone of extreme agitation. 'A state prisoner! alas! then am I a state prisoner?' 'Oh, no, madame, no such thing;' and these people swore that I was not one. But there is some excuse for them; they belonged to the police, and perjury and

* M. Feuillet de Conches has, among his curious collection of autographs relating to the affair of the Diamond Necklace, a series of reports from the Marquis de Launay to the Baron de Breteuil, which give, day by day, a list of the persons who visited the cardinal during his confinement in the Bastille.

bearing false witness is no small part of their employment. Yet they used such kind expressions that, knowing my innocence, I flattered myself I was not deceived. One of them said to me: 'Madame, I wish we were arrived at my house, where I could accommodate you with a bath and a bed; for as it is now so very early I'm afraid we shall not be able to get an interview with the Baron de Breteuil, who has given me orders if we arrived too early to conduct you to my house, and to wait upon him about eleven; therefore be composed and try to sleep a little.' All this time I remained upon my seat; but soon after, they desired me to conceal myself in the bottom of the *voiture;* this was when we arrived at the Porte St. Antoine, where they endeavoured as much as possible to place themselves in such positions before me that I might neither be seen by any one nor observe the turning of the Bastille. Finding myself rather warm, 'Let me see,' said I; and looking out I discovered the Bastille. 'How!' exclaimed I, with agitated surprise; 'is it to the Bastille then that I am going? Oh! you are all impostors!' They endeavoured to pacify me, and begged me not to make a disturbance; told me that they were not their own masters; that they had received their orders, but that they were absolutely ignorant of the motive for which I was taken to the Bastille, and that they were persuaded in a very few days I should be liberated.

"By this time we arrived at the first bridge leading

to the governor's house. The postillion knocked, and many *invalides* came out. The post-chaise belonging to the police drove up to the governor's door, who came out himself in a *robe de chambre* to the carriage to give me his hand, begging me at the same time to excuse his *déshabille*. He then conducted me into a large hall. Soon afterwards, the king's lieutenant arrived with a large book, wherein he entered the date of my arrival, and afterwards presented it to me to sign my name, which request I complied with. During this ceremony, which only occupied a few minutes, the governor was in the court with the *exempts*, who were giving him an account of every circumstance which occurred in the execution of their orders. This over, the governor returned, and asked me if I would take any refreshment, adding, 'We shall take great care of you, madame.' I then asked him into which apartment I should go to receive the Baron de Breteuil, remarking at the same time that I hoped he would come at eleven, as the *exempts* had informed me. 'Oh, there is not the least doubt of it, madame,' replied the governor. He then called Saint-Jean, the turnkey, to whom he gave my papers, to place them, as I have since heard, in the archives; after which the governor desired the king's lieutenant to conduct me to my apartment. Some little conversation passed relative to the place of my destination, of which the lieutenant seemed uncertain. 'Oh,' said the governor, '*La Comtée* is the best; it is very light.' He then put me in charge of the king's lieutenant, whose arm I took, persuaded that I should be shown into some other apartment, and for a far different purpose. As I went along I saw some soldiers (*invalides*) enveloped in blue cloaks, with large hoods over their heads, and long bands hanging down. As I passed them I was not a little surprised to see them turn their backs towards me, it being the rule when any prisoner arrives for them to turn themselves round lest they should take too much notice. I began to laugh with the lieutenant at the novelty of this, and particularly at these grotesque figures in their masquerade. . .

"We passed on till we arrived at the court, the staircase of which led to the tower of *La Comtée*. After ascending this we arrived at the apartment destined for my reception, all the gates of which were very large, and moreover open. St. Jean, who was to be my turnkey, attended me thither.

"Struck with such a dismal change of situation, so very different from what I had ever been accustomed to, I could not help expressing my dissatisfaction to the lieutenant. 'If this is the place,' said I, 'which the governor pleases to call my apartment, to be sure I am greatly obliged to him.' I then went to look at the bed, which was indeed a wretched one; told him that it would be impossible for me to sleep in so miserable a bed as that, and demanded if he could not accommodate me with one as good as the cardinal's? He replied, very politely that he really did not comprehend my meaning. . . .

"My disapprobation of the bed, however, was attended with favourable results, for the turnkey substituted for the one which I had great reason to complain of an excellent feather bed with fine sheets and curtains. Thus accommodated, and extremely fatigued, I attempted to get some rest; but I was scarce in bed when the lieutenant, with my own and another turnkey, arrived. The two turnkeys examined my clothes and my pockets, out of which they took all the contents, consisting of several little articlès, particularly a gold *étui* set with pearls, another of tortoiseshell, a small ivory box ornamented with gold, having on its lid a miniature with a gold rim, containing a small mirror and some rouge, an English pocket-knife, a knife with a tortoiseshell handle and gold blade, my purse, containing eighteen louis and about nineteen livres, and a gold repeating watch with a diamond chain.

"Indignant at such humiliating treatment, which I could not patiently endure, I remonstrated with some asperity, and threatened to inform the Baron de Breteuil, whom I was simple enough to believe I should see. They were however regardless of my threats, and having executed their orders, departed through those dreadful doors which with their horrid bolts were closed upon me, and the sound pierced my very soul. . . .

"About eight o'clock the turnkey came to my door.

I spoke to him, but he paid no attention to me, and departed without saying a word. I rose to examine my dismal habitation, and traversed the room in every direction backwards and forwards. I opened the window to see if I could discover anybody, or make myself sufficiently conspicuous for any one to see me. I climbed upon the sill, and held my face close to the bars, but I could discover nothing; as for people, it was impossible to distinguish them."*

At noon the lieutenant of the Bastille came to fetch the countess as she thought to an interview with the Baron de Breteuil, instead of which she was conducted into the presence of the lieutenant of police and the Commissary Chénon, who commenced examining her respecting the Diamond Necklace, and ended by accusing her of having first obtained possession of and afterwards absconding to a foreign country with the missing jewel. Madame de la Motte, perfectly unabashed, says that she laughed outright in the commissary's face at what she styles the "ridiculous absurdity" of such an accusation. Her examination was continued day by day, and when completed, the commissary, as the countess artfully states, "gabbled over something which she scarce understood," but which she nevertheless signed. "It was this cunning dissembler," she remarks, "who made me sign those odious things which I was supposed to

* "Life of the Countess de la Motte, by herself," vol. i. p. 389, et seq.

have said myself, and which were so detestable that when they were read by his majesty he spat upon them, saying, 'Fie upon the filthy creature!'"*

The countess, who in early life was glad to feed upon broken victuals passed through a trap-hole in the miserable hovel that sheltered the Saint-Remi family at Fontette, appears not to have entirely approved of the *cuisine* of the Bastille. What more particularly annoyed her, however, was that she, who had been latterly accustomed to gold and silver plate, should now be expected to dine off vulgar pewter. According to her own account, she preferred enduring the pangs of hunger to submitting to such an indignity, and sent the dishes away untouched. The turnkey, she tells us, somewhat surprised at this proceeding, "said in a rude manner, 'So then you don't choose to eat, don't you?' 'No,' replied I, 'I don't choose to eat, and I desire to know if you serve the cardinal off pewter? Inform the governor that the Valois are quite as nice as and entitled to equal respect with the Rohans.' The turnkey was astounded. He looked at me respectfully, and mildly answered that he was ignorant who I was; then begging my pardon he departed, and returned shortly afterwards with a better dinner served in beautiful dishes with silver covers." †

Poor Madame de la Tour, Count de la Motte's sister,

* "Life of the Countess de la Motte, by herself," vol. i. p. 408.
† Ibid. vol. i. p. 416.

having applied to the Marquis de Launay for permission to visit the countess in the Bastille, was arrested by two *exempts* on leaving the governor's house, and forthwith conducted to a cell in the gloomy old fortress, where she was kept confined for a period of six months, in spite of the efforts of her husband and family to procure her release. This was paying rather a heavy penalty for her feelings of sympathy towards an incriminated sister-in-law.

Before the countess had been immured in the Bastille a fortnight, we find her attempting a rambling exculpation of herself in a document which bears no address, but was no doubt intended to produce an impression on the Baron de Breteuil, and which she describes as " Explanatory reflections on the accusations made by Monseigneur le Cardinal de Rohan."

" Does Monseigneur le Cardinal de Rohan believe me ass enough not to have disappeared immediately if I had desired to retain the Necklace under some pretext, as he accuses me of doing ?

" Does Monseigneur le Cardinal believe that I caused the Necklace to be sold here under the eyes both of the vendor and of himself, and that I should have been able, had I been guilty, to have so far deluded them as to remain at Paris so tranquilly as I did, knowing all the while the date of payment ? Should I not rather have taken a safe departure before the moment of payment arrived ? Monseigneur le Cardinal de Rohan was at Saverne for six weeks. Could I not have profited by his absence to join my husband in England with my whole household, and have remained there?

"Instead of which my husband was there by his orders, and returned as agreed upon with Monseigneur le Cardinal. Would it have been possible, with me living almost at his door, for him not to have given me something during four years, or at least to have taken care of me and mine, since all I had was my pension of 800 livres? The expenses of my house were always heavy enough to make it requisite for the cardinal to give me large sums to keep it up; and at this time I solicited more than ever both at Versailles and at Paris. Every day I required *voitures de remise*, which were very dear; I had, too, a house at Versailles to reside in when there. How, moreover, let me ask, should I have done the bidding of a sovereign without anticipating great returns from it, since sooner or later this intimacy would certainly have been discovered? How could I have exercised so little precaution, I say, as to remain in Paris, where, if guilty, I should have had to have taken the utmost care to appear more at my ease than under ordinary circumstances, fearful of being suspected by Monseigneur le Cardinal, whose people, and especially M. le Baron de Planta (whom he also brought as a witness against me), came continually to my house?

"Will Monseigneur le Cardinal dare to deny all the facts which I have advanced in my examination, and which will at least convince him that I have been forced to this, and that it has only been in self-defence? But he accuses me wrongfully. I must tell the truth to prove my innocence, and to prove that he was not in a position to use me as a servant, as Monseigneur le Cardinal pretends, in an affair of such importance, since it concerned the person of the queen. Moreover, I do not know any one who is attached to her.

"I have the honour to be, with submission,

"COMTESSE DE VALOIS DE LA MOTTE DE LA PÉNICIÈRE.

" At the Bastille this Monday, 29th August, 1785."*

Another letter is extant, bearing date Sept. 13, 1785, evidently written by the countess during her confinement in the Bastille, though it has no signature to it, and which, couched in terms of extreme familiarity, is addressed to the Duke de Guines, a very grand gentleman of the court, and, what is more, one of the queen's most intimate friends. In this letter, in the midst of the most absurd and nonsensical details, the countess introduces the names of her sister and of Cagliostro and his wife, on the two last of whom she seeks to turn the accusation directed against herself.† The duke, who pretended not to understand the drift of the letter, sent it to the Baron de Breteuil.

* Autograph letter of Madame de la Motte's, in the Imperial Archives.
† Anonymous autograph letter of Madame de la Motte's, in the collection of M. Feuillet de Conches.

XXV.

EFFECT PRODUCED ON THE PUBLIC MIND BY THESE ARRESTS.—THE ENEMIES OF THE QUEEN.

It is impossible to conceive the sensation produced throughout France, and indeed throughout Europe generally, by these arrests and the extravagant rumours to which they gave rise. Marie-Antoinette in various ways had unfortunately made numerous enemies—through her efforts, for instance, to get the Duke de Choiseul appointed prime minister; through her too decided partiality for particular favourites, for whom she secured both places and pensions; and through what was affectedly styled her want of prudence—in other words, her open disregard of the rigid formalities of French court etiquette. Arrayed against her were many of the oldest families in France, each of whom cherished some particular grievance of its own. The consequence was, there were many hostile interests at work intent upon destroying her reputation and bringing about her ruin if need be, even at the expense of the monarchy itself, so that the great fraud of the Diamond Necklace was altogether regarded in the light of a political event, and no time was lost by the different inimical factions in twisting it to serve their own purposes, without the slightest regard being paid by any one of them to the real character of the act itself.

We will here interrupt the course of our narrative to examine at some length into the origin of this widespread animosity against the queen, and to trace the causes of its rapid extension through all classes of French society. To do this it will be necessary for us to go back to the very outset of her career.

When Marie-Antoinette, then a young girl of fifteen, first set foot on French soil, nothing could exceed the enthusiasm with which she was welcomed. Her progress from Strasbourg to Versailles was one long ovation. At Versailles, save the dauphin's old maiden aunts, who made themselves sufficiently disagreeable, and the king's mistress, Madame Dubarry, who could not tolerate this fair and pure young spirit, every one was more or less charmed with her. The old king, worn out by excesses, and weary of the deceptive flattery which he daily had to listen to, was captivated, not merely by her personal graces, but by her frank and lively nature, her open unaffected ways. The women may have secretly envied her, but the men could not help adoring her. She far excelled the young female members of the royal family in beauty. At the time of her marriage her form was not fully developed : her stature was short, and her figure altogether small, though perfectly proportioned; her arm was finely rounded and of a dazzling whiteness, her hand plump, her fingers tapering, her nails transparent and rose-coloured, her foot charming. When she grew taller and stouter the foot and hand remained perfect, her figure only became a little inelegant, and her chest a trifle too broad. Her face formed a rather long oval; her complexion, which was really dazzling, displayed the most tender shades of colour, from pearly white to delicate rose tint; her eyes were blue, soft, and animated, and shaded by long, full lashes; her nose was aquiline, and slightly tapered at the end; her mouth was small and delicate and well arched, her lower lip prominent, after the Austrian type; her neck was slender and a trifle long, but well set; her forehead was convex, and furnished with too little of her beautiful chesnut-colour hair. The *coiffure* of the empire would have accomplished marvels for her, for the hair turned down over her forehead would have given to her face a regular beauty.*

Though the young dauphiness was addicted to reverie, and displayed a fondness for retirement in the society of a few chosen friends, she was far from being of a reserved disposition; indeed, she was a good deal given to gaiety of that light, playful, almost pert character which imparts movement and life to all around. She

* M. F. Barrière.

forced every one to laugh with her. She cared nothing for the restraints imposed by the barriers of etiquette. If it did not please her to walk in stately fashion, she would run and skip about, regardless of her train or her ladies of honour. In winter-time she would scamper over the slippery ground, dragging after her the youngest lady of her court, whose duty it was to hold up her train, and delighted while glancing behind at the score of racing trains which etiquette required should follow in procession. In the old king's days she was known to have even laughed out loud in the royal box at Preville's funny face, to the great scandal of those who only deigned to smile.*

At the very first court she held after she became queen, provoked by some pleasantries on the part of one of her ladies, and the ridiculous figures cut by certain ancient court dames who had come to pay their respects to her, she could not refrain from laughing at them behind her fan. This naturally enough gave great offence to these antiquated dowagers, who vowed the queen had mocked at them, that she had not a proper respect for age, and was utterly wanting in propriety. The name of "*moqueuse*" was given to her in consequence.†

The young queen, with the full sanction of her hus-

---

* "Histoire de Marie-Antoinette," par E. et J. de Goncourt, pp. 39, 102.

† "Memoirs of Marie-Antoinette," by Madame Campan, vol. i.

band, went early one morning to see the sun rise from the highest point of Marly gardens—a harmless enough proceeding, one would think, but which nevertheless gave rise to most disgraceful calumnies. On another occasion she displayed her skill as a charioteer, by driving about Marly in a cabriolet, preceded merely by a single officer of the king's body-guard. This spectacle astonished the old courtiers, who had never seen a queen handle the reins before, and who therefore pronounced the proceeding highly unbecoming, if not, indeed, improper.

Marie-Antoinette, who was fond of dancing, organized a series of fancy dress balls in the *Salle de Comédie* at Versailles, into the spirit of which her brothers-in-law and their young wives entered most heartily. Being herself a good dancer, she was glad to secure good dancers for these entertainments, but had to undergo no end of reproaches because she, a young queen of twenty years of age, had appealed to the minister of war to grant leave of absence to certain officers, favourites at these fêtes, who had been ordered to rejoin their regiments. Everything she did was wrong. She was condemned for being present at the summer night promenades on the terrace of the château of Versailles, then open to the general public, when, attired in a plain white cambric dress and a simple straw hat, she and Madame Elisabeth, and perhaps her married sisters-in-law, would mix unobserved among the crowd, or, seated on a bench, would listen to the music performed by the king's guards; watching and commenting meanwhile on the secret flirtations which under cover of the night were carried on on these occasions.

The foregoing incidents seem to have been harmless enough, but the same can hardly be said of her excursions to the *bals de l'opéra,* when " lost in their vortex, she was happy or trembling under her mask," and whither she would resort attended merely by a single lady of the court and with her servants in undress grey liveries. On one of these occasions her carriage broke down, and she was obliged to have recourse to a public vehicle. On entering the theatre she is reported to have exclaimed to her friends, " It is I, come in a *fiacre!* Isn't it droll?" One can well conceive an incident like this giving rise to much unpleasant scandal, and can sympathise in the reproaches which her brother the Emperor Joseph addressed to her on her frequent presence at these entertainments.

It was the misfortune of Marie-Antoinette to have made for herself a host of enemies almost from the very first day she was called upon to share a throne. Among others, of her brother-in-law, the Count de Provence, who, attached to her at the outset of her career, took to quizzing her, and criticising her conduct, and even to caricaturing her, while preserving an outward appearance of friendship towards her, soon after she became a queen. The Prince de Condé, allied to the Cardinal de

Rohan by marriage, was embittered against her because she very properly declined to receive his mistress, Madame de Monaco, at court. A warm friendship had sprung up between Marie-Antoinette and the young Duke de Chartres, afterwards Orléans *Égalité*, on her first arrival in France; but after a time, Louis XVI., who disliked the duke, and made a point of insulting his friends whenever he got the chance, availed himself of the duke's known immorality to forbid the queen associating with him on the same familiar terms as heretofore. The consequence was, the duke, who was unaware of the real cause of his disgrace, conceived a strong dislike for the queen, who on her part retaliated by saying many spiteful things respecting him. Dislike grew into hatred, and hatred grew bitter and more bitter, until at last the duke pursued Marie-Antoinette with a relentless vengeance that was positively diabolic, and which only terminated with her life. Dissolute old De Maurepas, prime minister, and all his kin, and more particularly his nephew, the Duke d'Aiguillon, a former creature of the Dubarry's, and now a creature of the Duke d'Orléans, and whose disgrace at court had been brought about by the queen's influence, were arrayed against her on account of the persistent exertions she made to get her favourite, De Choiseul—whom Catherine of Russia used to style the coachman of Europe, as when in power he directed all the cabinets—appointed prime minister in De Maurepas' stead. M. de Vergennes too, whose handsome Greek wife the queen would not consent to receive, cherished a steady hatred of her—all the more dangerous because it was concealed—and even wrote regular reports respecting her to Louis XVI., which the king kept secret, and which only came to light on the discovery of the famous "*armoire de fer*" in the wall of the royal closet in the Tuileries, a few months before the king's death.

At the head of the enemies the queen had succeeded in making among her own sex were, Mesdames Adelaide and Louise, two of the king's aunts, the former of whom had for a while exercised a certain control over her nephew, and was now jealous and irritated beyond measure at the influence which the young queen had acquired over her husband. Since their exile to Lorraine, however, these old ladies had been comparatively powerless for mischief. A far more dangerous enemy of the queen was the stiff old Countess de Marsan, herself a Rohan, and cousin of the cardinal, for whom in past years she had secured the post of grand almoner, who during the late reign had been governess to the king's grandchildren, and who had been from the very first greatly scandalized at Marie-Antoinette's freedom of manners: the dauphiness's most innocent acts being magnified by this old prude into crimes. If she glanced at any one it was set down to coquetry; if she chanced to laugh, it was either unbecoming, or else her gaiety was all forced; if she wore her hair loose she was compared to a bacchante; and even her simple white muslin dresses were pronounced to be stage costumes, worn solely to create an effect. The Duchess de Noailles, who had been Marie-Antoinette's chief lady of honour from the moment of her arrival in France, and Madame de Cossé, her lady of the bedchamber, threw up their posts on the Princess de Lamballe being appointed mistress of the queen's household, and both enlisted themselves among the malcontents, which comprised, in addition to those we have already mentioned, the powerful families of Conti, Montmorency, Clermont-Tonnerre, La Rochefoucauld, and Crillon.

XXVI.

LITTLE TRIANON, AND THE QUEEN'S SOCIETY THERE.

THE enemies of the queen at the moment the Necklace scandal burst upon the public were many and formidable; the real friends that she had capable of defending her were but few. The Baron de Breteuil was well enough disposed towards her, still it was not so much the shielding of the queen's reputation as compassing the downfall of his enemy, the Cardinal de Rohan, that he had at heart. The Abbé de Vermond, who had been Marie-Antoinette's instructor, and was now a sort of secretary to her, had only his fidelity to recommend him. He could influence the queen, but wanted the head to direct her wisely. Specious M. de Calonne was too busy raising new loans to supply a continually emptying royal exchequer to trouble himself about necklaces or cardinals; besides, no particular friendship existed now between the queen and him. He no longer gallantly told her that if what she required was simply difficult it was already done, and if it was impossible, that it should be done. The Duke de Choiseul had been dead these several months past. Those intimate friends of Marie-Antoinette's with whom her daily life was chiefly spent, and who formed what was styled her society, shared her unpopularity to some extent, for it was the favours heaped upon certain members of the Trianon set which had estranged so many of the old nobility from her. Moreover, with the exception of the Count d'Artois and the Duke de Coigny, there was not a man of influence among them who could do her real service in the hour of need.

The *habitués* of Little Trianon—"the queen's society," as they were styled—comprised, first, her youngest brother-in-law, the Count d'Artois, who danced with her, hunted with her, acted with her, and entered generally into the spirit of her amusements; then there was his wife, the countess, exceedingly short of stature, with a complexion as fresh as a rose, and a prepossessing if not a pretty face, yet with a nose which, as Marie-Antoinette wickedly remarked, had never been finished; at one time, too, there were the Count and Countess de Provence, the latter an elder sister of the Countess d'Artois, and the reverse of good-looking. Louis XVI. in his blunt way once told his brother that his wife was by no means handsome, to which the Count de Provence quietly replied, "Sire, I find her to my taste, and that is quite sufficient."* Then there was the

---

* "Les derniers jours de Trianon," par M. Capefigue, p. 25.

queen's sister-in-law, Madame Elisabeth, her true and loving friend until death; next there were the Polignacs, foremost among whom was the Countess Jules, the queen's most particular favourite, who was very handsome, with expressive blue eyes, a ravishing mouth, beautiful small white teeth, a nose just a trifle *retroussé*, a forehead perhaps a little too high, magnificent brown hair, a skin almost as white as alabaster, low shoulders and a well set neck which seemed to give height to her small figure. A touching sweetness formed the foundation of her physiognomy—looks, features, smiles, everything with her partook of the angelic. She had, moreover, wit and grace, and a natural ease and *abandon* which were positively charming. Negligence was her coquetry, dishabille her full dress. It has been said of her that she never looked better than when in a loose morning gown, and with a simple rose, perhaps, in her hair. When the queen first took notice of her, she and her husband, with their two young children, were living in a very humble style (we have heard what Madame de la Motte had to say of her poverty)[*] on a miserable income of three hundred and twenty pounds a year. A pension of six thousand francs was immediately granted her, and ere long she was appointed governess of the royal children, with a salary of fifty thousand francs, and her husband named postmaster-general, and master

---

[*] See *ante*, p. 77.

of the horse to the queen, with a salary of eighty thousand francs; in addition to which a joint pension of eighty thousand francs was conferred upon them, besides other considerable emoluments which brought their income almost up to three hundred thousand francs.* The count, who through the influence of the queen had been raised to the dignity of a duke, seems to have been an amiable sort of man, very generally liked, for he had not allowed his good fortune to spoil him. His sister, the Countess Diane, one of Madame Elisabeth's ladies of honour, was given, we are told, to gallantry and intrigue; her son by the Marquis d'Autichamp—the same wicked rake who was so anxious to escort Madame de la Motte from Lunéville to Paris—entered the Russian service, and was killed at the battle of Austerlitz.† Her personal appearance was the very reverse of engaging. She was compared to a brown owl (she was a southern brunette), with all its feathers in disorder, and to a paroquet, with a crooked beak and round eyes surrounded by dark circles.‡ Nevertheless, she had only to open her mouth to have face, form, toilette, the little she had received from nature, and the little she herself did to render herself pretty, entirely forgotten. It was impossible to know her and not to be

---

* "Weber's Memoirs of Marie-Antoinette," vol. ii. p. 263.

† "Lettres et Documents Inédits de Louis XVI. et Marie-Antoinette," par M. Feuillet de Conches, vol. iii. p. 318.

‡ "Souvenirs de la Marquise de Créqui," par le Comte de Courchamps.

prepossessed in her favour. Her arch way of looking a subject, her piquant turn of thought, which was almost epigrammatic, her sudden changes from gaiety to sadness, from irony to sensibility, her audacity, which nothing could intimidate, her daring and contagious recklessness, made her a general favourite in the society over which she to some extent dominated. A woman like her was invaluable to a court already depressed with melancholy, to put life into the conversation, to dissipate dull thoughts, to defy alarm, to prophesy fine weather, and display a perfect disregard for the future.

The young Princess de Lamballe, one of the earliest friends Marie-Antoinette made in France, ranked next to the Countess Jules de Polignac in her favour. Extremely beautiful, as amiable as she was handsome, and left a widow when she was only eighteen—her husband, son of the old Duke de Penthièvre, who received Madame de la Motte so courteously at Château-Villain, having fallen a victim to early debauchery—a peculiar interest attached to her. A native of the sunny south, she nevertheless possessed all the northern graces. The sweet serenity of her countenance was its great charm: there was tranquillity even in the flash of her eye. On her beautiful forehead, shaded by her long fair hair, not a cloud, not a trace existed of the early grief she had been called upon to suffer. Her mind had all the serene beauty of her face. She was gentle, affectionate, full of caresses, always just, always ready to make sacrifices, devoted even in trifles, and disinterested above everything.

No one occupied a more prominent position in the queen's society at Little Trianon than the Baron de Besenval, a handsome-looking man past the middle age of life, tall and well proportioned, with sharply-defined profile and large well-formed nose, quick, intelligent eye, and small mouth curled up in a mocking and disdainful pout. Of cultivated tastes, full of insolent grace, perfectly content with himself and ever ready to laugh at others, pleasure was the sole pursuit of his life until the death of Louis XV. brought him into closer contact with the Count d'Artois, colonel-general of the Swiss guards, in which corps Besenval, himself a Swiss, held a command. Of the count he made a friend, got presented through his influence to the queen, whose confidence he secured and whom he almost directed; was appointed lieutenant-general of the army, grand cross commander of St. Louis, and inspector-general of the Swiss guards, without seeming at all astonished at his good fortune. In the hour of danger, however, he was found singularly wanting, and it was soon evident that he was not the man to save the monarchy or stem the tide of revolution. His conduct while in command of the army of Paris has been very generally and deservedly condemned.

M. de Vaudreuil was another prominent member of the Trianon coterie, who, entering early in life the highest and most exclusive society of Versailles, had come to the conclusion that human nature, as it was to be found in courts, was neither so very beautiful nor so very great as was commonly represented. Intellect charmed him, and above all that intellect which sparkled with wit. He was the friend of all clever men, spoke but rarely himself, but would lie in wait behind the hubbub of the talkers and suddenly discharge his arrow right at the mark. What made him a favourite with the queen was the fact of his being the best private actor of his day. When young he had been remarkably handsome, but the small-pox had destroyed his good looks. Suffering from disease of the lungs, and subject to nervous twitchings of the body and to frequent fits of depression, he had all the immunities of a sick person accorded him. The good nature of the Duchess de Polignac and the indulgence of his friends caused them to tolerate his caprices and whims. His disposition changed daily according to his bodily ailments; still he was not without certain vigorous virtues, for he was noble, generous, frank, loyal, and a devoted and constant friend.

Next on the list of the queen's favourites comes M. d'Adhémar, whose musical skill and admirable voice had procured him the applause of the master of the king's music. He wrote verses and songs, acted well, and accompanied himself on the harpsichord. His was but a little mind; nevertheless, under a guise of modesty and humility he nourished grand schemes of ambition, and eventually succeeded in securing for himself the English embassy, in connection with which we shall hear of him again. His complaisance was proverbial; he courted every one, offended no one, made innocent jokes in an undertone of voice, and never lost his temper. It will be understood what manner of man he was when we remark, that the women spoke to him when they had nothing to say, the men when they had nothing to do.

The remaining *habitués* of Little Trianon were the three Coignys: the Duke de Coigny, the queen's most constant friend, whom the Triànon set desired to make her lover, which the Duke d'Orléans maintained he already was—styling the young dauphin "*Le fils de Coigny;*"* the Count de Coigny, a big, good-tempered man; and the Chevalier de Coigny, an agreeable flatterer, whom all the women strove to secure to themselves, and who was a favourite wherever he went; the Duke de Guines, the "Versailles Journal," as he was styled, who knew and repeated all the scandal of the court, ridiculed everybody, and was consequently disliked by everybody, was an excellent musician, and prided himself immensely on having played the flute with the great Frederick; the Prince d'Henin, a philanthropist, at court like a fish out of water; the Bailli du Crussol, who made jokes with a most serious air;

---

* "Louis XVI.," par Alexandre Dumas, vol. iii. p. 167.

the Count de Polastron, who played the violin in a ravishing style, and his pale and languishing wife—the amiable "Goddess of Melancholy," as she was called; the Count and Countess de Chalons; the Count and Countess d'Audlau; the sensible, witty, and good-natured Madame de Coigny; the Duke de Guiche, captain of the king's guards, and his young and lovely duchess, daughter of the Duchess Jules de Polignac.* Besides the foregoing, there were a few distinguished foreigners, such as Prince Esterhazy, the Prince de Ligne, the Count de Fersen, a prominent member of the Swedish aristocracy, who was styled by the women the "Beau Fersen," and who in subsequent years drove the *berline* in which the royal family sought to escape from France, and eventually lost his life in an *émeute* at Stockholm in the year 1810; and the Baron de Stedingk, the intimate friend of Fersen and a great favourite with Marie-Antoinette, who said to him, on parting with him in 1787: "Remember, M. de Stedingk, that under no circumstances can any harm happen to you;"† implying that her influence, which she believed to be paramount, would be exercised for his protection in whatever quarter of the world he might chance to be, and little dreaming that in a very few

* "Histoire de Marie-Antoinette," par E. et J. de Goncourt. Most of the foregoing particulars respecting the queen's society at Little Trianon have been derived from this work.

† "Mémoires Posthumes du Feld-Maréchal Comte de Stedingk," vol. iii. pp. 17, 74.

years there would not be another woman in all France so powerless as she.

Having made acquaintance with the queen's society at Trianon, let us now see what Trianon itself was like; that Little Trianon to which Marie-Antoinette retired to escape the splendours, the restraints, the intrigues, and, most of all, the slanders of the court, and enjoy the society of friends of her own choosing; a retirement which unhappily gave rise to new calumnies —calumnies which it does not seem in nature for one woman to invent or propagate of another, but which Madame de la Motte more than insinuates in her lying "Mémoires Justificatifs," and which have outlived the other hideous slanders of which Marie-Antoinette was the victim; that Little Trianon, where Madame de la Motte asserts most of her pretended interviews with the queen took place, and where she affirms Marie-Antoinette was accustomed to receive the Cardinal de Rohan, who, according to the countess's statements, would come late at night disguised as a valet, and spend hour after hour with the queen in a small pavilion in the gardens while she remained outside on the watch.* On one occasion the Cardinal de Rohan certainly did go to Little Trianon, and in a partial disguise, but it was by bribing the gatekeeper that he gained admission to the grounds. It was at the time

* "Life of the Countess de la Motte," by herself, vol. i. p. 312, et seq.

when both building and gardens were brilliantly illuminated in honour of the visit of the Grand Duke and Grand Duchess of Russia, who were travelling about Europe under the titles of Count and Countess du Nord. The cardinal, who professed great anxiety to see these illuminations, promised the gatekeeper to remain in his lodge until all the company had left for Versailles; instead of which, when the man's back was turned, he slunk into the gardens, and, with his cardinal's red stockings showing below his overcoat, took up the most prominent position he could select, where he waited for the royal family and its suite to pass. The queen saw him and recognised him, and next day gave orders for the instant dismissal of the gatekeeper; but Madame Campan, who had been informed of all the circumstances, appealed to Marie-Antoinette in the man's behalf, and succeeded in getting him retained in his post."*

To console Marie-Antoinette for not having appointed her favourite, the Duke de Choiseul, prime minister, Louis XVI. is said to have given her the Little Trianon, which skirts the park of Versailles and adjoins the gardens of the Great Trianon, to do as she pleased with. "You love flowers," said he: "ah! well, I have a bouquet for you—the Little Trianon."

The repairing and embellishing of this miniature

* "Memoirs of Marie-Antoinette," by Madame Campan, vol. i. p. 242.

palace, the alteration and enlargement of its grounds, with a host of artists and gardeners subject to her sway, was for the next year or two Marie-Antoinette's greatest delight. The building, erected by the architect Gabriel for Louis XV., is of a square form, and each of its sides has a frontage of only seventy feet. It is in the Italian style, and its different façades are ornamented with Corinthian columns or pilasters and enriched friezes and cornices. The depraved old king in the last years of his life was enamoured with this "little corner of his grand Versailles." It was to his taste, for here he could live in retirement and at his ease. In addition to its flower garden, laid out in the formal French style, there was a botanical garden, which Louis XIV., at the time he lived at the Great Trianon, caused to be planted with exotic trees and shrubs of multifarious tints and perfumes then almost unknown in France.

The principal entrance to Little Trianon leads immediately to the grand staircase with its handsome gilded balustrade, in the interlacings of which the initials M. A. are prominently displayed. Facing the landing, as if in menace, is a head of the Medusa, which proved powerless however to keep out scandal. After a small ante-chamber comes the *salle-à-manger*, decorated with paintings of the four seasons by Dejunne, and bathing and fishing subjects by Pater, and the re-joined *parquet* of which shows traces of the opening through which

Loriot's flying table was accustomed to ascend at the orgies of Louis XV. In this apartment commence the ornaments upon the panelling—crossed quivers surmounted by wreaths of roses and garlands of flowers—executed by order of Marie-Antoinette. The little *salon* near the *salle-à-manger* displays in relief upon its sides emblems of the vintage and the attributes of the genius of comedy. Hanging from festoons of grapes are bunches and baskets of fruit, masks and tambourines, flutes and guitars, and beneath the marble beards of the goats that support the mantelpiece more bunches of grapes are entwined. At the four corners of the cornice of the grand *salon* are groups of cupids at play. Each panel, surmounted by the emblems of literature and the arts, springs from a stalk of triple flowering lilies, garlanded with laurel and with a wreath of fullblown roses by way of crest. Four paintings by Watteau —of those graceful Decameron-like subjects in which he excelled—are on the walls of this apartment. In the little cabinet which precedes the queen's bedchamber the finest arabesques run over the woodwork; here are cupids bearing cornucopias overflowing with flowers, cooing doves, smoking tripods, and crossed bows and arrows hanging to ribbons. Bouquets of poppies intermingled with thousands of small flowers, all most delicately rendered, are scattered over the panels of the bedroom; the bed with its light blue silk hangings, the chairs and couches *en suite*, and the console tables, looking-glasses, clock and chandeliers being, it is said, much as they were in the days of Marie-Antoinette.

The most elegant façade of the little palace, with its four fluted Corinthian columns and its four flights of steps in the form of an Italian terrace, looks over the French garden, with its flower beds of geometric shape and the flowers themselves planted in straight lines. In the centre of this garden, which is bordered by cool green arcades formed of trees clipped into shape, is a small pavilion with groups of cupids surmounting each of its four entrances. This was the summer dining-room of both Louis XV. and Marie-Antoinette. At the end of one of these leafy arcades is the theatre where the queen and her friends performed alike comedies and operas. Sculptured in high relief above the principal entrance is a cupid grasping a lyre and a crown of laurel, with torches, trumpets, and rolls of music lying at his feet. The interior decorations of the theatre are white and gold; the orchestra stalls and fronts of the boxes are covered with blue velvet, the panels being decorated with cupids suspending garlands of flowers. On either side of the stage two gilded nymphs gracefully twist themselves into candelabra, and above the curtain two other nymphs support the escutcheon of Marie-Antoinette.

At the back and to the right of the little palace is the queen's production, the English garden as it is called, laid out with an absence of formality which almost rivals the productions of Nature's self. The waters apparently wind according to their own fancy, the trees and shrubs seem to have been sown at the will of the wind. Nearly a thousand varieties of trees, some among them being most rare, join their shade and mingle the different tints of their leaves, which vary from the lightest and deepest greens to dark purple and cherry red. The flowers appear to have been planted at hazard; the ground rises and falls at its will; paths wind and go out of the way with provoking pertinacity; stones have been converted into rocks, and small patches of grass made to resemble meadows.

From a hillock in the midst of a thicket of roses, jasmine, and myrtle, rises a belvidere, from whence the queen was accustomed to take in a view of the whole of her domain. This octangular pavilion, with its four windows and its four doors, and its eight sphinxes crouching upon the steps, has repeated eight times over, in figures upon its skirtings and in emblems over its entrances, the allegory of the four seasons, carved by perhaps the cleverest chisel of the century. The interior is paved with coloured marbles, and coloured arabesques run along its walls, with more bows and arrows and quivers, more bouquets and garlands of flowers and musical instruments, together with cameos and cages hanging from ribbons, and little monkeys and squirrels that scratch the sides of a crystal vase or play with the fishes. In the centre of the pavilion, a table, from which hang three rings, rests upon three claws of gilt bronze; this is the table at which Marie-Antoinette breakfasted, for this belvidere was her morning *salle-à-manger*.

From here she could overlook her grotto and the group of artificial rocks; the waterfall, and the trembling bridge thrown across the little torrent; the lake, and, under the shade of the shrubs, the embarking and landing-places, with the galley dotted all over with *fleurs-de-lis*; the temple of love open to all the winds, with its statue, by Bouchardon, of Cupid trying to trim for himself a bow out of the massive club of Hercules; the groves that skirt the river's bank; and, finally, at the most remote part of the garden—the background, so to speak, of the picture—the hamlet where Marie-Antoinette had the king disguised as a miller and the Count de Provence as a schoolmaster. Here are the little houses of the village nestled together like members of one family. The queen's is the prettiest of them all, for it has vases filled with flowers, and grape-vines in front of it. On the opposite side of the lake, and near to the water's edge, is the white marble dairy, with its four goat's-head fountains, and close beside it, and near to a weeping willow planted by the queen's own hand, is the tower of Marlborough, so called from the nursery song which the young dauphin's *bonne* used to sing to him. Nothing is wanting to this pretty village of the stage, neither the curé's house nor that of the bailiff; nor the mill, with its wheel which actually turns; neither the farmhouse, with the stone troughs for the cattle, and the little barns to store away the corn, nor the thatched roofs, the wooden balconies, the little diamond-paned windows, and the flights of steps at the sides of the cottages. Marie-Antoinette and Hubert Robert, the painter, had thought of everything, even of painting rents in the stonework, cracks in the plaster, with here and there beams and bricks jutting out of place, as if time would not wither with sufficient rapidity this peasantry of a queen.*

Marie-Antoinette put aside all regal authority at Trianon. Here she was no longer queen, but merely the mistress of the establishment, which was like an ordinary country-house, with its small retinue of servants and all its unrestrained habits. When the queen entered the *salon*, the ladies neither quitted the piano nor their embroidery-frames, nor the men their games at billiards or backgammon. The king would come to Trianon on foot, and unattended. The queen's guests arrived at two o'clock to dinner, and returned to Versailles at midnight. Marie-Antoinette's occupations and amusements were exclusively those of a country life. Attired in a white muslin dress, a lace shawl, and

---

* "Histoire de Marie-Antoinette," par E. et J. de Goncourt, to which interesting work we are indebted for the larger portion of the present chapter.

a straw hat, she would run about the gardens, or visit her farm, where she would take her guests to drink her milk and eat her new-laid eggs. Or she would conduct the king to a summer-house, where he could read his book undisturbed until she summoned him to a lunch on the grass; after which she would amuse herself by watching the milking of her cows, or with fishing in the lake, or, seated on a rustic seat, would occupy herself by winding up the distaff of some young villager.

Private theatricals were at this time in great favour with the queen, whose *troupe* comprised the Count d'Artois, M. de Vaudreuil, M. d'Adhémar, the Duke and Duchess de Guiche, the Countess Diane de Polignac, and M. de Crussol: occasionally the Baron de Besenval, the Countess de Polastron, and Counts Esterhazy and de Coigny had parts assigned them. The Count de Provence and his wife considered these diversions beneath their rank, and the king moreover disapproved of them. On one occasion, when the "Devin du Village" was being played, and the queen was singing an air in it with more than her accustomed taste, all at once a whistle was heard from the back of one of the boxes. Marie-Antoinette soon perceived that it was from the king himself that this interruption proceeded. Advancing to the footlights, she bowed profoundly, and said, with a smile: "Sir, if you are dissatisfied with the performers you can leave, and your money will be returned to you."* She then resumed her song, which she was permitted to finish without further interruption. Beaumarchais' comedy of the "Barbier de Séville," for which, Madame Campan tells us, Marie-Antoinette was studying her part at the time she made the disclosure to her of the conversation she had had with Böhmer respecting the Necklace, was the last piece performed by this aristocratic *troupe*. It was played on the 19th of August, 1785, the very day on which the Countess de la Motte was lodged in the Bastille.

* "Les derniers jours de Trianon," par M. Capefigue, p. 84.

END OF VOL. I.

Milton Keynes UK
Ingram Content Group UK Ltd.
UKHW010307170224
437973UK00007B/673